Inner Contradictions
of Rigorous Research

ORGANIZATIONAL AND OCCUPATIONAL PSYCHOLOGY

Series Editor: PETER WARR
MRC Social and Applied Psychology Unit, Department of Psychology,
The University, Sheffield, England

Theodore D. Weinshall
Managerial Communication: Concepts, Approaches and Techniques, 1979

Chris Arygis
Inner Contradictions of Rigorous Research, 1980

Inner Contradictions
of Rigorous Research

Chris Argyris

Harvard University

1980

ACADEMIC PRESS

A Subsidiary of Harcourt Brace Jovanovich, Publishers

New York London Toronto Sydney San Francisco

ACADEMIC PRESS, INC.
111 Fifth Avenue, New York, New York 10003

United Kingdom Edition published by
ACADEMIC PRESS, INC. (LONDON) LTD.
24/28 Oval Road, London NW1 7DX

Library of Congress Cataloging in Publication Data

Argyris, Chris
    Inner contradictions of rigorous research.

    (Organizational and occupational psychology)
    Includes index.
    1. Research––Social aspects. 2. Science––Social
aspects. 3. Social action. I. Title. II. Series.
Q180.55.S62A73   306'.4   80–17327
ISBN 0–12–060150–8

PRINTED IN THE UNITED STATES OF AMERICA

80 81 82 83   9 8 7 6 5 4 3 2 1

To Phillip
with admiration and love

Contents

Preface

This book comes at a time when scholars are giving increasing attention to making social science more applicable. A smaller but growing number of social scientists are also seeking to use social science knowledge to provide maps that would lead to more liberating alternative ways of life.

Both groups appear to agree that applicability will be enhanced by the presence of at least three conditions. The first is that attention should be paid to observing everyday life activities so as to understand the ecological context within which human action occurs. The second is that sound observation requires theory to inform its design and to interpret the results. As Lewin pointed out, there is nothing as practical as theory. The third condition is that we use methodology that assures us that the results are credible and that we are not fooling ourselves. While there are a variety of views on what is proper methodology, I believe it is safe to say that the majority of social scientists hold to an empirically rigorous methodology that shows a high degree of internal and external validity.

Embedded in these three conditions are several implicit assumptions that should be made explicit. The first is that the knowledge produced by social science researchers is additive. We shall see that this assumption, which lies at the heart of most research activity, is rarely fulfilled, a well-documented point seldom taken seriously by empirically oriented researchers.

A second assumption is that there is nothing inherently contradictory within the three conditions mentioned previously. One purpose of this book is to suggest that the methodology of rigorous research developed to enhance the internal validity of the knowledge produced may not only detract from its external validity but may also detract from its internal validity.

Another assumption is that social scientists should study the universe as it exists (or more accurately, as we conceptualize it to exist). This book will suggest—as its second purpose—that such a focus makes it less likely that social scientists will produce genuine alternatives, or identify some of the innermost mechanisms by which the status quo is maintained.

Both of these purposes focus on inner contradictions, contradictions that exist when mechanisms designed to achieve a state of affairs also produce counterproductive states of affairs. For example, rigorous methodology may facilitate and inhibit internal and external validity. Or, studying the world as it is will not provide a complete picture of the world as it is.

While the operative scope of these inner contradictions is not clear, what seems relatively certain is that they apply in those relationships where human beings are interacting with each other (face-to-face) and where they are embedded in a larger social system for which they are acting as agents. This analysis is limited to these conditions.

Literature from personality, child development, individual testing and selection, industrial engineering, group dynamics, communications research, leadership, intergroup relations, and bureaucratic and organizational structures is explored to illustrate that most results provide an incomplete and nonadditive picture of the status quo and reinforce it by not considering alternative worlds.

A beginning step is taken to develop some of the foundations of an "action science" that can be used to understand the status quo, to develop new alternatives, and to be applicable in both domains. The approach begins with the assumption that research must produce knowledge that is falsifiable (which in turn implies a concept of causality) and elegant (that is, increasing comprehension with decreasing number of concepts and untestable assumptions).

The approach departs from some of the more traditional views by placing heavy emphasis upon (relatively) observable data, upon the development of normative models in order to create a dialectical inquiry, upon concepts with low precision and relatively high accuracy, and upon closing the information gaps that necessarily will exist with intervention.

The book is written for social science researchers who are interested in developing more applicable knowledge as well as in offering society alternative universes. It will be especially relevant for social and behavioral scientists who are conducting research in applied settings.

I should like to express my gratitude to John Musser and the General Service Foundation for supporting a portion of a year's sabbatical during which I wrote this book. Professors Clayton Alderfer, Lee Bolman, Richard Hackman, and Donald Schön have given me much helpful advice. Mrs. Judy Galper helped enormously in the typing of the manuscript.

CHAPTER 1

Introduction

The primary purpose of my research has been, and continues to be, to provide knowledge and skills with which people can design a higher quality of life (to be defined throughout the book). I have been especially concerned with such issues as changing values and actions, with designing social systems that are more effective and efficient, and with focusing on difficult or yet omnipresent human issues such as conformity, low trust, games of survival whose price is a lower sense of integrity, and double binds.

Most of these problems tend to be basic to the fabric of society, to the sanity of individuals, and yet they are frequently undiscussable by the parties who create them. Why do individuals create such problems when they so overwhelmingly abhor them? Is society or are organizations the culprit? Or are people programmed to create these problems even if they prefer not to do so? My research suggests that both alternatives may be the case.

Anyone who tries to conduct research in field settings is continually impressed with the complexity, emotionality, and pressure that exist in everyday life. Compounding this problem is the fact that few people have either the material resources or the time to understand, as well as they wish, the setting in which they must act.

How do people go about trying to make sense out of the complexity they face? Donald Schön and I have been trying to answer this question. It appears to us that people have theories of action that they use to design and implement their values, attitudes, and actions. The values and attitudes are always related to the theories that people espouse. Many of their most important actions, as we shall see, are rarely related to their espoused theories. People apparently may hold values and attitudes different from those that they actually use when they take action. Not only may there be a discrepancy between espoused theories and actions (an old idea), but people may use theories of action of which they are unaware and over which they have little control.

There is another interesting aspect concerning these theories. There appears to be a large variance in the theories in which people believe, a large variance in how they behave, but almost no variance in the theories that they actually use. More about this and other related issues in Chapter 2.

Social scientists may also be said to hold theories of action about how to conduct research. They, too, tend to have a variance of views about the nature of rigorous research; they, too, tend to vary their research strategies; and they, too, tend to utilize a similar theory to inform their actions. In Chapter 3, I hope to show that the theory individuals use to make sense out of, and to manage, their everyday lives is consonant with the theory of action (but not necessarily the espoused theory) that the scientists employ when conducting rigorous research.

If the theories of action that are used in everyday life are congruent with the theories of action used to conduct rigorous research, then would this not enhance the applicability or external validity of the research results? The answer appears to be yes and no. It probably enhances external validity for the more routine issues; it inhibits the external validity for the nonroutine and more important issues.

The problem is that the theories people use to design and take action have embedded in them features that, as we shall see (1) inhibit the production of valid information; (2) inhibit effective action, especially for the threatening, nonroutine issues; and (3) make it unlikely that the actors will be aware of these consequences. The features that are embedded in the theories that inhibit the production of valid information for the difficult issues also exist, I hope to show, in the theories that inform the production of much of the rigorous research. Hence, if there is congruence between these theories that may lead to a high external validity for research findings, there is also the probability that scientific research will contain the same threats to validity as those that exist in everyday life and that researchers will be unaware of the degree to which this is the case.

In Chapter 4, I suggest that the congruence between the theories people use in everyday life and those used by the researchers may result in social science research becoming unrealizingly limited to the service of the status quo. This possibility especially concerns those social scientists who believe that the purpose of social science should be not only to understand and predict but also to generate new and liberating universes. In Chapter 5, I try to document how the social scientists, even some who are concerned about creating alternative universes, provide advice to the citizenry that remains within and reinforces the status quo.

Although I raise questions about the methods of rigorous research, this is not a polemic against empirical research. I adhere as strictly as I can to the underlying notions of science, namely: public disconfirmability, some notion of causality, and the idea of elegance (i.e., theories that have the greatest comprehension with the least number of concepts and untestable axioms). I adhere to these features because they help to guarantee that social scientists will not knowingly strive to kid themselves or their fellow citizens; that social science knowledge will always be put to continual test; and that social science knowledge will be usable under on-line conditions.

The latter point is especially important in defining the domain of this book. I am focusing on the *knowledge that people can use to design and execute their actions in face-to-face relationships, ranging from dyads to complex systems.* This inquiry, therefore, is not directly relevant to neurologically or physiologically based mechanisms over which people have little control. Nor is it directly related to social science knowledge designed to define policies for society or any subsystem. Those policies—as long as they remain policies—are espoused theories of action. It is the gap between the policy and the effective execution or implementation of it that is of special concern in this book.

An outline of the purposes and features of action science[1] is presented in Chapter 6. These features are designed to overcome some of the inner contradictions embedded in rigorous research methodologies as well as the apparent compulsion for social science research to be limited to the status quo. In Chapter 7, I present the reasoning processes of action science as well as several primitive examples of action science models. Needless to say, Chapters 6 and 7 represent only the briefest outline, and the ideas are very primitive. The brevity and primitiveness are primarily due to my ignorance and limited experience. I believe that new models for social science research should be developed in parallel with actual research. Chapter 7 not only indicates how far I have gone but, more importantly, how much more research is needed.

1. I believe that Dr. William Torbert was the first to use the term "action science." W. R. Torbert, *Creating a community of inquiry: Conflict, collaboration, transformation* (New York: Wiley, 1976).

Reactions to the Perspective

I have had an opportunity to discuss my position with patient and helpful colleagues. Their reactions are germaine because they may capture the concerns of some of the readers of this book.

1. Philosophers of science (e.g., Kaplan, 1964) provide a definition of a scientific method that is broad enough to include the one explored in this book. Hence, from the point of view of gaining acceptance, would it not make sense to emphasize that the ideas in the book fit under the expanded view of normal science? Why create an antithesis when it is not needed?

I would be glad to take whatever strategic position increases the likelihood that the ideas in this book will be taken seriously by empirically oriented social scientists. In my limited experience, however, many practicing social scientists tend not to take philosophers of science seriously. The question is how to alter the practice of empirical research, that is, how to alter what is actually going on where researchers are working. To repeat, the action science perspective that I present is congruent with these basic features of normal science, namely, causality, public disconfirmability, and elegance. The differences will be found to exist in the technology for producing valid knowledge, the meaning of precision and accuracy, and the ultimate purpose of scientific inquiry.

2. Increasingly scholars are raising questions about the applicability of scientific knowledge. They are already struggling to find ways to make applied research more acceptable in the scientific community.

I am aware of the increasing interest in the applicability of research. However, I should like to differentiate several approaches being taken.

First, there are the thoughtful social scientists who are trying to find ways of making social science more applicable by making it more likely that scholars (especially younger ones) will find it more attractive. These scholars write articles admonishing their peers to take on more applied interests. Many of them design courses and experiences for graduate students that focus on conducting useful applied research. For the most part, these scholars appear to conceive the problem as decreasing the barriers to the conduct of applied research (Altman, 1976; Bloom, 1975; Cronback & Suppes, 1969; Deutch & Hornstein, 1975; Heller & Manahan, 1977; Kiesler & Turner, 1977; Lazarsfeld & Rietz, 1975; McGuire, 1973; Ring, 1967).

I support these efforts. However, many of these scholars do not appear to view the existing technology for the conduct of rigorous research as being a barrier to the applicability of knowledge.

There is a second group of social scientists who are questioning the technology of rigorous research and its relevance to everyday life. Some of them are suggesting that a more historical dialectical approach is required (Asplund, 1972; Gergen, 1978; Mitroff & Kelmann, 1978; Normann, 1973; Sampson, 1975, 1977; Zuniga, 1975). Others are making similar suggestions but appear at times to add a Marxist ideology (Israel, 1972; Moscovici, 1972; Zuniga, 1975). Nevertheless, both subgroups appear to be asking for more fundamental changes in research methodologies than are being recommended by the first group.

The second group takes the position, as I do, that all descriptions of reality are normative because social reality is an artifact. When we make *is* statements about the universe, they are statements about how the universe "expects" us to behave. This is not a new perspective. As Asplund (1972) has pointed out, the old masters in sociology (Durkheim, Pareto, and Weber) intertwined descriptive and normative views to the point that it was, "impossible to remove the moral factor without distorting the meaning and changing the nature and quality of the test [p. 260]." I believe the same is true for the old masters in psychology such as McDougal, Freud, and Lewin. As Asplund concludes: "Whereas modern positivistic science has tried to keep theory and practice apart, classical social science was both theoretical and practical [p. 261]."

Both perspectives should be supported and expanded. They will help to create an ongoing dialectic which, in turn, may provide us with more illumination about how to get from here to there. Peter Warr's plea for a more human psychology (1973) and his "aided" experiments may be a way to begin to bridge these worlds. In an aided experiment, the investigator is an observer and change-maker. The investigator is himself a variable because he may have to encourage, inform, persuade, while at the same time he is studying his chosen situation (Warr, 1977, p. 4).

I also agree with members of this group who argue that not only does normal science (Kuhn, 1970) methodology distance itself from the basic features of life but it also develops knowledge that reinforces that status quo. There are few, if any, liberating alternatives produced by normal science methodology because the theory of action implicit in the conduct of rigorous research is consonant with the theory of action of most individuals; that is, it is consonant with the status quo. I do take the normative position, along with scholars such as Habermas (1972) and Moscovici (1972), that the aim of knowledge is not only to systematize that which exists but also to invent that which does not exist as yet (Moscovici, 1972). Indeed, I hope to show that by creating a dialectic between the existing and nonexisting worlds, one learns more about the inner structure of the status quo.

3. Conducting research that combines diagnosis and re-education takes a long time, can be very expensive, and may require teams of social scientists. Hence, action science may be difficult to implement.

Action science does take longer because the re-education of individuals and systems may require several years. This more longitudinal imperative, however, can be, as I hope to show, an advantage in that it will provide opportunities for repetitive tests of hypotheses and simultaneously increase the external validity of the findings.

As to expense, I believe that the cost of action science is significantly lower than that of many normal science projects. But if the cost ever were to become as high or higher, it would not be a problem, for the clients would probably be willing to bear the costs because action science would also be of value to them. The problem of competent action science is more one of where to find the competent people than where to locate the money.

Some readers may wonder if being financed by the client does not increase the probability that the researchers may be inhibited in the questions they can ask and the confrontations that they are able to mount on the underlying values and assumptions. Elsewhere I have tried to show that the empirical data do not support this fear. For example, researchers financed by the National Science Foundation and the National Institutes of Mental Health develop theories of organization that remain within the values of traditional management theory. Yet, researchers in the same field who have been paid by management have developed theories that are significantly more confronting of management values and assumptions (Argyris, 1972a). It is ironic but true that the social scientists who have confronted management are significantly more respected by top executives and administrators than, for example, industrial and testing psychologists who remain within the criteria defined by the system.

4. A fourth reaction to my position is also a practical one: It is difficult to get access to ongoing group and organizational settings where it is possible to observe and tape record and where it is possible to develop individual and organizational re-educational activities.

There has been a big change in the last two decades in the openness of people at the top. I do not know of any highly competent action scientist who is lacking in opportunities. Indeed, there are quite a few who are able to utilize their status to help younger researchers gain entry. In my experience, the key issue is the ability of the researchers to deliver on their promises and not to be frightened by powerful people who become defensive on having their root values confronted.

5. Many of us are not trained to conduct action science research; does this fact not make my argument unreasonable?

I agree that it is more difficult to conduct research where one does not have unilateral control, where the researcher is expected to be of help in overcoming real problems yet is not expected to succumb, and is not respected if he does, to the anxieties of clients trying to learn.

Field research and intervention, or "aided experiments" as Warr calls them, require a rather high degree of competence in dealing with stressful issues, on-line confrontations, and crisis requests. They also require a more explicit theory because, if the researchers are to deal with emotionally laden and tough issues, it is important that they be able to draw upon a relatively clear and comprehensive theory of individual and system as well as a map of how to get from here to there.

The issues of entry, competence, and resources are valid, but they may also be self-fulfilling. It may well be that as the researchers' action science competence increases, the entry possibilities and resources will also increase. It is my belief that opportunities that make it possible for doctorate and postdoctorates to add to their maps and skills need to be designed. The experience to date is that as competent people become available the opportunities for research are easily located. Their freedom for inquiry is as great as or greater than that they would have if they were conducting normal science studies with no intervention phase envisaged.

Reflecting further on these dialogues with my colleagues, there appeared to be a consistent sequence of objections. First, the audience appeared to take sides. There were those for and against the position. Those against the position first attacked it as being antiscientific. But, as Donald Campbell pointed out in a taped debate with the author at Northwestern University (November 1977), the core of this approach is experimentation. The approach is more a new theory of learning, suggested Campbell, than a plea against the experimental method, broadly conceived.

Next, the questioning by the audience reflected their concern that I appeared to be asking researchers to become more normative and less descriptive. I responded that my position was that description of reality was the first step in all research. However, all descriptive statements are also normative, and all normative statements must be subject to public disconfirmability.

The attention then tended to turn to financial and time costs. As these concerns were alleviated, the discussion always took a more personal twist. Researchers spoke about their preferences to separate understanding from action, about their fears of encounters that were likely when intervening, about fears of lack of skills, of being manipulated, and of being rejected.

The core to a long-range solution of the problem resides, I believe, in the deeply held attitudes, fears, values, preferences, and skills of researchers. It is these features that probably influence us to become researchers in the first place. We probably select the professional role of researcher in order to live within these personal constraints. If this be the case, then the unfreezing and re-education that will be necessary will not be accomplished by books but, however, by carefully designed learning experiences. Books like this one may, however, make it clear why such learning experiences are necessary.

CHAPTER 2

The Individual and the System[1]

The very way we choose to describe human nature and social systems depends upon the purpose of the description. The purpose of most social science research is to understand, to explain, and to predict individual and system behavior. The outputs of such research are usually in the form of generalizations that describe the empirical relationships among the variables being examined. These patterns of empirical relationships can be formulated as models or, eventually, theories.

It is the thesis of this book that the purposes of science must go beyond understanding and predicting. The essence of individual and social system activity is action. Action is behavior whose meaning is constructed by the actors and that is designed to achieve intended consequences.

The proper role of social science is to produce knowledge that informs human and systemic action. Such knowledge requires valid propositions about the relationships among variables (understanding and explanation) and evidence of their validity (prediction). But it goes beyond these requirements in that it purports to generate propositions about how to effect intended events. Knowledge for the purpose of understanding a particular phenomenon can be quite different from that required to understand the same phenomenon in order to effect specified events. For example, maps that executives develop to understand and predict problem-solving activities with their subordinates when they are dealing with difficult issues turn out to be quite different (indeed, they even can be contradictory) from the maps they create when they have to show the maps to their

1. In this chapter I draw heavily on the work by Donald Schön and myself (Argyris, 1976b, 1976c; & Schön, 1974, 1978).

9

subordinates or, more importantly, when they have to use these maps themselves to manage the same problem-solving activities (Argyris, 1976a, Argyris & Schön, 1978). I have previously described how the maps that top news executives developed to deal with hiring a particular controversial news executive and with a cabal among the reporters to take over the paper were quite different from the maps they created and used when these events actually took place (Argyris, 1974a).

Individuals

Let us begin the descriptions of the nature of human beings with the axiom that they are meaning-creating, action-taking organisms. Designing and taking actions to achieve intended consequences (conscious or unconscious) and monitoring to learn how well the intended consequences are being achieved are basic life activities. The environment in which these two basic life activities occur is much more complicated than the information-processing capacities of human beings (Simon, 1969).

If individuals are to remain sane, they must make their world manageable and controllable. There are several ways to do this. First, people may delimit the scope of the environment to which they pay attention by constructing or enacting their reality (Weick, 1969). Unlike Weick, however, we believe that people design and create the meanings to which they will attend. The individuals accomplish the construction of their reality through the use of theories of action. Theories of action act like executive computer programs that can be used to generate subprograms to fit unique situations. Theories of action are theories of design and of execution of action (Argyris, 1976b; Argyris & Schön, 1974).

But if people faced continually different environments every time they wanted to act, effective action would be very difficult to manage. The second activity, therefore, is to create systems that, when in operation, can constrain and control the variance possible in human action. These systems acquire a life of their own which makes it possible for them to remain stable while the individuals can come and go (Argyris & Schön, 1978). The systems acquire a life of their own because individuals choose to give them these supraindividual properties. Individuals choose to give systems these supraindividual properties in order to make life manageable or in order for them to be effective human beings. Hence, the age-old philosophical problem: To be free is to actively select the constraints on our freedom.

Individuals with their theories of action combine with systems (with their systems' theories of action) to create an order that is more manageable and lawful. The order also increases the probability that individual and system events will be determined, that is, that they will be causally determined. Human beings may now seek systematic patterning of the consequences of their actions.

The reader may have noticed by now that the requirements for effective human action are similar to the requirements for conducting scientific research. For example, scientists create their own meanings to make the environment manageable; they create temporary social systems (e.g., experiments) in order to meet the requirements of producing systematic knowledge. The constraints on processing information and managing life that exist for human beings also exist for scientists. The interesting question is how scientists qua scientists have resolved this basic problem.

Scientists have created a rigorous methodology to inform them how to solve it. This rigorous methodology has embedded within it a theory of action that is similar to the theory of action most human beings appear to hold. A difficulty arises, as we shall see, because the theory of action most people hold is counterproductive to inquiry that scientists value. This may be one reason why many of us who study human behavior may not be significantly more competent in our daily lives than those less informed by scientific knowledge. The scientific knowledge (even though more rigorous) may simply inform nonscientists of a theory of action that they already know and use *and* that is one of their major problems.

Let us return to the observation that scientists and human beings may have the same information-processing capacities and challenges in designing their actions.[2] However, let us now turn our attention to the nonscientist and say that most people act as scientists, albeit "naive" scientists, in order to make sense out of life.

Describing individuals as naive scientists identifies us with a social psychological-sociological-anthropological approach with an emphasis upon cognitive features of life. It also indicates a principal bias of social scientists. We describe human beings as naive because they do not use the rigorous technology we as scientists use. I should like to

2. Included in this perspective are Bandler & Grinder (1975); Berger & Luckmann (1967); Broadbent (1971); Bruner, Oliver, & Greenfield (1966); Cicourel (1973); Geertz (1973); Heider (1958); Kelley (1955); Kelley (1971); Lewin (1951); Miller (1956); Polanyi (1967); Salancik & Pfeffer (1978); Schutz (1967); Simon (1969); Watzlawick, Veavin, & Jackson (1967); Weick (1969)*; Weizenbaum (1976)*; Wexler & Rice (1974).

*For a thoughtful review of the psychological features see: Daniel M. Wegner & Robin R. Vallacher, *Implicit psychology*. (New York: Oxford University Press, 1977).

argue a somewhat different perspective. The technology of rigorous-
ness currently followed by normal science contains within it threats
to validity and serious limitations to applicability. The characteristics
of sloppiness and vagueness that characterize human design and action may lead to less precise but more accurate, and hence more
effective, human action. If this is true, then we may be "naive," and
the everyday citizen (including scientists when they act as citizens)
may be wise.

Let us begin by asserting that people hold maps in their heads
about how to design, implement, and monitor their actions. These
maps contain propositions not unlike those used by normal science,
for example, "If you want to motivate people to perform, then pay
them well and inspect their output closely." However, few people are
aware that the propositions or theories they use to take action are
not the theories they explicitly espouse. Even fewer people are aware
of the theories they do use. The conclusion is not simply that people
do not behave according to their *espoused theories*. If people have
theories-in-use that are the source of the design and the implementation of their actions, and they tend to be unaware of their theories-
in-use, then how can they manage their behavior effectively?

It is possible to conceptualize the theories-in-use that people hold.
Let me first introduce Model I. The components of Model I include:
(1) the *governing values* or *variables* that human beings strive to
satisfy; (2) *the behavioral strategies* that they use to take action yet
satisfy the governing values; and (3) the *consequences* of these actions on the *behavioral environment*, on *learning*, and on *problem-
solving effectiveness* (Figure 2.1).

Human behavior, in any situation, represents that solution most
consistent with people's governing values or variables. The four most
prominent governing variables identified to date are: achieving the
purpose as the actor defines it, winning, suppressing negative feelings,
and emphasizing rationality.

Human beings associate behavioral strategies with their governing
values or variables. The primary strategies are to control unilaterally
the relevant environment and tasks, and to protect themselves or
others unilaterally. The underlying behavioral strategy is control over
other people. Although people vary widely in how they control
others, using concepts whose meaning is defined and controlled by
the action is one of the most powerful ways to achieve such control.

Unilateral control inhibits candid communication and can produce
defensiveness in the actor and in others. Defensiveness is an act of
protection. Model I theory-in-use informs the actors how to design

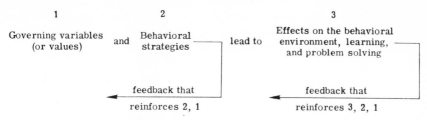

FIGURE 2.1. *Components of a theory-in-use.*

and use defenses unilaterally, no matter whether it is being used to protect themselves or others.

The purpose of a defense is to protect individuals by maintaining or reinforcing their immediate construction of reality. When the threat is not too great and the vulnerability not too high, individuals are able to maintain their immediate construction of reality yet remain open to being confronted. However, when the vulnerability and threat are high (i.e., they have no available map to deal with the situation as it currently exists), people will seek strategies that defend them from further threat.

These microtheories-in-use, which are typically created early in life, cannot be used to deal with present environmental reality accurately. But that is not their purpose. The purpose of these defenses is to protect the individual. In order to protect themselves, individuals must distort aspects of the environment and of themselves to maintain a sense that they can deal with the world competently. Such distortion can vary in scope and depth. It is also usually coupled with defenses designed to keep the individuals unaware of their defensive reactions.

The more people expose their thoughts and feelings, the more vulnerable they become to the reactions of other people because the others are programmed with Model I theories-in-use that require them to win and not lose. Inquiry without the requirement for action minimizes the threat from public exposure. Inquiry also minimizes the likelihood that individuals may expose aspects of themselves to themselves because the inquiry tends to be at the level of espoused actions and beliefs, not at the level of theories-in-use.

Action facilitates public exposure of the espoused theory and the theory-in-use. Therefore, action calls into play the defense structure of individuals, and that in turn may trigger the defenses of the social system in which the actors are embedded. The defense structure modifies and reduces the scope of attention paid, and the space of free movement available, to the individuals.

It cannot be too strongly emphasized that the distinction between espoused theory and theory-in-use is *not* the distinction between beliefs, attitudes, and actions as Chemers and Fiedler (1978) suggest. Making this distinction misses the fundamental point that a theory-in-use is the theory that informs the actions; it is not the actions themselves. There can be a wide variance in actions, but so far we have found almost no variance in the theories-in-use. If behavioral strategies (or actions) contain the genotype meanings, then the theory-in-use is the executive program that produces the behavioral strategies. Or, an operational definition of a gimmick is action based upon a theory other than that which one actually holds.

Model I is a model of *single-loop learning*. Single-loop learning is any detection and correction of error that does not require changes in the governing values or variables. This means that the use of Model I seriously limits the actor's learning capacity, especially when the issues are important, ambiguous, and threatening. It is precisely under these conditions where learning is critical that single-loop learning is not likely to be effective.

The reason for this ineffectiveness may be made clearer if we think of conditions that may inhibit or facilitate the detection and correction of errors.

Knowledge that

Facilitates error	Inhibits error
Ambiguous	Unambiguous
Unclear	Clear
Inconsistent	Consistent
Incongruent	Congruent

The more the problem being dealt with contains information whose features approximate the left ends of the continua, the more likely it is that errors will tend to occur. If the information about a particular issue is ambiguous, unclear, inconsistent, and if the problem is a threatening one, then given the governing values of Model I, the actors will hesitate to confront the ambiguity, lest they embarrass others and themselves. People programmed with Model I theories-in-use, who are dealing with difficult threatening issues, will therefore tend to reinforce the ambiguity and inconsistency of the information. This tendency to reinforce the conditions that facilitate errors are *primary inhibiting loops* to learning. They are "built into" individuals and they have important consequences for the systems people create and maintain.

The System

What kinds of learning systems will people create when they are participating in a group and/or acting as agents for families, schools, government bureaus, municipal entities, hospitals, etc.? Briefly, they may be described as O-I learning systems (see Figure 2.2): that is, systems that build upon, but conform to, Model I (Argyris & Schön, 1978).

The first feature of organizational learning systems is the primary inhibiting loop just described. People programmed with Model I will create primary inhibiting loops even if the system in which they were embedded were to encourage them to do otherwise. (To date we have found few learning systems that encourage inquiry that goes beyond Model I constraints.)

The primary inhibiting loops of the O-I learning system lead to a set of *secondary inhibiting loops*. They are created by: (1) the systematic blindness of people using Model I to their impact upon others and to the degree to which they are limited to single-loop learning; (2) the competitive win-lose dynamics; (3) the interdepartmental rivalries; and (4) the organizational politics or games played by people to protect themselves. These factors combine to increase the probability that however much ambiguity, lack of clarity, inconsistency, and incongruity exist in the information about a given problem, they will be reinforced and strengthened.

Primary and secondary loops lead to deception, lying, hiding, and other types of protective behavior. Such behavior is punishable in most organizations. Hence, the primary and secondary loops have to be camouflaged, and in order to ensure survival, the camouflage has to be camouflaged. These layers of camouflage are in themselves acts of deception. They will act to keep information about threatening issues ambiguous, vague, inconsistent, and incongruent, thus strengthening the primary and secondary loops as well as each individual's Model I theory-in-use.

The result is a condition where *double-loop learning* is highly unlikely. Double-loop learning is the detection and correction of error that requires changes in the governing values of Model I and O-I; such changes are not required in single-loop learning. For example, detecting and correcting errors in win-lose dynamics, or in the intergroup rivalries, are examples of single-loop learning. Refining the games people play or redesigning the camouflage are also examples of single-loop learning. Double-loop learning occurs when the actors examine the governing values that lead to win-lose dynamics, intergroup

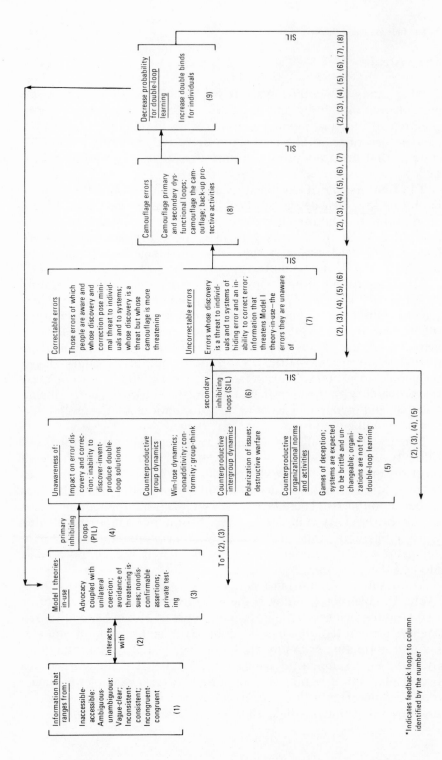

FIGURE 2.2. *Model 0-1: Organizational learning systems that inhibit error detection and correction.*

rivalries, and camouflage, with the purpose of reducing their undiscussability. Double-loop learning would most probably lead to the reduction of these actions. There can be conditions under which win-lose dynamics, etc., are functional. For example, confronting actors' reasoning processes can, under certain conditions, lead to win-lose dynamics *and* more valid information. Hence, the key criteria in double-loop learning are that the phenomena be discussable and the resulting alterations be related to changes in the governing variables.

Double-loop learning is unlikely in practice because such actions could destroy the O-I system. It is ironic but true that people come to believe that what is necessary for more effective problem-solving (double-loop learning) is also dangerous and unthinkable. We have found that most "mature" systems contain the paradox: The very actions needed to correct error can make the situation worse, thereby enhancing error.

Under these conditions people resign themselves to the belief that systems are not for double-loop learning. This resignation may make life easier for those participants choosing to be uninvolved and minimally responsible. They create a double bind for those who choose to be responsible and involved in the health of the system. If they demonstrate and criticize the O-I learning system, they run the risk of opening up the organization's Pandora's box. If they hide the issues, they violate their own sense of integrity and responsibility.

Models II and O-II

Our research suggests that in order to begin to change O-I learning systems, individuals must first learn how to double-loop learn themselves. There is no way to bring about the use of Model II simply by changing the environment. Recall that people construct their reality and that they typically construct it with Model I. Hence, they have to be helped to learn Model II before they can take advantage of environmental and societal changes to encourage the development of Model II and O-II learning systems.

It is not easy to learn Model II because people who are programmed with Model I: (1) think they have the skills to behave according to Model II but do not; (2) unrealizingly inhibit their own and others' learning (because the only theory-in-use they have is Model I); (3) create O-I learning systems during their learning seminars, thus reinforcing the factors that they are trying to overcome; and (4) become frustrated with the slowness of the learning and the high degree of interdependence that is required.

The governing values or variables of Model II are valid information, free and informed choice, and internal commitment. These are not themselves opposites of Model I governing variables. Similarly, the behavioral strategies required to satisfice these values are not the opposite of Model I. For example, Model I emphasizes that individuals are expected to be articulate about their purposes, goals, and so forth, and simultaneously to control others and the environment in order to ensure achievement of their goals. However, in Model II, the unilateral control that usually accompanies advocacy is rejected because the typical purpose of advocacy is to win. In Model II, articulateness and advocacy are carried out in ways that encourage others to confront the actor's views and, where necessary, to alter them. The goal is to produce the most complete, valid information possible in such a way as to maximize the participants' internal commitment to their position. Every significant action in Model II is evaluated in terms of the degree to which it helps the participants to generate valid and useful information, including relevant feelings, and to solve problems so that they remain solved without reducing the level of problem-solving effectiveness.

The behavioral strategies of Model II involve sharing problem solving with those who have competence and information as well as with those who may be relevant in deciding or implementing the action, in the definition of a task, or in control over the environment. Face saving is resisted because it is seen as a defensive counterproductive activity. Any face saving action that must be taken is planned jointly with the people involved, with the exception of individuals vulnerable to such candid and joint solutions.

Under these conditions, individuals would not tend to compete in making decisions for others or in outdoing others for self-gratification. They would try to find the most competent people for the decision to be made and would try to build viable decision-making networks in which the major function of the group would be to maximize the contributions of each member so that, when a synthesis was developed, the widest possible exploration of views would have taken place. Finally, if new concepts were formulated, the meaning given to them by the formulator and the inference processes used to develop them would be open to scrutiny by those who were expected to use them. Evaluations and attributions would be the result of directly observable data after the concepts were used. Also, the formulator would feel responsible for presenting evaluations and attributions so as to encourage open and constructive confrontations.

If the governing values and behavioral strategies just outlined are used, then the degree of defensiveness in individuals and that within, between, and among groups should tend to decrease. This would act to decrease the primary and secondary loops, making it possible to confront ambiguity, lack of clarity, and inconsistency in a manner of inquiry that would reduce these features of knowledge and increase the probability for the detection and correction of error.

Summary

The key purpose of life is to make it meaningful. The more effective we are in making life meaningful, the greater our sense of competence and confidence. The greater our sense of confidence and of competence, the higher our self-esteem. The higher our self-esteem, the lower our vulnerability under stress. The lower our vulnerability under stress, the more likely that we can manage our lives effectively.

We continuously invest life with our meanings. This is another way of saying that we enact (establish, create) our world, be it in the organization, at home, or in any other setting. Enacting is a very complicated process. It involves at least the following: (1) discovering problems; (2) inventing solutions to the problems; (3) producing the solutions; and (4) evaluating our effectiveness by checking for errors and correcting them.

Because every situation is unique, the possible meanings are infinite and cannot be known ahead of time. This makes life unmanageable unless corrective action is taken. In practice, we make life manageable by limiting the number of meanings that we consider appropriate. We do this as individuals by developing a theory-in-use. Therefore our theory-in-use is our design of how and what to discover-invent-produce-evaluate in life. Our theory-in-use is our master program for how to design and implement more specific subprograms in specific situations.

But even the specific situational theories-in-use (subroutines) that we design cannot be complete. The amount of information that would be needed to design a complete subroutine would be enormous. Therefore, individuals will always face information gaps. The way to close an information gap is to be able to produce effective on-line inquiry with others. Under the latter condition, we may encourage others to solve problems, but the way we respond to their participation will provide cues to the others as to whether or not we are seeking to control and to win.

A second major mechanism by which we make life manageable is to socialize others into theories-in-use that are similar to ours. We accomplish this objective by creating learning systems that reinforce our theories-in-use. So theories-in-use combined with learning systems make life manageable.

But there is a price we pay for the manageability acquired in these ways. We limit the scope and depth of the learning that we as individuals, and our organizations, can do. For example, it is not possible for individuals to design meanings that are not embedded in their theories-in-use. This means that people cannot discover-invent-produce actions that are beyond or violate their present theories-in-use. (The same is true for organizations.)

People cannot knowingly design to create error. To design an error would be to expect a mismatch; an expected mismatch is not a design error. To produce an intended mismatch is an example of a match between the actor's expectations and the outcome. Such a condition of match is not an error. Design errors are only unintended mismatches.

Yet it is an observable fact that people produce errors. One way to explain this puzzle is to hypothesize that when individuals produce errors they are unaware of this fact. But what causes the unawareness? It appears that one cause is related to the nature of skill. People must be skillful if they are to go through the stages of discovering a problem and then inventing and producing new actions under on-line constraints. What do we know about skillful action?

1. It is economical, effortless, and on target because people have internalized a set of rules. These rules must be consonant with their theories-in-use. (Remember, no one can produce actions incongruent with their theory-in-use.)
2. In order to adhere to the rules and use them in an on-line manner, people must have accurate cues as to when the rules are, and when they are not, required.
3. There are two sets of cues individuals utilize. External cues come from the environment. Internal cues come from their inner experience. But individuals' inner experience is organized by their theory-in-use. Hence, whatever theory-in-use individuals hold, that is the one they will use to create the rules for producing skillful action and for identifying the internal cues as to when the action is appropriate.
4. No theory-in-use is adequate for every situation. As pointed out previously, there will always be gaps in our information. In order to minimize error, we must be capable of changing and

redesigning our actions as the external situation changes. But once learned, a theory-in-use acts to interpret external cues in a way consistent with the theory as it exists. This makes the theory-in-use resistant to change and the actor unaware of the need for change.

The very fact that skillful behavior is both tacit and automatic inhibits conscious reflection on, and alteration of, programs of skillful action. Thus, incompleteness, and therefore the probability for error, are intrinsic to the nature of skillful behavior in a Model I world.

Skills enhance the conditions for error because, when individuals behave skillfully, they also tend:

1. To be blind to incipient errors that have not yet become large enough to be identified by their internal cues or to be unignorable by other people (in which case the others might give us feedback).
2. To be the last to know about their errors and, hence, to feel blind and incompetent.
3. To be in the bind that, in order to learn new skills, they require new internal and external cues. It is highly unlikely that outsiders will supply the external cues unless the actor asks for them. But it is also highly improbable that the actors will ask, because their internal cues will not alert them to ask (Argyris & Schön, 1978). Even if the actors know that their internal cues are inadequate, it is not possible to shut them off because to do so implies that they have a new set of cues to put in their place.
4. To learn new skills by having new cues and to learn new cues by having new skills. This chicken-egg condition means that learning is not going to be neat and linearly progressive. Rather, learning will be repetitive and iterative and full of embarrassment, confusion, and failure. It also means that individuals will have to learn at their own pace.

Implications for Research

When individuals participate as subjects in research, they bring to the research setting their Model I theories-in-use, their predisposition to see and to create contexts that are congruent with O-I learning systems, and their Model I skills. These factors combine to make it highly likely that if their skills are not threatened in the research situation, then their perceptions and responses will be automatic and faithful to Models I and O-I. The probability that their skills will be threatened, as we shall see, is low because the research context generated by normal science is congruent with Model I and O-I and, in order to obtain high reliability for instruments, it is necessary that subjects be able to complete them with relative ease.

This argument has important implications for the design and conduct of research. They are:

1. Individuals may not be aware of important distortions in their perceptions, errors in their actions, and inner contradictions created by their theories-in-use. Hence, even if they wish to be "good" subjects, they may provide researchers with data that are unknowingly invalid. If social scientists are also programmed with Models I and O-I, then this may increase the likelihood that they will not be able to identify important distortions and inner contradictions (because they are programmed with them also). It is desirable, therefore, that research be designed and executed in ways that strive to minimize the features of Models I and O-I that set off these tacit and automatic threats to validity.

2. It is also important that research be designed and executed in ways that make explicit these tacit threats to validity. In order to assess threats to validity that are created by unrecognized distortions and inner contradictions, it is necessary to interrupt the automatic responses that people make in everyday life as part of the skillful actions they have learned. The way to interrupt the skillful actions is to show that they are no longer appropriate. In order to show this, one has to place research subjects in a situation where their Model I theories-in-use and the O-I learning systems are no longer effective. In order to accomplish that objective, the researcher has to make requirements of the subject so that skillful execution will require a different theory-in-use and a different learning system.

3. This interruption of skills must occur at the production phase of the experimental process. It follows that the individual will also experience the interruption in the discovery and invention phases.

Research whose effective execution requires that the subjects only *discover* their distortions and the inner contradictions is not adequate. We have found, as we shall illustrate in the next chapter, that people produce significantly different information about the same issue depending on whether the purpose for learning was discovery, invention, or the production of new actions. The last of these three requires understanding of the first two and provides the best guarantee for discovering threats to validity.

It is also useful, therefore, to design research that gives subjects the opportunity not only to understand or discover but also to invent and to produce solutions that require different theories-in-use.

CHAPTER 3

Inner Contradictions
of Rigorous Research

Four fundamental requirements of rigorous research are that the propositions produced be as much as possible: (1) descriptive of the social universe as it is; (2) precise; (3) unambiguous about causality; and (4) comprehensive in coverage and additive. In this chapter, I should like to show that, when individuals as subjects interact with the conditions researchers typically create to approximate these requirements, inner contradictions and threats to validity are created and that they not only go unnoticed, but that part of the cause of this unawareness is the requirements themselves.

Primary Objective of Normal Science

The primary objective of normal science is to describe the social universe as it exists. The first inner contradiction is that, if researchers focus primarily on describing the social universe as it is: (1) they will not be able to describe many of its important features; (2) their propositions will contain errors and be incomplete or inconsistent; and (3) these features will not be detectable partly because they adhere to the axiom of being descriptive. The contradiction is assumed to be relevant when the focus of our inquiry is upon knowledge that purports to be useful to individuals and systems in designing and taking action. In Chapter 2, I argued that most people hold Model I theories-in-use, that they are not effective in double-loop learning, and that they are blind to their degree of ineffectiveness. The blindness occurs because their actions are skilled and hence tacit, because others do not provide them with feedback about their impact, and because the Model O-I learning systems reinforce the blindness. As long as people interact in a Model I and O-I social universe, their skills will be "appropriate," and hence their blindness will not be confronted.

If the purpose of social science research is to describe the social universe as it is, then there is little likelihood that subjects' skills will be interrupted. This is the case because research will focus on Model I and O-I features of the universe (because that is the universe's overwhelmingly predominant feature) and, as we shall see later, because the theory-in-use of rigorous research methodology is itself congruent with Model I.

Subjects may make errors and/or produce a variance in their responses, but all of them are likely to be confined to Model I. In other words, if they produce error, they will not try to correct it by altering the governing variables of their theories-in-use or those of the learning system in which they are embedded.

It follows that propositions about how people or systems react when their governing variables are threatened and when their skills are counterproductive will rarely, if ever, be produced by conventional rigorous research. Yet such propositions are part of the social universe as it is. Moreover, they represent the domain of propositions that are of central concern to those who are interested in providing societal options that are significantly different from those that exist presently.

One way to produce this knowledge is to place people in situations where the skills they have mastered through acculturation are no longer effective and where the Model O-I learning system is no longer rewarded. But such conditions rarely exist in the world as it is. In order to create them, researchers must design new types of environments. In order for people to choose freely to enter them, they must believe that it is in their interest to do so.

A universe where Model II theories-in-use and O-II learning systems are valued would be an example of such an environment. One reason why people may wish to enter these environments is to learn how to overcome the inner contradictions and barriers to double-loop learning that are endemic to the social universe as it exists.

It is not, therefore, accidental that the examples of the inner contradictions come from instances where people have, for whatever reason, tried to create a social universe different from the presently existing one. For example, six company presidents were helped to learn Model II theories-in-use. They understood Model II, committed themselves to producing it in their actions, and dedicated themselves to the long learning process involved. Donald Schön and I developed a model to help them achieve these objectives that was consonant with much of the prevailing thinking about cognitive learning processes (Argyris & Schön, 1974). We specified how we could help people use their understanding of Model II to design new behavior, to discover the error in their designs, to design new solutions, to produce the new designs, to correct the error, etc. The implicit assumption in our approach was that motivated mature adults could discover, invent, and produce Model II behavior because they understood Model II and were motivated to learn it. We also assumed that, for highly motivated adults, learning it was primarily a matter of experiment and practice with the new behavior.

Neither of these assumptions proved valid. The difficulty was that people programmed with Model I tended to be unable to discover, invent, and produce Model II behavior *and* were unaware of this fact. Also, their fellow students were unable to help them in ways that would lead to progress in learning, and they too were unaware of this fact. Thus, we had a situation where each actor was unaware of her or his inability to discover, invent, and produce coupled with fellow students who would create O-I learning conditions that reinforced each actor's unawareness of how unhelpful they could be (even though they were motivated to help and thought they were doing so). The result was a state of unawareness on everyone's part, reinforced by an unawareness of the unawareness.

Another layer of unawareness was discovered when the executives attempted to use Model II in their organizations. Each had practiced his or her "back home" behaviors until he or she could produce them under stress and under varying conditions with subordinates. Yet when they tried to produce these behaviors in the actual "back home" situations, they learned that some of their own responses as well as those of others that they were sure would occur, did not, and others they were sure would not occur, did. These deeper features of the universe began to surface when the executives tried to move toward Model II. In order to do so, they had to overcome their automatic Model I responses. These responses were automatic because they were skilled. Being skilled responses, they were also largely tacit. Being tacit, they were not consciously focused upon by the actors; hence, they were automatic. Moreover, none of their peers could help them because they had helped to create an O-I system that rewarded the skilled responses and reinforced their automaticity (Argyris, 1976a).

In other words, the model that we had developed about learning in a Model I world was incomplete and naive, but we could not have discovered that until we placed people in a situation where their Model I skills and the O-I learning environment were questioned. Once we did this and began to learn about the automaticity of responses, about the unawareness, about the inability of peers to help, it was easier to see that, although people may understand Model II skills (e.g., advocating with inquiry, making disconfirmable statements), they could not produce them. The problem was that, even though they wished to move toward Model II, the only theory-in-use they had was of a Model I kind. This led them, beginning with their perceptions, to respond automatically in a Model I manner. They were locked in and were unaware of the fact.

There are also abundant illustrations of the same phenomena at the systemic level. Take the "alternative schools" that were fashionable during the late 1960s and early 1970s. Five cases were studied where the teachers and the students volunteered to join the schools; the curriculum and grading systems were jointly controlled; the charter was Model II; and the experiments failed. It appeared that a major difficulty was that the teachers thought that Model II was the opposite of Model I. If they could be nondirective, caring, and minimally competitive, then they could set the stage for progress. Some students felt the same way. They soon began to learn the difficulties of getting something done under a mode dominated by inquiry, caring, and nondirectiveness. A larger proportion of the students appeared to interpret the espoused theory of Model II to mean an oscillating Model I. They would let the teachers "have it" and expect the teachers to do the same. The individual now vacillated between opposite to Model I to oscillating Model I theories-in-use. Soon the schools developed O-I learning systems with all the intergroup rivalries, games, camouflages, and double binds commonly found in traditional organizations. This, in turn, discouraged the teachers and the students. The former withdrew; the behavior of the latter became more Model I; and hence a self-sealing process was created. Eventually all the participants felt that the system was failing and experienced a sense of helplessness about correcting the situation (Argyris, 1974b).

In other words, the teachers and the students wanted to create Model II and O-II organizations but were unaware that they could not do so. The "alternative schools" soon became Model I and O-I systems, a prediction that they could have made had they been aware of the foregoing reasoning. Some readers may point out that the examples actually illustrate that it is possible to study the unintended consequences of having skills interrupted.

Several responses appear relevant. First, the knowledge was produced unintentionally by human beings. They learned how they were capable of harming themselves after the fact and were unable to correct this. Under these conditions, we as social scientists would be relegated to studying these factors as, or after, people harm themselves. This places us in the position of profiting from others being hurt and of being reactive. We would study these counterproductive activities when others created them.

Experience to date indicates that most explanations of failures of "alternative schools" evolve from economic, legal, political issues and from the lack of clarity about objectives and how to implement them. Scholars lament the fact that in the early history of the schools, usually one or two people played dominant roles, and they did not know how to implement their objectives. These explanations are valid, but they remain within Model I assumptions, namely, if people were clear about their objectives and/or if people knew how to implement their objectives, there would have been more success. The question is why this was true for so many cases. What prevented people from correcting the situation once they realized what was happening?

Researchers themselves may also be wedded to the status quo (Model I) and, like the teachers, be unaware of this fact. For example, Fiedler (1974, 1975) has placed a great emphasis upon contingency: Different leadership styles are required for different situations. The first difficulty of this view is that all of the advice that flows from research is Model I advice. Attributions are made that are never tested, yet asserted as valid. Fiedler, Chemers, and Makar (1975) state, for example: (1) that a leader like General Patton could not change to become an effective leader of a sensitivity group (yet there are many such cases on record); (2) that it is best to recognize the situations in which the person is successful and unsuccessful and strive to avoid the latter while seeking the former (the individual cannot change); and (3) that the underlying reason for the leader to become more effective is so that he can get his subordinates to do what he wants them to do.

Fiedler, Chemers, and Makar (1975) also recommend deception and secrecy as well as the manipulation of anxiety in order to lead subordinates. For example, the authors of the manual describe approvingly an air force commander who had "close" personal relationships with his men. The latter's performance began to deteriorate. He diagnosed the cause as being that he had been "too familiar." As a result, he stopped socializing with the men. This, the authors assert, created anxieties in the subordinates. "These anxieties soon became translated into more careful work and greater efforts to perform good maintenance. . . . When a boss withdraws from social contact, he makes it difficult for the subordinate to assure himself of his boss's approval in a way except by good performance [pp. 2-8]." Hence, we have a theory whose fundamental axiom is contingency, recommending behavioral strategies whose theory-in-use is noncontingent.

A second difficulty is that, in order for leaders to determine the most appropriate leadership style, they must diagnose the situation as well as their leadership style. Instruments are provided for that purpose. The ones available presently have all the complications described in the next section. But even if this were not the case, it is well known that frame of mind influences the responses that people give. Not all conditions are equally effective in minimizing intended or unintended distortions. Hence a leader, in order to obtain valid information about the context, requires a particular context, namely, one that is favorable to inquiry, candidness, and honesty. These conditions in turn require trust, security, and low fear of being punished. We conclude, therefore, that the leader is in the difficult position of trying to create a condition for inquiry that is noncontingent in order to diagnose the contingent condition.

A third difficulty is related to Fiedler's pessimistic view about the alterability of human action. He recommends to the practitioners that they match the individual's style of leadership with the task and other conditions. One difficulty with this suggestion is that the conditions may vary within a given unit and over time. Does that mean the leader is to be moved in and out? Second, and more important, the theory takes a normative position on the unchangeability of human beings without data to support the position. I can agree with Fiedler that behavioral change seems difficult. But given the Model I and O-I features of the world, this is not surprising. Indeed, those who strive to go beyond behavioral change to change a theory-in-use are facing even more difficult problems. Before we tell the world that people are unchangeable, ought we not to study this assertion as thoroughly as we did the contingency conditions?

The issues that we have described are serious, yet not much attention has been paid to them until recently when these researchers attempted to write a book on how to implement their views. It is during the phase of implementation that the inconsistencies previously described surfaced. One wonders what would have happened if Fiedler and his co-workers, early in the program of research, paid as much attention to the use of their results as they did to producing the results. The reason this was not the case, I should like to suggest, was that they were following the axiom that normal science should be descriptive. Only after decades of descriptive research would they be ready to focus heavily upon application.

The Scandinavian Institute of Research contains leading scholars who are aware of the importance of implementation. Early in their history they questioned the axiom of describing the universe and ignoring normative research (Rhenman, 1973). From the start, they were interested in action research that focused upon double-loop issues (Normann, 1977; Rhenman, 1973).

One key aspect of their work is to discover the "dominating themes" of an organization and to explore their appropriateness. For example, in one organization they found:

Dominant themes	Appropriateness of themes
1. Top management thinking is based on the assumption of continued expansion.	1. The market has "matured" and expansion may be severely limited.
2. Every market is treated in the same way.	2. Different markets require different approaches.
3. The same structure is used for all businesses.	3. Different businesses require different structures.

The researchers then asked themselves: Why do these dominant themes not change? Why does top management not see the dysfunctionality of their dominant themes? The research team's diagnosis was that the president was a dominating leader. For his subordinates to question his dominating theme would be for them to run a risk. Part of the climate was to find scapegoats to explain the failure of the company (rather than to challenge the dominant themes). There was a tendency for the top to hide the real explanation of the difficulties and to hide the fact that they were hiding their facts.

The actions developed by the Institute team included:

1. Develop a report with a diagnosis that included enough of the president's view so that conflict and polarization between them and the president would be minimized.
2. Develop a new set of organizing concepts for the top to conceptualize reality. For example, they concluded that in a com-

pany where the president played such a key role, if they could
help him to diagnose himself validly and if they could give him
new concepts, then he could use these ideas to move forward.

For example, one consultant said that if they give the president
new and appropriate concepts, "We can trust him to take the right
steps." Another consultant added, "I think you are right. But we also
need to help others to see the situation . . . (we must) push them to
see the new ideas. . . . (we must) give them new insights." The first
consultant agreed, but wondered if such a strategy might not create
more internal top management problems between the president and
his subordinates.

If one were to examine the processes of thinking that these notes
suggest, it would appear that the Institute members acted congru-
ently with their espoused theories. They analyzed the dominant
ideas, identified their dysfunctionality, and suggested new ones.
However, they were faced with a dominating president who they believed might resist their diagnosis. His leadership style (or his theory-
in-use) was continually on their minds while developing a strategy,
but it did not become part of their overt strategy. For example, the
team members never chose to help the president become aware of his
theory-in-use related to leading the company. One reason that they
did not do so was that it was not a part of their intervention theory
(espoused or theory-in-use). If the intervention theory assumes that
people are able to alter their behavior if they are given new maps and
new languages, then the task of the interventionists is to develop
those maps and languages as competently as they can and offer them
to the client. The assumption is, given the right information, the
client "can be trusted to take the right steps." According to our perspective, this will not be the case. The president's theory-in-use is
Model I. Hence, he will tend to create primary inhibiting loops and
tend to be unaware that he does so. Whatever advice or maps are
given to the president, he will perceive them through the filters of
Model I and his attempts to use them will remain constrained by
Model I. Moreover, he will tend to be unaware of these incongruities
and limits, but his subordinates and interventionists will be aware of
them. However, both are programmed not to bring them to the surface.

The second reason why the interventionists may not have broached
these issues with the president might be their belief that if they focused on their client's dominating leadership style, he might become
so upset that he might not listen to their diagnosis. In my opinion,

the interventionists would probably be correct in assuming that the client could become defensive. But, with Model II skills, they should be able to help him deal constructively with the defenses and make progress in solving the important problems.

But what if the client chose to fire the interventionists? This is a risk which the interventionists should take. If the client is not able to deal with them in a way that he will learn, there is doubt in our minds about the quality of the relationship that he will create with his subordinates. These people, we may recall, have been the recipients of the leadership style. For many years they have been suppressing their reactions and, therefore, know that they have been withholding information from the client and deceiving themselves. It is doubtful that, under these conditions, insight into the dominant business themes will lead to the progress that is necessary.

In making the president's theory-in-use undiscussable, the consultants began to act the way that the president's subordinates acted toward him. Moreover, their strategy of "creating," "giving," and "pushing" the client to see the new concepts would place them in a dominant relationship with the president. They would then be in the difficult position of recommending to the president that he not dominate while at the very same time they would be dominating the president and the top management group. In other words, although the client's espoused theories differed significantly from those of the consultants, their theories-in-use were similar (i.e., of a Model I kind).

What would lead the consultants to utilize a Model I intervention strategy when they espoused a Model II strategy? One answer is that the consultants were unaware that they were doing so. A second answer is that, although the Institute espoused Model II strategy, its theory-in-use was Model I and its members tended to be unaware of the discrepancy.

Some anecdotal evidence that lent credence to both of these hypotheses was gathered and fed back to the members of the Institute. Two key members involved in the first case agreed immediately that the additional factors were key items. They wondered why, if they were aware of these factors, they did not include them. One response was that they did not know how to cope with these factors. They knew how to define appropriate dominant themes, but they did not know how to help people to discuss the undiscussable. This inability suggested the hypothesis that, if there were threatening issues within the Institute, the subordinate researchers would not tend to expose them candidly. Either they would describe them in abstract or oblique terms or they would suppress them. During an

all-day discussion among members of the firm, the younger professional researchers confirmed the hypothesis and gave many examples to illustrate their point. At another meeting, several other cases of serious communication problems among the professionals were brought up by the younger members. The underlying theory-in-use for dealing with these issues was to hide the potentially threatening information from the superiors. The superiors, not knowing the true situation, continued to act as they did before. This closed the loop and drove the issues even further underground. Hence, the Institute had its own vicious circles.

One way the younger professionals dealt with these unresolved issues was to hold private discussions among themselves (in groups of two or three). During these sessions they discovered that each had similar feelings but that no one had more information. Consequently, one of the dominant themes of such discussion was to attempt to analyze and second-guess the motives of the senior professionals. One such theme that began to develop was that the seniors wanted the junior professionals to conform to their image. These dominant themes, under the conditions previously described, tended to become self-sealing, so that whenever the seniors behaved in ways that were perceived as ambiguous, unclear, or inconsistent, the juniors tended to read into the behavior whatever would follow from the dominant themes.

The senior members espoused motivations that were the opposite of those described earlier. Indeed, there were many instances where the seniors behaved in ways that the observer inferred were consistent with providing the juniors more autonomy. Yet the juniors were misinterpreting these actions. Some of the key senior members were so intent on encouraging autonomy that they consciously withdrew from everyday management of client relationships. The juniors were partially concerned about the withdrawal because they did not feel as competent to deal with clients as they felt they should be. Given their lack of confidence and their increased sense of aloneness, they turned, as quickly as possible, to learning the perspectives and skills of the senior members. Hence, a situation arose where the juniors were striving to become like the seniors. The notion that withdrawal leads to autonomy has been shown to be commonly held by people with a Model I theory-in-use. The logic is: If I am controlling, then I will withdraw and leave the other more free. The assumption is that one alternative to Model I is the opposite of Model I. But, as we have seen, this is not the case.

In summary, the primary objective of social science research is to understand and predict the universe as it presently exists. An inner contradiction is embedded in this purpose because some of the most profound aspects about the universe cannot be observed unless we interrupt the social activity in the universe. In order to do so, we must develop models of universes that presently do not exist, produce knowledge about lawful behavior in those universes, produce knowledge about how individuals or systems can move from here to there, and create conditions under which subjects will choose to become participants in such studies. We have not been as aware of the inner contradictions and the requirements as is required for the production of complete descriptions of reality because of the blinders inherent in the subjects' and our Model I theories-in-use.

Another critical factor that reinforces the unawareness and the gaps described earlier is the distancing from the everyday action context that occurs through our attempts to describe reality as precisely as possible. We now turn our attention to that issue.

Descriptions of Rigorous Research

The descriptions of rigorous research should be as precise as possible. The task of rigorous science is to develop generalizations about individuals and systemic behavior that go beyond any single case. Normal science descriptions should be in the form of generalizations about invariant relations among existing variables. These propositions can be combined into models (and later theories) whose characteristics include (a) precise definition of the concepts; (b) explicit identification of the interrelationships among the concepts; and (c) explicit connection of the concepts with empirical reality through the use of coordinating definitions and operational definitions. The models should be as parsimonious as possible, combining comprehensiveness with simplicity.

The most frequent and valued strategy to achieve the foregoing characteristics in normal science is to quantify. "And the history of science, . . . may be said to be the development of the possibilities inherent in quantitative conception and measurement. Each new departure has been a fresh attempt to rid the world of scientific knowledge of whatever is incapable of quantitative statement and to discover methods of measurement less and less at the mercy of a particular observer and his situation [Oakeshott, 1966, pp. 176-197]."

The scientific method is, then, a quantitative method, and it is this because science is the pursuit of a world of stable, communicable and impersonal experiences (Oakeshott, 1966).

In order to assign a quantitative value to anything, one must define clearly the properties or features of the phenomenon to which the numerical value is supposed to correspond. The very process of identifying certain features clearly and unambiguously so that they may always be represented by a particular numerical value also requires abstraction. The processes of selection and abstraction basic to quantification therefore necessarily lead to meanings that are distant from the immediate empirical reality in which we are embedded. But selection and abstraction are also necessary for managing life whether one wishes to quantify or not. A theory-in-use involves selection and abstraction as well as the process of distancing ourselves from the empirical world in which we are embedded in order to be able to manage our lives. There are important differences, however, between the distancing required for research quantification and the distancing required for making life personally manageable. The latter distancing utilizes abstractions that are not precise yet they are accurate and are directly connective to the level of action, be it the individual or social system.

Cohen (1971) and Scribner and Cole (1973) provide insights into why this may be the case. All human beings are socialized to their particular culture. Successful acculturation occurs when the individuals have been taught to organize reality (which is an act of distancing) in such a way that they do not ignore the *particularistic, concrete* aspects of their culture. The teaching process in socialization is powerful, ongoing, and managed continuously by the socializers. Its power comes not simply from being omnipresent but also from the fact that the rewards and punishments used are related to the deepest personal features of our lives. For example, in internalizing kinship, people must understand the particularistic criteria in recruitment and in the evaluation of behavior. This is best expressed in the fundamental dictum that "your brother is your brother, and you must get along and cooperate with him, regardless of how you feel about him." The function of socialization is to prepare individuals "for responsiveness to particularistic criteria [Cohen, 1971, p. 25]."

Therefore, socialization focuses on getting people to understand and internalize the world in which they take action by connecting them, as much as possible, with the immediate, concrete, emotional realities of everyday life. People who, in the final analysis, construct their own reality are helped to shape the reality of the local or *action context* (i.e., where the action takes place) by the particular type of conceptualization and language learned through acculturation.

The conceptualization and language of the action context has identifiable properties. They include particularistic (a short ladder of inference), subjective, emotionally laden, and implicitly logical features, and the processes for disconfirming tend to be private (Argyris, 1977). The educational processes by which knowledge for action is learned tend to be highly context-centered. For example, the expectations for performance are phrased in terms of who the person is rather than what he or she accomplishes and are characterized by such "learning through looking" mechanisms (Cazden & John, 1971) as empathy, imitation, and identification (Scribner & Cole, 1973).

We can now see why William James called the action context a blooming, buzzing confusion. It is full of subjective, imprecise, overlapping meanings whose identification is made more difficult by the emotionality in which they are embedded. Yet this is the context with which all human beings must deal. How do they do it? First, they learn to do it over a long period of time, usually through the socialization processes. Hence, the problem of dealing with the action context is decomposed and dealt with piecemeal. As the individuals become more acculturated, they also learn the appropriate behavioral skills. As the learned behavior becomes skillful, it also becomes tacit. As it becomes tacit, it is no longer in immediate focal awareness. This does not mean that people lose touch with the meanings of the action context. Quite the opposite. They are aware of them, but they take these meanings for granted. It is precisely because they are able to take them for granted that they can operate effectively within the action context.

Social scientists, especially those with field interests, have long been aware of the taken-for-granted feature of much socialized action. Hence, it is standard procedure not to rely primarily on questionnaires or interviews that are limited to producing espoused-level information. It is common practice to observe the participants and then to ask questions. Geertz (1973) has provided excellent examples of how asking an informant a series of questions unearths several levels of description, all of which are valid. He called it "thick description." This thick description, which is so characteristic of the action context, tends to be missed or oversimplified by procedures to quantify data.[1]

In order to assign a quantitative value to an empirical phenomenon,

---

1. It should be pointed out that "thick description" does not include the description that is obtained by placing people in different universes and interrupting their skills.

one must define clearly and unambiguously a property to which the numerical value is to be coordinated. In our case, the properties are meanings. Most empirical phenomena at the action level contain clusters of meanings that are, as we have seen, subjective and difficult to replicate unambiguously in some objective manner. Nevertheless, it is necessary that one meaning be selected *and* that the meaning be easily reproducible with a high degree of reliability. In order to achieve these requirements, social scientists usually select from the cluster one meaning that is easily reproducible. If it is difficult to find such a meaning, then one can be created. This meaning is usually called the "operational definition." For example, the operational definition for "cohesiveness" (a very complex cluster concept) can be several surrogates, such as the number of times the word "we" is used.

There are two important results of this meaning-selection process. First, as Brunswick (1955) pointed out, variables are uncoupled from their natural cluster. Second, the individualistic, subjective, complex meaning that is in good currency in the action context is lost. We have created knowledge that distances itself from the action context in a way that makes it difficult for it to illuminate the action context.

Let us dig further into the problems related to distancing by examining the leadership studies of the correlational mode. A key research program has been the Ohio State Leadership Studies (Blum & Naylor, 1968, pp. 421-424; Fleischman, 1973; Korman, 1966). In order to develop a leadership behavior questionnaire, an original pool of 1800 items was selected and studied empirically. Several factor analyses were made that resulted in 150 items. Further refinement of the 150 items indicated two distinct groupings of supervisory behavior. They were labeled "Consideration" and "Initiation of Structure."

This inventory, like any other similar instrument, locates the subject's behavior on these two dimensions. A leader may be high on one and low on the other, low on both, or high on both. So far, we have an accurate description of the status quo. But what would happen if, for example, a supervisor wished to alter his behavior? Could he utilize the questionnaire to help him change? What is the relatively directly observable action context information that he will need if he is to alter his behavior? For the supervisor to be told that he is high or low on "Consideration" and/or "Initiation of Structure" is to give him feedback that is typically not based on observable behavior. Even the Leadership Behavior Description Questionnaire (LBDQ), which is filled in by subordinates or by others who have observed the supervisor, is made up of statements that are inferences from behavior.

Let us assume the supervisor is able to obtain a copy of the Leadership Behavior Description Questionnaire and that he examines the items with the highest loadings on "Consideration." The items are:

1. He expresses appreciation when one of us does a good job.
2. He is easy to understand.
3. He stresses the importance of high morale among those under him.
4. He makes those under him feel at ease when talking with him.
5. He is friendly and can be easily approached [Blum & Naylor, 1968, p. 422].

These items do not give cues regarding the actual behavior involved in "expresses appreciation," "is easy to understand," "makes those under him feel at ease." The variance of behavior that could be perceived to accomplish these may be very great. In one study, "friendly and easily approachable foremen" (upon observation) turned out to be foremen "who left the men alone and rarely pressured them" (Argyris, 1960). In another study "friendly foremen" took the initiative to discuss "difficult issues" with the men (Argyris, 1965). Lowen, Hrapschak, and Kavanaugh (1969, pp. 246-247), in an attempt to prepare scripts related to "Consideration" and "Initiation of Structure," found it difficult to understand precisely the behavioral content of these categories, especially "Initiation of Structure." They wondered about the applicability of the concepts in the evaluation and education of supervisors.

A second example of distancing in meaning can be found in the work of Dunnette and Campbell (1969), who conducted a thorough research study in order to develop a new career index for a particular organization. After a systematic series of research studies, nine dimensions were chosen to describe the relative effectiveness of managers. The items were primarily of the inferred category variety. For example:

"Maintains harmonious relationship with sales associates."
"Avoids and counteracts harmful turnover among sales associates."
"Exercises tact and consideration in working with sales associates."

There were no items that described behavior in relatively directly observable categories, so that the question arises, for example, how (in actual behavior) does an individual "maintain harmonious relationships?" Dunnette and Campbell are aware of these questions, and have attempted to make the instrument more operational by developing scales that have actual incidents defining the levels of effectiveness. But we are still unclear as to how a manager behaves so that he impresses a customer to buy more than he or she would ordinarily buy. How does he "smooth things over?" By withdrawal or by compromise? These can be significantly different behaviors.

There is another fundamental question. Distant knowledge that separates itself from the action context is usually concerned with truth. The knowledge to be used in action contexts is concerned, as we have seen, with truth (in the sense that it must be publicly disconfirmable) *and* effectiveness. The latter is the ultimate, and the former is the penultimate criterion in the action context. Distant knowledge leads the researchers to become unintentionally distant from the problems that they aspire to solve. For example, the Dunnette-Campbell research implies that withdrawal or compromise are effective behaviors. Yet Blake and Mouton (1969) contend that the strategies for being a successful salesperson (as identified by Dunnette and Campbell) may lead to long-run difficulties. For example, maintaining harmonious relations can be accomplished at the expense of quality of openness; being tactful and diplomatic can lead to a lowering of salespeople's levels of aspiration.

Another example is the list of the patterns of behavior involved in leadership as given by Stogdill (1974, p. 143):

- Representation—Speaks and acts as representative of a group.
- Demand reconciliation—Reconciles conflicting organizational demands and reduces disorder to system.
- Tolerance of uncertainy—Is able to tolerate uncertainty and postponement without anxiety or upset.
- Persuasiveness—Uses persuasion and argument effectively; exhibits strong convictions.
- Initiation of structure—Clearly defines own role and lets followers know what is expected.
- Tolerance of freedom—Allows followers scope for initiative, decision, and action.
- Role retention—Actively exercises leadership role rather than surrendering leadership to others.
- Consideration—Regards the comfort, well-being, status, and contributions of followers.
- Production emphasis—Applies pressure for productive output.
- Predictive accuracy—Exhibits foresight and ability to predict outcomes accurately.
- Integration—Maintains a closely knit organization; resolves intermember conflicts.

• Influence with superiors—Maintains cordial relations with superiors; has influence with them; is striving for higher status.

These definitions do not differentiate between types of theory-in-use. Does it make no difference whether the leader is considerate or reconciles conflicting demands through a Model I or through Model II theory-in-use? Is it not possible for a leader to tolerate freedom either by using Model II or by using the opposite to Model I? Yet the two theories are far apart in behavioral strategies and in consequences. Would it not make a difference if the leader were to maintain a closely knit organization through the use of a Model I rather than a Model II theory-in-use? What differences in behavior and consequences would occur if these behavior patterns were carried out in an O-I or O-II learning system? If one does not specify the theory-in-use, then how will it be possible to define how to educate leaders to achieve these patterns, or which to achieve, and how to unfreeze other patterns?

Dunnette and Campbell could respond to the question of their model by noting that the assessment of effectiveness is an empirical matter. If compromise or withdrawal are ineffective strategies, research will tell us so, and then the items can be altered. But where is research conducted but in the "real" world? If the real world is Model I, then the test will always be limited to a Model I world. If the tests are limited in this way, then not only is the supervisor maintaining the status quo but the research is producing knowledge that maintains the societal status quo, which feeds back to make the individual conclude that not changing may make good sense.

If the foregoing analysis is valid in the sense that citizens hold the same doubts and concerns as we do, then it is reasonable to hypothesize that they may come to the filling out of a questionnaire with these attitudes. The responses that people give in questionnaires and interviews are known to be influenced by the sense the questions make to them and by the degree to which they can profit from the results of the research. A question whose abstract definition appears to be distant from the subject's reality will tend to be seen at best as benign and at worst as annoying. Research results that are desirable to the subjects (e.g., learning about their leadership behavior) but whose applicability gap appears to the subject to be too great to overcome may also be annoying to the subject.

The subjects will tend to produce responses by using action context criteria and not distant context criteria. Hence, a questionnaire or interview that appears to them to be disconnected from their action context may also induce a sense of bewilderment. But if they wish to cooperate and because they probably hold Model I theories-in-use, they may be predisposed to withhold their bewilderment. They may also be unaware of their confusion. To the extent this is the case, their responses may be tinkering with the internal validity of the research.

But, if these distortions are not subject to further distortion, are we not describing valid behavior? The answer is yes, and therein lies the problem for three reasons. First of all, we are describing behavior that is unrealizingly distorted, and our scientific generalizations are, as is the actor, blind to the distortion. Second, it is blind spots like these that create many of the human communication problems that social scientists are trying to understand. It is one thing for subjects to be unaware that they are unaware of their distortion; it is quite another for scientific generalizations to contain the same ignorance. Third, subjects who wish to apply social science knowledge in order to become more effective or competent not only will tend to find it difficult to use the knowledge that is distant but also may find it dangerous because it is full of implicit distortions. At best, such knowledge may be used to maintain their status quo rather than to change it.

As Meissner (1976) and Taylor (1977) suggest, it is time that our research instruments reflect accurately the language of work. Meissner, for example, has suggested the limitations on verbal communication imposed by the technical constraints of the production process and has argued that working-class upbringing and experience limits the scope and complexity of verbal articulation. One result is that, when they are faced with a questionnaire or formalized interview, workers have to cast their responses in a literate code, one which they use with persons who do not normally share their experiences. Nearly three-fourths of over 3,000 industrial workers checked off "very satisfied" or "satisfied" in answer to the question, "How do you feel about your job?" Yet extended observations in the work place indicate employees' habitual griping, resentment of the boss, and ingenious arrangements for "beating the system."

A similar analysis can be made of the operational definitions utilized in the experimental leadership studies. In order to produce operational definitions whose ambiguity is low (and whose interobserver reliability is high), the researcher utilizes meanings that are questionable in the action context. Perhaps the most prominent example is Fielder's LPC measure. The reason this concept was used was that it appeared to be unambiguously definable (although doubts have been raised) and that it was empirically manageable. For the first several decades, the fact that the meaning may not have been directly usable by leaders was not of concern because Fiedler did not pay attention to this problem. However, recently he and his co-workers have published a manual on how to use the theory based upon LPC. As I have indicated earlier, the difficulties immediately surfaced when an action perspective was taken. Other examples include the string of leadership studies where the operational defini-tion of group cohesion was the number of times people said "we" or referred to the group.[2] In other studies, especially in schools, cohe-sion was measured in terms of statements about closures, friendliness, and warmth. All of these operational definitions can have the oppo-site meanings in action contexts. For example, teachers who tend to be uncomfortable with hostility may mask their low feelings of co-hesion and/or high feelings of rejection by using the terms for cohe-sion. Leadership has been measured by the numbers of times a person has spoken or by the number of people that seem to agree with the person's views. Yet, in a Model O-I world, that can be an effective game to neutralize leadership or, in more extreme cases, to get the leader in trouble.

Dale and Payne (1976) show that prestructured instruments can have important consequences on the quality and effectiveness of intervention. They suggest that prestructured instruments may act to prevent double-loop learning although they may be useful for single-loop learning. They also provide evidence that there may be a strong tendency for prestructured instruments to lead to authori-tarian manipulative interventions. The model of development they constructed focuses on three levels of awareness. The first two are existence (which concerns itself with safety, mastery domination, etc.) and relatedness (law and order, esteem of others, etc.). There is a great gap between the second and third level, which is growth (personal responsibility, self-set esteem, autonomous integration, etc.).

Dale and Payne (1976) point out that there may be significantly different conditions required for within-level (single-loop) and be-tween-level (double-loop) learning. The more one wishes to empha-size between-level learning, the more one requires instruments that: (1) present stimuli that are so novel that the subjects can recognize their validity (action-level validity) but cannot absorb them within

2. The early Lewinian studies used these operational definitions but did so, as I hope to show, in a profoundly different manner.

their existing patterns; (2) internalize the source of authority in the sense that the actors must not be able to assign the validity of the information to factors outside themselves; (3) provide maximum discretion as to what action to take; and (4) permit the actor to be in control of the monitoring process. These conditions can be shown to be rarely met by prestructured instruments. Hence, Dale and Payne conclude that such instruments may be most effective for within-level learning of the first two levels or stages of development.

The challenge is for basic research to discover instruments for double-loop learning that, because they are less structured, will be less precise *but* that should produce greater accuracy. Such instruments may have such features as being general yet personal; known by many yet subjective; accurate yet ambiguous in meaning. These features can give us clues to the research that is needed in order to illuminate how human beings are managing their worlds by combining less precision with greater accuracy. One is reminded of Von Neumann's perceptive generalization that an important difference between the computer and the brain is that the latter can operate accurately with a sloppy calculus and under conditions of a lot of noise (Von Neumann, 1958).

Lord Kelvin has been quoted as having said: "When you can measure what you are speaking about, and express it in numbers, you know something about it; but when you cannot measure it, when you cannot express it in numbers, your knowledge is of a meager and unsatisfactory kind; it may be the beginning of knowledge, but you have scarcely, in your thoughts, advanced to the stage of science, whatever the matter may be [Kaplan, 1964, p. 172]." This quotation illustrates a predominant belief among many social scientists. Indeed, those social scientists who are antimeasurement are so much so that they may ignore the valuable aspects of measurement.

The Kelvin quotation appears to be valid *if* the criteria for knowing are those that are congruent with distant knowledge. But is not the scientific method associated with distant knowledge? Yes, and the argument of this book is that such a method will produce research conditions that may be counterproductive to the generation of valid or validatable knowledge that is applicable by human beings or social systems in their respective action. Hence, another inner contradiction.

Let us recapitulate the position taken so far regarding relationships between precision and distancing. In order to quantify, it is important that the variables be stated in precise terms where each factor assigned to a particular quantitative value has one objective, easily identifiable, easily countable feature. This requires the uncoupling of a feature from a cluster of features. Hence, the theory-in-use meaning that exists at the action level is usually lost. The gain is in terms of generalizations that define the precise quantitative relationship among several variables. But because the gap between this precise but distant knowledge and the action context is large, the probability that the generalization can be used at the action level under on-line conditions is low.

There is a second problem related to precision. Much empirical social science research depends upon the existence of variance. If variance does not exist among variables, the quantitative technology available becomes irrelevant and the interest, on the part of many empirically oriented social scientists, is reduced. As we have stated in Chapter 2 and expect to document more fully in the next two chapters, we have found much variance in espoused theories and in actual behavior. There is, however, significantly less variance in the genotypic meaning (behavioral strategies) and almost no variance in the theory-in-use that informs them. If this generalization holds, then the variance that much of normal science is focusing upon is within Models I and O-I. If the variance is within Models I and O-I, then the generalizations that are produced are limited to that world. In order to test this assertion, science would have to create the conditions of a good dialectic. The good dialectic requires that another model that has significantly different governing variables and behavioral strategies be developed. But because normal science is descriptive and because Models I and O-I comprehend the I and O-I universe adequately, it is highly unlikely that normal science would concern itself with new and rare models.

As we shall see in the next two chapters, the lack of a dialectic and the unawareness of the restrictedness of much of the variance have profound effects on the applicability of science and the kinds of advice that it produces. The overwhelming number of generalizations are limited to a Model I and O-I world or to the opposite of Models I and O-I (the latter being illustrated by T-groups and personal growth laboratories [Argyris, 1967a, 1972a]). Moreover, the advice given reads, I believe, as if the foregoing is not the case. We will read (especially in the latter part of Chapter 5 and in Chapter 6) of scholars who imply that they are generalizing to a world whose features are congruent with Models II and O-II and of others who imply that Models I and O-I are necessary for social order. An example of the former will be the scholar who recommends the nonneurotic use of power as a good idea. He provides examples of such nonneurotic use of power that suggest a leadership strategy whose theory-in-use is to keep secret one's intentions while manipulating people. (An effective leader gets the subordinates to do what he wants them to do without their realizing his influence or, better yet, with their thinking that they are origins when in reality they are pawns.) An example of the latter view that Models I and O-I are the basis for social order will be the social psychologist who traces back the necessity for a Model I obedience to the nature of order in society.

If we are correct, why do these anomalies exist? This is an important question that requires much research. At this time, all I can do is hazard the following hypothesis based upon the research conducted by Schön and myself. Most social scientists hold a Model I (or the opposite to I) theory-in-use (although we may espouse a quite different theory of action). People who hold Model I theories-in-use also have Model I skills. These skills are internalized programs whose apparently effortless execution requires that the program remain tacit. Indeed, the actors can lose their skill by becoming conscious of the programs. Moreover, most of us live with others who are also programmed with Model I. Together we create an O-I world. Whatever little possibility there may be for the social scientists to become aware of these problems is reduced even more by the technology and the criteria for precision as well as by the kinds of generalizations that normal science values.

A priori Precision with Unilateral Control

The function of empirical research is to produce the knowledge that is needed for us to choose among competing theories or models. It is important that research be carried out in a way that minimizes the probable errors that are associated with these inferences. There is available a long lineage of advice about how to satisfy this requirement. One can begin conveniently with Mill. He defined several principles or canons about the conditions required if causality was to be inferred validly from empirical research. Two of the most basic canons are the method of difference and of concomitant variation. Cook and Campbell (1976, p. 225) define these canons to state that: (a) the cause must precede an effect in time; (b) the treatment or treatments have to co-vary with the effect, for if the potential cause and effect are not related, the one could not have been a cause of the other; and (c) there must be no plausible alternative explanations of b other than a.

Researchers and logicians have developed rules and procedures that must be applied if causality is to be inferred with minimal probability of error. For example, Stebbing (1943) identified these activities as follows: The research must formulate the question to be explored before the research is begun. The question should be precise enough to guide the inquiry. The problems that are complex should be decomposed into their component parts. Research can be conducted on each part, and eventually the results can be synthesized into a more complete understanding. All the conditions that can influence the outcome of the research should be identified and constantly monitored. The relevant factors should be varied one at a time. Whenever possible, the factors that are viewed to be irrelevant should be varied to determine the reality of such irrelevancy. The utmost safeguards must be exercised so as not to introduce unnoticed factors that may be relevant to the result.

Campbell and Stanley (1963) have pointed out that important errors may unrealizingly occur in social science research even if the foregoing advice is followed. These errors are threats to the "internal" validity of the experiment. Errors may be introduced by: (1) events that took place between the pretest and posttest, and when these events are not part of the treatment; (2) changes that would occur naturally as a result of the subject's growing older, wiser, stronger, etc.; (3) learning that may occur by taking tests or instruments several times; and (4) bias that can occur because of selection.

The responsibility for carrying out the rules and procedures lies clearly on the shoulders of the researchers. Thus, Festinger (1957) asserts that the investigators create the exact conditions that they want and in which they manage all the variables. The investigators create a setting where they can control rigorously the conditions so that they can strive to make an intended consequence occur (Zelditch & Hopkins, 1961). Weick (1965), in a review of the definition of a laboratory experiment, concludes that there are several commonalities, among which are the following: (1) The experimental events occur at the discretion of the experimenter; (2) there exist controls to identify sources of variation so that potential alternative explanations are minimized; (3) the experimenter determines the groups and the treatments to which the groups will be exposed, in what order, and at what time; and (4) the experimenter determines the measurements to be used as well as when they will be used. Edwards (1954) notes that rigorous research occurs when:

1. The research is deliberately undertaken to satisfy the needs of the researchers, and the pace of activity is controlled by the

researchers to give them maximum possible control over the subjects' behavior.

2. The setting is designed by the researchers to achieve their objectives and to minimize the possibility that any of the subjects' desires can contaminate the experiment.

3. The researchers are responsible for making accurate observations, recording them, analyzing them, and eventually reporting them.

4. The researcher has the conditions so rigorously defined that he or others can replicate them.

5. The researcher can systematically vary the conditions and note the concomitant variation among the variables.

These conditions are remarkably similar to those top management defines when designing an organization. Top management (researcher) defines the worker's (subject's) role as rationally and clearly as possible (to minimize error) and as simply as possible (to minimize having to draw from a selected population, thereby reducing the generalizability of the research findings); he or she provides as little information as possible beyond the tasks (thereby minimizing the time perspective of the subject) and defines the inducements for participating (e.g., a requirement to pass a course, a plea for the creation of knowledge, or money). Indeed, if Edwards's description is valid, the rigorous research criteria would create a world for the subject in which his or her behavior is defined, controlled, evaluated, manipulated, and reported to a degree that is comparable to the behavior of workers in the most mechanized assembly-line conditions.

In effect, researchers are required to be extremely precise by using a theory-in-use (not an espoused theory) that makes them as *unilaterally controlling* as possible. The central features of this theory are similar to the conditions created by Model I theories-in-use. We know, however, that Model I theories-in-use create defensive behavioral environments and that these environments, in turn, increase the likelihood of producing invalid information.

The consequences will vary depending upon the subjects' reaction to being on the receiving end of Model I treatment. For example, those who prefer to be dependent and submissive and who minimize their sense of personal responsibility may be good, indeed too good, subjects. They are too good in that they may be overly cooperative. Those who react negatively to being unilaterally controlled may become uncooperative and "negativistic subjects." (For a review of the relevant literature, see Fromkin & Streufert, 1976.) But if they react this way and they, too, hold a Model I theory-in-use, then they will tend not to communicate to the researchers their feelings, feelings that could influence the meanings they report in their questionnaire responses or in their behavior.

Some subjects become apprehensive at the thought that the researcher may be evaluating their emotional adequacy. They may react by becoming overly sensitive to the directions given as well as to the behavior of the experimenter (Fromkin & Streufert, 1976). Still other subjects may try to second-guess the researcher. They may play games of minimal involvement that consist of their producing a minimally acceptable performance, getting their subject fee, and leaving as soon as possible. There are even a few cases on record where student subjects have attempted to unionize to better their working conditions (Argyris, 1968).

All these consequences are reminiscent of the secondary inhibiting loops and the games described in Model O-I learning systems. It appears that the proposition that Model I conditions create Model O-I learning systems may also hold for the conditions created by rigorous research. According to Model O-I, if the subjects experience the research setting as ambiguous, inconsistent, vague, etc., and if these qualities are seen as related to key aspects of the research, then they will tend not to confront these ambiguities openly. If they do broach them, and if they are central to the underlying design (double-loop), then the researchers will tend to delay dealing with them because they cannot conduct rigorous research and change the underlying conditions in the middle of the experiment.

We may also predict that it will be the positively motivated or "good" subjects who will feel frustrated. The ones who are there to fulfill a request by a teacher or a superior, to obtain payment, or to fulfill a promise to a friend will not be particularly upset. Thus, the involved feel the double bind described in Model O-I. It is in the form of "if I broach the issue, I may upset the researcher or the other subjects in the experiment. If I suppress it, I will feel frustrated, and such feelings could influence my responses." The result may be that the involved and uninvolved subjects learn to distance themselves. They become "appropriately" responsive. But to do so means that the range of possible reactions to the experimental conditions will be limited.

Therefore the structure of rigorous research not only inhibits the potential for people to be proactive but also probably encourages the subjects' collusion with the experimenter to accept the role of being reactive. Perhaps this is why Allport (1969) found that much of social science research conceived of human beings as being reactive.

Consequences of Rigorous Research Procedures

Internal Validity

I believe it is possible to show that these features have important consequences for internal and external validity. In this section I will discuss their impact upon internal validity (did the experimental manipulation take hold as the researcher intended) as well as upon the degree of certainty with which internal validity can be ascertained if the foregoing argument is valid.

Let us begin by recalling certain assumptions and basic propositions of the theory of action perspective:

1. We share the view (with the many social psychologists and sociologists listed at the outset of this chapter) that it is important to understand the meaning of action to the actor and to the observer. Meanings and intentions are the causal springs of individually designed social action. In this connection, Ginsberg (1978) cites James Jenkins (whose work for decades was based upon an associationistic perspective) as having had to move toward the centrality of meaning when he later found that subjects recognized sentences they had never seen before if the sentences reasonably accurately described events that had been described by other sentences that they had seen (p. 107).

2. Menzel (1978) notes that different perspectives can produce different meanings. Our approach does not deny this possibility; it asserts that each individual (or system) can hold meanings at the espoused and theory-in-use levels. People programmed with Model I theory-in-use and embedded in O-I learning situations tend to have poor knowledge of the meanings they produce. Their ineffectiveness is partially due to their lack of competent reflection and to the self-sealing processes created by Model I. The lack of reflectivity and the self-sealing processes are, in turn, reinforced by O-I learning systems. Hence, individuals (and systems, through their agents) are not particularly valid reporters of their meanings. Indeed, when it comes to communicating threatening or double-loop issues, individuals' performance in producing and effectively implementing their intentions is not very high.

3. To complicate matters, people can produce different meanings for the same subject but for different purposes. Recall the presidents who produced different meanings for how they would deal with their vice presidents (and vice versa) when the purpose was to discover and inquire, different meanings when they attempted to invent solutions,

and significantly different meanings when they attempted to produce the meanings during the seminar through role-playing and simulation. To complicate matters even further, they produced different meanings when they attempted to produce their strategies with their vice presidents in the backhome organizational context.

4. These differences in meaning do not tend to occur as frequently when individuals are discovering, inventing, and producing actions that are congruent with their existing theories-in-use. In the case of the presidents, the gaps between discovery, invention, and production were not found until they returned to their organizations and tried to design and execute Model II behavior.

In this chapter, we have attempted to show that: (1) the conditions of unilateral control embedded in rigorous research procedures create, for the subjects, conditions of dependence, submissiveness, and short time perspective; (2) the abstractions required for precision and quantification tend to lead to instruments whose meanings are not based on the action context experienced by subjects in their everyday life (hence the meanings may be confusing, unclear, and ambiguous); and (3) the axiom that the purpose of science is to understand or explain while prediction and control are tests of our understanding and explanation leads to a social science of the status quo. The more the citizens become aware of this fact, the higher the probability that they will associate being a subject with helping to generate knowledge about the world as it is and not as it might be. This realization may have an explicit or tacit impact upon subjects' actions and responses.

All of the foregoing conditions may combine to create a sense of distancing between the researchers and the subjects. On the assumption that both are programmed with Model I, then we also predict that the dependency, submissiveness, short time perspective, status quo, and distancing will be undiscussable. Because rigorous research is also based on a Model I theory-in-use, the researchers compound the undiscussability of these issues during the research, for discussion could lead to questions about the design and about their unilateral control. Such a process could confound the experimental manipulation and lower the internal validity.

The probable impact of these conditions upon internal validity can be mapped as follows. The consequences previously described, coupled with their undiscussability, could lead people to misperceive the experimental manipulation and/or to unrealizingly distort what they report in instruments and during interviews as well as what they exhibit in their actual behavior as related to the way they understand the experimental manipulation.

One way to illustrate this point is to note first the inherent and irresolvable dilemmas in the deception designs of experiments that logically prevent unambiguous inferences (Ginsberg, 1978, pp. 99-100). A deception means that the researcher covers up the real definition of the routine and incidental behavior. The real definition construes the behavior as one that the subjects would avoid performing if they knew its real meaning to the research. The dilemma is that researchers can draw an unambiguous inference "only if the critical behavior of the subject actually represents an instance of (the researcher's) private definition; but if it does represent such an instance, and the subject sees this, he will respond disingenuously. If the subject does not see the investigator's private meaning of the critical behavior, then that behavior may not be an instance of the private definition, and if the behavior does not represent a clear instance of the private definition, how can we be said to have dealt with our variable of interest [Ginsberg, 1978, p. 99]?"

This dilemma occurs because deception is based upon censorship of issues that effect the researchers' control over the situation. But such censorship is endemic to all Model I theories-in-use and O-I learning systems. Thus, the dilemma of deception is created naturally by human beings in their everyday life. Model I theories-in-use lead to ongoing unawareness. Because the research conditions are consonant with Model I, it follows that the censorship and blindness that is endemic to Models I and O-I will now be affecting the subject. Under these conditions, we cannot know with adequate certainty the meaning that the experimental manipulation has had for the subjects because they themselves may not know. Recall that individuals programmed with Model I are not valid reporters of many of their experiences.

The reader may point out that one way to overcome these problems is to create control groups. But control groups are not an adequate response. A control group is itself designed in accordance with the procedures of rigorous research; hence, it too is Model I and, hence, the unilateral control, dependence, distancing, etc. It is these conditions that we have suggested can lead subjects to distort unrealizingly.

For example, the principal investigator of one of the more rigorous studies of T-groups reported that several female students told him that they were perturbed and angry at being subjects in his T-group experiment. They volunteered because the experiment was advertised as dealing with interpersonal and group issues. They became confused and angry when, every time they attempted to talk about these issues, the "trainer" steered them away to neutral issues such as baseball, dancing, etc. It was not until they discussed it with each other that they realized some of the students were in the experimental groups while others (including themselves) had been assigned to the control groups. That was why the "trainer" permitted them to talk about anything except what they came to discuss. Because the issue was undiscussable, they remained quiet (presumably to get paid). They also reported that they expressed their hostility by filling out the instruments invalidly but, of course, not saying so.

Nor are these difficulties overcome if the control group is one where no new condition is introduced. Natural ongoing control groups have Model I and O-I distortion mechanisms built into them. The planned control group simply reinforces the conditions of every-day life because it is designed on the basis of Model I and O-I.

To sum up, all these multilevel conditions for distortion of which the subjects are unaware make it very difficult to establish unambiguously that the behavior observed or that reported in instruments was not influenced by some third factor. The analysis does not purport to provide a compelling argument that such influences will always occur, but, as Cook and Campbell (1976) point out, the burden of proof regarding internal validity is upon the researcher.

External Validity

Fromkin and Streufert (1976) and Weick (1977a) suggest that the congruency between the experimental conditions and Models I and O-I may be translated into an opportunity precisely because so much of the world may be consonant with Models I and O-I. The research results would be more relevant because they have been generated under conditions that are congruent with the noncontrived "real" world. The external validity may be high.

There are several difficulties with this suggestion. First, recall that it is in the nature of the I and O-I world to limit and/or distort valid inquiry into its underlying, double-loop issues. Hence, science would be opting for a world that limits inquiry and understanding of critically important phenomena. Second, science also would be incorporating the forces that inhibit valid inquiry into its propositions and, in the case of double-loop issues, would do so unknowingly. What is the value of high external validity to science when this feature is incorporating the same systematic ignorance and unawareness as that in the world as it presently exists? Third, as we shall see in Chapters 4 and 5, one consequence of systematically incorporating the ignorance and unawareness is that research tends to remain in the service of the status quo. If the universe has built into it features that inhibit double-loop learning and if these features are unrealizingly included in our scientific propositions, then science will not be informative about liberating or double-loop options. Finally, as we shall see in Chapters 5 and 6, research that obtains its external validity from the fact that it incorporates the inquiry-inhibiting features of the present world can lead to advice that contains important inconsistencies. Recall, for example, Fiedler's illustration of an effective army officer being one who covertly manipulates people or, as we will read, the social scientist who equates the nonneurotic use of power with covert manipulation of people and appears to be unaware of this possibility.

Weick describes the heart of the issue: "definitions of the situation in rigorous research are *not* negotiable; if they become so, the resulting study is unethical [Weick, 1977a, p. 2]." The reason the study may become unethical is that if the researcher becomes more compassionate, the result may be experiments that are uninterpretable, hence unethical. I agree with Weick that it would be unethical knowingly to conduct experiments that are uninterpretable. But, as I hope I am showing, the interpretability of rigorous research is problematic because of the efforts of theories-in-use to achieve rigor. This is an inner contradiction that cannot be wished away by assuming that the present technology for rigor is the only technology that can be developed. The assumption may turn out to be valid but a conclusion about the issue should be based upon empirical research.

It is not coincidental, I believe, that the examples Weick uses to illustrate the problems represent the experimenter as moving from a Model I position toward Model II. The experimenter is pictured as masking "the desire to influence the subject (by) presenting an ambiguous set of demands which multiply, rather than narrow, the potential meanings that are imposed on the situation [Weick, 1977a, p. 2]." Such a covert strategy is Model I. In the next example, the researcher abbreviates the questioning of the participants and lengthens the amount of time spent trying to restore trust and repair damage. Weick is correct that this behavior could lead to alternative explanations not being discovered. The example he uses, however, is of a researcher who was Model I during the research and became "compassionate" after the research. Such role-playing, I believe, will build greater mistrust than trust. Such a researcher does not repair damage; he or she adds to it. We agree on the basic issue, namely, that research results must be interpretable and that alternative explanations must be made explicit. Not only does science require these conditions but so do the human beings who may use the knowledge that we produce.

I believe that the problem with Weick's argument is that it is based upon the assumption that rigor as defined by normal science is the only way that it can be achieved. I, too, am interested in rigor (i.e., where threats to internal and external validity are minimized). It is precisely because I have come to question the theory-in-use of how to gain rigor that I believe the interpretability of many normal science research projects is problematic.

Completeness

Embedded in the norms of social science research is the objective of knowledge becoming as complete as possible. Given the criteria described in the previous sections, variance among variables is the key to determining causality. This has led researchers to develop an impressive array of statistical procedures that have become hallmarks of rigorous research.

One result of this state of affairs is that social scientists are taught to look for problems where there is variance. Indeed, they construct their reality by focusing on variance. Data that manifest little variance are suspect. This is important in our case because, as we have indicated in Chapter 2, there is almost no variance in the theories-in-use people hold. Being acculturated to normal science norms, it took much unfreezing to come to the conclusion that constancy and consistency in a world full of variance may be a more important feature of life than variance itself.

In an attempt to seek variance, we may be focusing on the more phenotypic aspects of reality (behavioral strategies) and less on the genotypic (theories-in-use). Such a focus can, as we shall see, produce findings about relationships that are valid and massive in number. Their enormous number may almost assure their unusability under real-life conditions because they would be too difficult to store, retrieve, and utilize.

For example Mann, Indik, and Vroom (1963) have attempted to map the theoretically expected and empirically found relationships of the day-delivery unit and the night-sorting teams in a metropolitan plant at a particular point in time. They aspired to depict "the total systems of interrelationships [p. 2]" for both units, which in turn represented a subpart of a larger system.

Each map contains 39 variables and over 60 different empirical relationships. It appears highly unlikely that people would be able to store all the information in their brain and even less likely to retrieve it. But the maps could have served as external memories to which the subjects could refer when they needed the information. Assuming the maps might have been used as external memories, the question then arises as to their value for designing actions. Most of the correlations account for less than 25% of the nonrandom variance. There are a few that are higher, but those appear to be measuring almost the same domain. For example, there is a + .79 correlation between the station manager's participation in problem solving and the subordinates' reports that their opinions were requested.

The second problem is that most of the variables that might have been used to design behavior are stated so abstractly that they do not differentiate between theories-in-use. Also, many variables represent psychological states that are difficult to assess in an on-line manner (e.g., need for independence, authoritarianism). Still other variables are features that the actors could hardly influence (e.g., intelligence, education, age). These latter variables are as highly correlated with the other variables in the map as those that actors could alter. In other words, the uninfluenceable variables are as powerful as those that are influenceable.

The third problem with the map, one that is acknowledged by the authors, is that the territory the map depicts was susceptible to change. They emphasize that the maps are snapshots. The fourth problem is that these variables represent only a small part of the life space of individuals or the behavioral settings called "day-delivery" and "night-sorting." If the production, delivery, dispatch, and other functions were to be mapped, a terribly complex picture would emerge. The complete picture (assuming it had none of the limitations described earlier) would immobilize attempts to design action in an on-line manner.

Social scientists may appear unaware of the consequences of completeness and rigor even when they raise them implicitly. For example, Stogdill (1974) recommends the continued use of the "complex designs developed for investigation of conditional relationships [p. 425]." The simplest form that he recommends would require 300 manipulations (of 25 experimental and 6 criterion variables) if each of the variables were unitary (which Stogdill doubts is the case). He concludes that the work must be done but cautions that no one researcher is likely to investigate the relationships between more than a few of the variables. The interesting point from our view is that

Stogdill never asks about the impact of all that data upon the actor who wishes to be informed from social science. This research program by itself could lead to the publication of several volumes of findings.

However, when Stogdill (1974) reviews the literature he states:

> The above summaries indicate that a wide variety of factors contribute to emergence of the leadership role. The status, personality, and behavior of the leader himself; the size, structure, task, and composition of the group; the norms and goals of the group and the leader's identification with them; . . . [p. 415] . . . . All of these factors affect the leader, or the aspirant to leadership, in varying degrees, but it seems unlikely that he can be more than vaguely aware of their operation. Thus, it is not surprising that many individuals who attempt leadership find themselves bewildered by their lack of success. Nor is it surprising that those who obtain this status find the task difficult indeed [p. 414].

Here we see Stogdill informing the reader that there are many factors involved in the emergence of leadership, that it is difficult to be aware of them, and that it is not surprising to fail to be aware of them or to succeed by not consciously using them. The practitioner might understandably wonder about the value of social science research. Stogdill reaches these conclusions because he is following assiduously the rules of normal science. He is careful to identify the complexities involved, to be appropriately modest, and thereby to warn the reader against overreliance on the research to date. The point is that such conclusions and recommendations are embedded in the consequences of rigorous research. It is not a random event that, in most summaries of empirical research (including leadership), there is a consistent theme. As research results accumulate, their relevance and applicability seem to diminish.

So far we have been discussing the attempt by researchers to conduct research studies that produce knowledge that is as complete as possible. The same aspiration holds for an entire field of endeavor. One of the most fundamental assumptions in the practice of scientific research is that the results from separate studies will be additive or cumulative. Yet, as Finkelman (1978) has recently shown, with the exception of very few research programs (most toward the biological end of the spectrum), social science research is noncumulative. For example, the field of learning has dominated experimental psychology for four decades, yet he quotes Koch as concluding that there is little agreement on the definition of learning or, even at the crassest descriptive level, on the empirical conditions under which learning takes place. Stogdill (1974) came to a similar conclusion after reviewing the research on leadership.

Summary

The rules and technology developed to minimize threats to validity have included an emphasis upon descriptive research designed to understand and predict, which is guided by the Model I strategies of: (*a*) a priori precision; (*b*) accuracy that is unilaterally controlled; (*c*) meanings that are also unilaterally controlled; (*d*) distancing the researcher from the subject; and (*e*) minimizing the expression of information other than that intended by the experimental manipulation, which leads unintentionally to O-I learning systems that are counterproductive to the production of valid information.

These conditions are consonant with the Model I theories-in-use that subjects tend to hold. It is not surprising that they will respond with the Model I skills and competences they have. Many of these skills can lead to distortions of which subjects are aware (but make certain they do not communicate) or distortions of which subjects are unaware and cannot communicate.

These conditions not only influence external validity but also can influence internal validity, the quality that Campbell and Stanley call the *sine qua non* of research (1963, p. 5). The conditions of distancing and unilateral control may affect internal validity because they may trigger actions or responses to questionnaires that are related to the tacit Model I mechanisms that lead to unintended distortions. These distortions will significantly influence the answer to the question, "Did in fact the experimental treatments make a difference in this specific experimental instance?"

Finally, the conditions created to minimize threats to internal and external validity may lead to the unintended exclusion from our models of important qualities about the world as it is and make it highly unlikely that research will explore double-loop alternatives at the individual or system levels.

Implications

The technology for the conduct of rigorous research contains requirements that can create unrecognized threats to validity because it ignores the implications that were discussed in Chapter 2. Instead of designing research conditions that do not bring to the surface automatic Model I responses, we create research conditions that are consonant with Models I and O-I. This increases the probability that the unrecognized threats to validity embedded in Models I and O-I will become operative in our research context.

Instead of creating conditions that interrupt the Model I skills people have, we unknowingly act to reinforce these skills by constraining the purpose of social science research to describing and understanding the world as it presently exists.

Instead of creating conditions where individuals must *produce* a new set of skills, our research requires that they discover and (under some conditions) that they invent new solutions that are within the domain of Models I and O-I. Rarely, if ever, do we require subjects to perform in accordance with theories-in-use they do not hold. The distortions and inner contradictions that exist in the present world, and that do not surface unless people are required to produce new action, therefore will go unrecognized.

As a result, normal social science will tend not to be centrally concerned with conducting research that provides genuinely new alternatives (i.e., those that require new theories-in-use and new learning systems). Moreover, social scientists who are also programmed with Model I theories-in-use and who are embedded in O-I learning systems will tend to be unaware that their results may be counterproductive to the world of which they are part. I will discuss the former problem in Chapter 4 and the latter problem in Chapter 5.

Describing Reality and the Status Quo

So far, I have tried to illustrate how the technology of rigorous research may lead to distancing. The distancing, in turn, can inhibit the production of valid information and hence constitutes a threat to validity. In this chapter, I should like to step back to explore the almost axiomatic assumption that social science research should describe reality for the purpose of understanding and prediction. Embedded in this requirement, I will suggest, is not only an additional threat to validity but also a serious bias against research that may be described as emancipatory (Habermas, 1972). The argument put simply is as follows: If most people hold Model I theories-in-use and if most learning systems are O-I, then the requirement to describe reality will inevitably restrict the researcher's attention to reality as it exists—the status quo. Moreover, since Models I and O-I assure no learning of the double-loop variety, then it is highly unlikely that descriptive research might by accident lead to generalizations about new (double-loop) states of reality.

This argument does not imply that new options are not known. People advocate worlds whose properties are significantly different from Model I and O-I, worlds where, for example, double-loop learning and trust can be enhanced. These options are worth study if social science is to help human beings consider new alternative universes. To date the study of new options has been left by scientists to the politicians, to religious zealots, and to revolutionaries. Indeed, one way to disparage research on double-loop options is to characterize it as falling into one of these domains.

Cognitive Balance Theories[1]

I should like to begin an illustration of how the objective of being descriptive may lead to a science of the status quo by examining cognitive balance or consistency theories. These theories have been selected because they are central to modern social psychology. The theories make two important assumptions. First, cognitive balance or consistency enables individuals to predict accurately and thus behave more effectively in their interactions with others (Deutsch & Krauss, 1965; Secord & Backman, 1964). Second, it is assumed that there is a basic tendency for individuals to strive to reduce such imbalanced states as cognitive dissonance and inconsistency. Brown, in a review of several of these theories, concluded that they assume "human nature abhors imbalance" and "imbalance in the mind threatens to paralyze action [Brown et al., 1962, pp. 77-78]."

But why should imbalance be so abhorrent? One possibility is that in a Model I world, action to correct imbalance may be very difficult to take without violating the norms against discussing threatening issues. The individuals who attempt to correct an interpersonal incongruity may find themselves raising issues that have been hidden, discussing attributions that have been unilateral and covert, and experimenting with behavior that, in itself, is not supported by Model I. Under these conditions, imbalance or incongruity in interpersonal relations may well become a state to be avoided or reduced as quickly as possible.

A second reason why imbalance may be abhorrent is also related to the findings stated previously—that in a Model I world individuals tend to have a low frequency of interpersonal success. If interpersonal success is low, individuals in those systems may tend to have little confidence in themselves and others in solving interpersonal issues. If this is so, would not imbalance, incongruence, or dissonance tend to create anxiety within the actors? But because interpersonal anxiety is an issue of feelings and because expression of feelings violates Model I, the incongruence will tend not to be resolved effectively, and individual anxiety will tend not to be reduced; hence the abhorrence of imbalance.

Under these conditions, the basic assumption of cognitive balance theories that, given dissonant relations among cognitive elements,

1. This discussion of cognitive balance and attributions represents a summary of Argyris, 1969.

pressure will rise to reduce the dissonance and to avoide increase in dissonance (Festinger, 1957, p. 31), makes good sense. In other words imbalance-reduction theories are a valid model of how individuals in a Model I world would tend to behave given the experience of imbalance in interpersonal relations.

On the other hand, there is evidence that in a Model II world individuals may *value* inconsistency as a basis for learning. Instead of attempting to reduce dissonance, their strategy may be to maintain it or increase it in order to learn (Argyris, 1969, 1976b, 1976c; Argyris & Schön, 1974, 1978). Hence, the conception of human nature as abhorring imbalance may not be as valid as has been presumed. This possibility would not appear likely if one studied reality as it is because the research that led to new conclusions was based on the creation of learning environments that were rare events and whose existence would not be tolerated in a Model I, O-I world.

Attribution Theories

Another example may be found in attribution theory. A central concern of attribution theory is its attempt to account, in a systematic way, for a naive perceiver's inference about an actor. "The perceiver seeks to find sufficient reason why the person acted and why the act took on a particular form [Jones & Davis, 1965, p. 220]." How is this done?

During the course of interaction, Person A observes specific behaviors performed by Person B. At the same time, Person A has, from past experience, a storehouse of knowledge about behavior of people in general as well as personal knowledge. In order to be able to comprehend all the discreet bits of data and behavior, A has some scheme of organization that allows him to identify many instances of behavior as similar in some sense and to store them all under one category. The category may take the form of a trait that he attributes to a person who performs these acts consistently. Getting work done on time, meeting appointments, etc., may fall into the category of dependability, and anyone who performs these behaviors with him is probably seen as dependable. The attribution process is essentially a matching between observed behavior and categories or concepts supplied by the past experiences of the observer (deCharms, 1968, p. 283). How is this process conceptualized in the work of Heider, Kelley, Jones, and Davis? Jones and Davis (1965) state:

1. The perceiver is imagined as a silent observer [p. 223].
2. The perceiver's fundamental task is to interpret or infer the causal antecedents of action [p. 220].
3. The actor is not conceived of as equal partner; as an "active" information giver, interpreter, and inferer of the causal antecedents of his behavior. His primary responsibility is to behave. It is the perceiver's primary responsibility to perform the analysis and make the attribution [p. 221].

These assumptions contain two links to the "typical" (Model I) universe described previously:

1. The perceiver-actor relationship is similar to the unilateral, "one-way" relationship described in the Model I. It is the former's responsibility to "determine," "evaluate," "assign intentions," and "make decisions" about subordinates' behavior.

2. The model of the "silent" perceiver going through the attribution activities is congruent with the consequences derived from Model I. There is little openness, little sharing of motives, little expression of feelings, little consideration of others as resources for gaining knowledge about interpersonal relationships, etc.

The conditions under which attribution theory holds are Model I. Hence, attribution theory is a theory of the status quo.

An interesting puzzle results from the concept of information value, a key concept in attribution theory. "An event is informative if it is one of a large number of equiprobable events. It is uninformative if it is bound to occur [Jones & Gerard, 1967, pp. 264-265]." In-role behavior is not informative; out-of-role behavior is informative (p. 266). From a theory-of-action perspective, in-role behavior is highly informative because it indicates that people are designing and executing similar plans. To put it another way, in-role behavior may indicate that different people have found it useful to deal with the same or different roles with the same theory. This should be of profound interest to social scientists because it gives us clues as to how individuals may strive to manage their lives and to maintain social order. The behavior (phenotypic) may vary, but the (genotypic) theory-in-use may remain constant.

If we were to focus on the theories-in-use, we would also learn to get at the initial causes of effectiveness and ineffectiveness because they inform the design activities and the diagnostic activities of all human beings. The other unintended consequence of the assumption made by attribution theory is that it will lead to studies of differences that, once obtained, have no impact upon the theory that informs the behavior in the first place.

It is my hypothesis that the reasoning that led to the assumption about what is informative came from the assumptions embedded in the quantitative procedures utilized in most of social science. These procedures are based upon the existence of variance, without which they are not usable. Scientists require variance whereas human beings, embedded in it in their action context, attempt to minimize it in order to make their lives manageable and their social order stable.

Obedience

Milgram (1974) conducted experiments where people could be induced to shock innocent subjects as acts of obedience. Milgram points out that there are important differences between obedience and conformity. Obedience occurs in a hierarchy where a superior has the right to prescribe behavior, and it represents compliance without imitation where the prescription for action is explicit and tends to embrace obedience ("I had to do it because I was ordered to"). Conformity, on the other hand, occurs in a nonhierarchical situation where there is no right to prescribe behavior, and it represents imitation where prescription is often implicit and where conformity tends to be denied (Milgram, 1974, pp. 114-115).

Milgram (1974) places much emphasis upon the existence of hierarchy for social order. Hierarchy is omnipresent because it is necessary for survival. "Challenges to the hierarchy . . . often provoke violence [p. 123]." The reason that hierarchy is important is that without it social organization is not possible. Subunits are integrated into wholes through the use of hierarchy. People, Milgram concludes, "are born with a *potential* for obedience which then interacts with the influence of society to produce the obedient man [p. 123]." Without obedience, there is no hierarchy; without hierarchy, there is no order; and people know this from early in life, indeed, they may be born with this capacity.

The idea that confrontation of hierarchy could lead to chaos is predictable from a theory-of-action perspective. Confrontation will be destructive because it will probably come in the form of Model I. Agents of such systems will fight to smother confrontation because they know that strong confrontation can destroy the O-I system. But why need we limit ourselves to these conditions? What if it were possible to confront hierarchy without destroying it? What if it were possible to confront hierarchy so that it could be altered in a way that does not destroy the social organism? Then Milgram's view that obedience is necessary if our hierarchical structures are to survive is open to empirical inquiry, making new options available.

Model II theories-in-use and O-II learning systems make these possibilities realistic. They encourage confrontation, especially of the double-loop variety. In a Model II, O-II learning system, the subparts have information for system effectiveness that is not held by the more comprehensive parts. When Milgram uses the cybernetic system as an analogy, he appears to ignore that most such physical systems are designed so that the subparts do not have more knowledge than the more comprehensive parts. Milgram's analysis appears to be constrained by Model I concepts.

Another set of difficulties arises with the suggestion Milgram (1974) makes to break the "inbred" reaction to obedience when such obedience is harmful. His solution is composed of two basic strategies. The first strategy is to increase the forces that would undermine automatic obedience. For example, subordinates may magnify or enlarge cues of pain to make the pain of innocent people clearer. Or they may increase implicit retaliatory threats or give contradictory orders.

There are at least two difficulties with these recommendations. First, the people in power in a hierarchy defend themselves by not seeing, or may find ways to hide the cries of pain and the cues that innocent people are being hurt, and to blunt retaliatory threats and contradictory orders. Milgram's recommendations may well presume more of an open society than exists. *If* people wanted Milgram's suggestions to work, why would they permit the hierarchy to hurt innocent people in the first place?

Another difficulty is that all these recommendations remain within a Model I theory-in-use. Hence, causes for obedience are not altered. Indeed, they may be reinforced. If increased retaliatory threats, order, cues of pain, and concern for innocent people are to work in a hierarchy, someone more powerful than the actor has to support these actions and reward subordinates when they obey.

The second strategy is related to reducing the binding factors. For example, help people to be less polite, reduce their sense of obligation to live up to the expectations of authority, encourage them to withdraw, and become less absorbed with the task. The difficulty with these recommendations is that they encourage people to become more like the opposite to Model I. Such behavior enhances the threat to the hierarchy.

There is another alternative that Milgram did not consider, which is to help people confront the hierarchy without destroying it. But such a possibility would require the existence of people programmed with Model II and hierarchies containing O-II learning systems. But, if our research is correct, these skills hardly exist. It is understandable why Milgram would have difficulty in recommending them. But this becomes a self-fulfilling prophecy. If social scientists do not produce new viable alternatives, then citizens will not be able to produce new options in their lives. If new options such as Models II and O-II are not produced, then social scientists who focus on the world as it is will not make recommendations about situations that are to them, at best, rare events and, at worst, untested pipe dreams. However, they may be rare, untested, and pipe dreams because the social scientists continue to consider the study of such options as beyond their mission.

Personal Causation

It is interesting to juxtapose the Milgram study with one by deCharms (1976) and his associates that was designed to enhance personal causality. Whereas Milgram is concerned about challenges to the hierarchy, deCharms focuses on helping people constructively to confront hierarchy (in this case the hierarchy in school systems). But deCharms and his group also do not distinguish between espoused theory and theory-in-use. If I understand them correctly, their "new" model is consonant with Model I. If that is the case, then the people whom they educate to be "origins" should become more proactive within the Model I constraints. Such an education should reinforce the obedience-requiring features of the hierarchy.

Richard deCharms and his students attempted to induce a greater sense of personal causation in a group of inner city, largely minority students. Personal causation is an underlying feeling of purpose. People strive to be causal agents, to be the primary focus of causation for, or the origin of, their behavior (deCharms, 1968, p. 269). If our hypothesis about the omnipresence of Models I and O-I is valid, then education to increase personal causation should approximate double-loop learning, especially when it is administered to children of the lower socioeconomic classes of our society.

A careful reading of the study suggests that it may represent a method of helping children who act like pawns (in our language, the opposite of Model I) to become more the origins of their actions (more Model I). Asserting that it may approximate a Model I educational purpose is not to criticize the project, for that may have been its purpose. The objective of this analysis is to show how a theory that *espouses* aspects of Model II may lead to an educational experience that more accurately approximates Model I, and that the rigorous design of the research may have played a role in this consequence.

First, a word about the concept of being an origin rather than a pawn. The children and the teachers were taught that origins are people who take personal responsibility, prepare their work carefully, plan their life to reach their goals, practice their skills, persist in their work, have patience to achieve long-range commitments, check their progress, and move toward perfecting their skills (p. 74). Origins are people who show more commitment to task, more work-oriented behavior, more concentration and attention, and more interaction with better students and the teacher (p. 118). They appear to strive to achieve their purposes as they define them, to win and not to lose, and to strive to be rational in the design and execution of their actions.

Now let us look at the educational program. In the educational environment there was first a phase of self-study to help people assess their predisposition to be pawns or origins. All the assessment instruments provide espoused-level data.

The next phase was to give people experiences in being pawns and origins. These experiences were in the form of games and exercises reminiscent of those used in *n* Achievement education. The important feature for our purposes is that either the educational experiences are written, and hence produce espoused-level data, or they are games whose achievement requires skills that people already have (e.g., building blocks, tossing rings into a basket, walking blindfolded). The point is that none of these actions requires skills of a theory-in-use different from Model I, with one exception, the Family Control Role Play. Here three people role-played a typical problem experienced by the families of the children who participated in the experiment. Unfortunately no transcripts were presented from which we can infer how the role-players acted toward each other. However, there is one sentence that provides a clue: "Throughout the discussion the participants talked about the difficulty of transforming conflict situations into cooperative problem-solving endeavors (deCharms, 1968, pp. 53-54]." This sentence describes a condition that has been observed many times in educational programs where people are helped to learn how to deal with difficult interpersonal issues. Another relevant observation is that the children were taught to become more competent in competing with others, in competing with one's self, in striving to do something that no one has ever done, and in doing something that will take a long time but will result in personal success

(p. 68). Again, these qualities appear to satisfice Model I governing variables.

The teachers utilized a manual they developed to induce origin behavior. They used the manual in ways that appear to be contradictory to the concept of origin. For example, the teacher was assigning responsibility when she required the children to do something to the manual. She said, "the manual wants to know [p. 114]." Teachers also advocated clearly that to be an origin was better than to be a pawn, although they appeared to do that by asking the students which is better, to be a pawn or an origin (p. 114).

Ideally, the authors state, people who are origins are those who are sensitive to others and allow them also to be origins (p. 78). Here is a requirement closer to Model II. Yet I could not find exercises designed to teach people the skills required. To be an origin in such a way that others can also be origins would be a skill that, in our experience, few adults appear to have. The closest this program came to teaching these skills was when people were asked to help others. The origin gave help when asked and when it was needed (p. 58). Otherwise, origins provided people with freedom to build and to create. Here we have the conditions that approximate the opposite of Model I. Instead of people being controlled, they are left alone to build whatever they wish or to perform in the games according to their level of aspiration and skills.

It is important to recall that all the tasks required in the games and exercises were simple enough that the children had the skills to perform them. If they lacked anything it would have been the motivation to be an origin. This is an important difference from education for Model II. In our experiences, even wealthy, well-educated, powerful, origin-oriented adults do not have the skills required to double-loop learn and to behave according to Model II (e.g., advocate combined with inquiry). The difference becomes relevant because the skills of being an origin in such a way as to help others be origins would be Model II skills. If we are correct that the teachers and the students were at best Model I (some preferred the opposite to Model I, hence pawns), then we should find no examples of Model II behavior. We can report that we found no such behavior. Indeed, the children who scored high on origin before the education began were children who advocated, controlled others, and took charge—all behaviors associated with Model I.

It should be pointed out that the study was not conducted with an action science bias or Model II in mind. This brings us to the research methodology. Much attention was paid to following rigorous research procedures within the limits of the clients and the concepts. For example, to fill out questionnaires with predesigned meanings would place the children in a pawn relationship. Therefore, many of the instruments were open-ended projective instruments. Such instruments create an optimally ambiguous condition where people can write what they wish. The analysis of their products is usually done by a scoring system that is not subject to distortion of the results by respondents. This means that the ladder of inference from the directly observable responses to the judgments about origins and pawns is quite long. Projective techniques purposely distance themselves from their respondents. The assumption is that such distancing makes it more probable that people will answer with less distortion. The other frequently used method was participation in games and exercises. In these settings, performance could be relatively easily connected to people's theories-in-use. As we noted earlier, their theories-in-use appeared to be Model I.

Returning to Milgram's work, one can conceive of the deCharms study as illustrating Milgram's theorizing about how to break the "inbred" reaction to obedience. DeCharms educated people to reduce the binding factors. For example, the students became more proactive, took on more responsibility for their learning, confronted (constructively) the teachers, and showed more commitment to the task. On the other hand, deCharms did not educate the students to reduce their sense of obligation to live up to the expectations of authority, nor did he encourage withdrawal and less absorption to the task. Personal causation theory sees these three reactions as predictable under conditions of unilateral obedience but also sees them as ultimately self-destructive. If the child chooses to withdraw from learning, it is he or she who gets hurt.

Milgram also suggests that people might be educated to increase the forces that would restrain automatic obedience. For example, they may be taught to magnify or enlarge cues of pain, to make the pain of innocent people clearer, to increase retaliatory threats, or to give contradictory orders. I believe it is fair to conclude that personal causation theory does not focus on the latter two strategies for reducing automatic obedience. However, one might infer that people who become more origin-oriented would be less inhibited about challenging poor education and standing up for their rights. Again, if I understand deCharms's normative theory, origins would do this from a base of credibility, which is why they behave like origins. This means, to refer to their own descriptions, origins are willing to be competitive, to strive to succeed, to reduce loss, and to work hard at their tasks. These qualities are congruent with Model I and hence reinforce the hierarchy (which is also based on a Model I theory-in-use).

Thus, it may be that the origin concept, as illustrated, remains within the constraints of the present world. This is not to imply a criticism of present practice and theory. First, it is not an easy feat to move children or adults from being pawns to origins. Second, doing so is progress in the sense that people will confront the hierarchy up to the limits that it permits. Our interest is in moving back the limits. But this cannot happen unless people have theories-in-use and are able to construct learning systems that can maintain the positive aspects of hierarchy and reduce its negative aspects.

Organizational Theory

To make matters more difficult, contemporary research and thinking about organizations is also limited largely to Model I or to pseudo-Model I. Elsewhere I have tried to show that the empirical work in the fields of organizational sociology, decision making in government bureaus, rational man theory, and the behavioral theory of the firm (Argyris, 1972a, 1973, 1976a) are consonant with Model I theories-in-use. The work of Blau (1970), Thompson (1967), and Perrow (1970) contains propositions about organizations that are primarily single-loop in that they remain within Models I and O-I. For example, Blau's basic findings about organizational size may be due to the nature of civil service regulations, whereas his concept of decentralization is embedded in scientific management theory. Thompson's view of organizations as a combination of rational and natural models of organization remains within Model I governing variables (rationality, the suppression of feelings, and the primary role of purpose or goals) as well as within the Model I behavioral strategies of unilateral control of superiors over subordinates. Neither Perrow nor Thompson nor Blau present any alternatives to the pyramidal structure. Nor do they indicate any interest in intervention that would lead to double-loop learning. The work of Simon (1969) also remains within the constraints of a Model I theory-in-use. The "relational concepts" that are at the core of Cyert's and March's behavioral theory of the firm are related to Model O-I win-lose games, intergroup rivalries, and coalition groups; hence, the theory remains within Models I and O-I. Turning to political scientists, Allison's work on decision making not only includes rational man concepts such as Schelling's and Simon's but also focuses heavily upon the internal politics and interpersonal relations of the O-I system (Argyris, 1973, 1976a). Moreover, most of these scholars focus primarily on espoused-theory data, do not differentiate between espoused theory and theory-in-use, do not present alternative models that may be used to overcome the dysfunctionalities that they have identified, and therefore do not concern themselves with interventions of how to move from the present state of organizational behavior to options that encourage double-loop learning.

These points have profound implications for the nature of organizational theories that are being produced and the interpretations that can be drawn from them. For example, the work by Burns and Stalker (1961) has been used to assert that in the social universe there is a "fit" or "balance" among individual needs, organizational requirements, and environmental demands. This fit theory is to sociology what cognitive imbalance theories are to social psychology.

Scholars tend to equate Models II and O-II with organic systems and Models I and O-I with mechanistic systems. Thus, organic systems are described as being open to learning, more flexible, and less concerned about rigid structures, whereas mechanistic systems are said to have opposite characteristics. Moreover, organic systems are thought to be functional in turbulent environments, and mechanistic systems more functional in stable environments. This view of the world ignores the possibility that mechanistic organizations that cannot double-loop learn not only may be unable to detect and correct error but also may be unable to detect their failures to detect and correct error. The result may be that actions can be taken within the organization that are wrong and that sow the seeds for creating a turbulent environment. Hence the "fit" of mechanistic systems to stable environments could lead to difficulties for the system (Argyris, 1972a).

If we examine the small amount of relatively directly observable data in the Burns and Stalker (1961) study, a case could be made that the organic systems are oscillating Model I systems. For example, one finds such statements as: (a) Weekly meetings between management and employees were largely "briefing sessions [p. 87]" because anything abnormal had been dealt with by other people and had been translated into the normal and routine; (b) Foremen were expected to speak up, but "it is also expected that persons of lower rank in the hierarchy of management will exercise their right to speak in a more discreet fashion than their seniors [p. 88]"; (c) In an organization, "the head of the concern stands for the concern and its relative success—he symbolizes or personifies it. The system and structure of management are both determined largely by him. Above all, he is the ultimate authority for appointments and promotion [p. 211]"; (d) An organization can be made more organic with centrally controlled flexibility. For example, "tight central control with the object of enabling production, resources, managerial and design efforts . . . to be changed quickly [by the top] as the situation demanded [p. 225]"; (e) Conditions that tend to make it difficult to raise questions and to voice criticisms (e.g., differences in status and power) were muted by games, such as everyone calling each other "chief" and the director calling everyone "governor" (p. 253).

For example, the following excerpt from Burns and Stalker (1961) is from an interview in an organic system:

> X: . . . Everybody is approachable by everybody else. It seems to me that it is almost a tradition here that that is so.
>
> Int: And it is not particularly cultivated? . . . or is it cultivated?
>
> X: It is natural, I suppose, to some extent. People with long service in the organization just naturally do it, you see, and people coming in from outside, I suppose, just follow on. They can't do anything else, you see, because . . .
>
> Int: You can't act stuffy among a crowd like that?
>
> X: No. No. You see, if the paint sprayer comes up with something and says, "Well, here you are, chief," there's nothing much you can do about it, even if you want to. Which he does, you see; everybody calls everybody else "chief" here, whoever they are. Except Mr. A. (a director)—he'll call everybody "governor."
>
> Int: Well, that's a nice way of smoothing over status differences. If everybody is "chief," then there are no differences between people to bother about.
>
> X: Yes, that's right. Nobody can complain [p. 253].

Apparently the device of calling everyone "chief" is seen as a genuine leveler and of "inestimable value." Whenever there is potential difficulty because of status differences, "the ability to pitch what one says into a half-jocular style that explicitly rejects the pressure or sanction one could bring to bear is of enormous value. The social technique of doing this—the accepted formula used in this firm—was trivial. The fact that it could be successfully employed was all important [Burns & Stalker, 1961, p. 253]."

Embedded in these assertions about organic systems are Model I top-down theories-in-use and O-I learning system. For example, in the statement, (a), top management decided what was to be translated into the routine; in (c) it is the top that personified success and defined the nature of the system and structure of management; and in (d) the organic flexibility was centrally controlled and manipulated. Examples (b) and (e) describe the games that people played in order to speak out yet to maintain the top-down authority structure.

Burns and Stalker (1961) did not present any data indicating that these games were discussable. Indeed, they imply that if these games had become discussable, it might have destroyed their effectiveness. They include one excerpt from an actual meeting among several foremen and a superior (pp. 255-256) that illustrates how "friendly intimacy" (the use of banter and irony) can help keep intellectually or emotionally difficult notions out of the discussion:

Chairman: *Any other points?* [Long pause.]

Foreman A: *There's a problem in my department. I've got two turners; they're good men but they make no bonus—but they'll not scrap any jobs. They've been in about four or five months now and I don't think they've scrapped a job between them. But they're not looking at their times.*

Chairman: *Then they're not good men, are they? . . . A good man is a man who makes a bonus and makes no scrap. Now these men make no scrap; but they make a bonus. Therefore they're only half good.*

Foreman A: *Well—what do we do?*

Chairman: *Well, we pay them by results. That's our accepted system here. . . . Suppose we pay these men a large bonus for not working hard. What happens to the other people?*

Foreman A: *You see, the ratefixer's been agitating at me to see if I could get these men—to see what was the matter with them that they're not making bonus.*

Chairman: *What is the matter with them?*

Foreman A: *Well, it appears to me, they're just made that way.*

Chairman: *Do they want to make any bonus?*

Foreman A: *Well, it doesn't seem to worry them—they never do, anyway.*

Chairman: *Why cross that bridge before we come to it, then?*

Dept. Mgr. A: *Isn't it quite clear that if these men are consistently not earning bonus, then they're not much use to us anyway?*

Foreman B: *Of course, these men are average men, and that's what bonus is fixed on.*

Foreman A: *They're good, these men.*

Dept. Mgr. A: *If they're average men, then they should be earning average bonus.*

[Chorus of dissent—confused argument about quality of the men's work.]

Dept. Mgr. A: *From the job point of view, they're first rate, that's the point. But they appear to be individuals with no great desire to earn more pennies. They also enjoy a fairly leisured existence and do high-class work.*

Foreman C: *I shouldn't like to say that the man who makes most bonus is the best man. Speed isn't always efficient—it's effective effort. . . .*

Dept. Mgr. A: *Surely the question really is, do we have the class of work suited to men of this description?*

Foreman C: *Evidently, according to the amount of scrap that's being produced around the factory, it's advisable to have a few of these men in the shop.*

Dept. Mgr. B: *They fill their part, really, I think.*

Chairman: *But people who make bonus don't make scrap.*

Foreman C: *It is the people who make bonus that make scrap—not these people who are slow but efficient.*

Chairman: *Are you talking about your department?*

Foreman C: *No. It's general through the factory. [Chorus of assent.]*

Foreman D: *You get this type of chap in every department—they aren't worried about money so much as turning out a good job. They've got pride in their work.*

Chairman: *They're not complaining they're not making any money, are they?*

Foreman A: *No, but this ratefixer, he puts a time on the job and they're taking far in excess of the time.*

Chairman: *Well then, they're below average. And they're quite happy about not making bonus, and we're quite happy—at the moment—to have our machines run at a low utilization rate. If the time comes when we're short of machines, then we'll have to consider doing something about it.*

Foreman A: *That's all I wanted to know—the general policy* [pp. 255-256].

Difficult topics can be discussed in these "civilized" ways because there is an acceptance of Model I and O-I. If our perspective is valid, then we should find that the same civilized manners lead to increasing difficulties in encouraging double-loop learning. Because organic systems are "sold" as encouraging double-loop learning, our prediction would be that the clients would soon discover that organic systems, as defined in this research, will not lead to double-loop learning. This may result, as has been the case in too many organizational development programs, in a backlash by the disappointed participants.

The point is that the reality that people experience on different levels not only may vary but also may be inherently contradictory. For example, according to Burns and Stalker (1961), the mechanistic and organic structures have the following properties:

Mechanistic structure	Organic structure
1. Great division of labor and specialization of tasks.	1. The person with the specialist knowledge goes wherever needed.
2. Clear hierarchy of authority.	2. Authority is vested in the person who can deal with the problem.
3. Precise definition of job, duties, rules, etc.	3. Continual redefinition of individuals' jobs as the situation requires.
4. Centralization of information and decision making.	4. Information and knowledge may be located anywhere in the organizational network.
5. Preponderance of vertical communication.	5. Preponderance of horizontal communication.

If people are programmed with a Model I theory-in-use, they will behave in either type of organization according to their theory-in-use. In the case of the organic organization, there will be a discrepancy between the structure and the behavior. For example, although authority is vested in the person who can deal with the problem (organic), that person will behave in ways that make clear who has the power (mechanistic). Although there may be redefinition of jobs (organic), as the foregoing material illustrates, there is a precise and unchanging definition of the rules of how to show deference (mechanistic). Although the communication may be horizontal (organic), the meanings produced within these communications will tend to be consonant with the vertical (mechanistic).

The author found similar results in studying matrix organizations. Although the structure of a matrix organization is organic, the actual behavior (as inferred from tape recordings of matrix meetings) was consonant with the mechanistic hierarchical organization. Such results suggest more than the possibility that there is a difference between the structure and the behavior. It suggests a set of problems of credibility of the structures and the participants if the latter behave incongruently with the requirements of the former (Argyris, 1967a).

A similar conclusion is possible in the case of organizational change described by Guest (1962) and later by Guest, Hersey, and Blanchard (1977). Guest studied the impact of a Model I manager upon his organization. The manager was replaced by another who was more participative. There are no data that I could find to illustrate that the new manager was anything but a less coercive Model I. His success may have been as much due to the fact that his superiors backed him up with financial and other resources and that the previous manager was so constricting that reducing the pressure on subordinates was beneficial. In this connection, the preponderance of subordinates' responses indicated that the new manager "got off our backs," "let us alone," "gave us our head," and "backed us up." This state may be characterized as going from Model I to the opposite of Model I. There is evidence that, under these conditions, people do feel better and their satisfaction does increase. But there was also evidence that the new manager was a "no-nonsense" executive who utilized a Model I theory-in-use after he had heard all the comments and/or when the issue being dealt with was an important one. What may be occurring here is that subordinates experience a less pressured world but one that contains the same underlying constraints to the examination of double-loop issues that existed before.

This hypothesis seems likely because we could find no evidence of double-loop problems being solved. The success occurred within the existing governing variables; indeed, all of the "hard" data to prove increased efficiency are related to the traditional organizational governing variables. The new manager helped the organization become a better single-loop learner. There is no evidence that the organization was either asked, or took on the responsibility, to solve double-loop issues. Nor does Guest assert that the organization did become an O-II or that it could perform double-loop learning.

But many organizational development practitioners evaluate this case as a successful example of organizational change and hence use it as an exemplar of what organizational development can accomplish. Elsewhere it has been suggested that much of the successful practice of organizational development may be where organizational single-loop learning is enhanced and the O-I learning system is not altered (Argyris & Schön, 1978). This conclusion, if valid, is troublesome because the literature of organizational development espouses Model II- and O-II-type organizations. Not only will this lead to frustrated and disappointed clients, but it may lead to clients who decide that double-loop changes are not possible. This, in turn, could lead to the profession's helping unintentionally to rigidify the society precisely in the state that it rejects (Models I and O-I).

A more profound problem may be the one illustrated by the work of Morse and Lorsch (1970). They found in a mechanistic organization that the managers felt very satisfied and committed and that they expressed a sense of competence and high motivation to perform work that was routine, highly predetermined, and under leaders who made the decisions. But why did the managers feel a sense of satisfaction, commitment, and competence under these conditions? Morse and Lorsch say because they accepted the orders, performed their jobs well, and therefore felt a sense of success and effectiveness. Another explanation may be that they, the managers, were obeying (in the Milgram sense) the dictates of a hierarchy and an O-I learning system.

Unfortunately, we cannot decide between the two explanations because the study used projective techniques. The difficulty is that what the employees see in a projective technique can be significantly influenced by the environment in which they are embedded. Their judgments about reality, and hence what they "project" onto the instrument, are influenced by the environment. For example, Morse and Lorsch (1970) report that the employees were satisfied, committed, and productive (in a Model I, mechanistically organized system) because they experienced a sense of competence. Competence, they argue, is a basic need. Because a basic need is being fulfilled, morale is positive.

The logic makes sense if the criterion for competence in the heads of the employees is not affected by the environment. But that criterion can be significantly influenced by the environment in which they work. If we examine the criterion of competence that Robert White (1959) uses and the one used by the managers, we find some important differences:

White's meaning of "competence"	Managers' meaning of "competence"
• Emphasizing novelty	• Emphasizing sameness and routine
• Having few predetermined rules	• Having many predetermined rules
• Producing further difference in sameness	• Staying within the differences permitted
• The subsiding of motivation when a situation has been explored and presents no new possibilities	• The continuing of motivation even when a situation presents no new possibilities
• Experimentation	• Minimal experimentation
• Striving toward autonomy	• Striving toward submissiveness
• Tending to vary behavior rather than to repeat it	• Tending to repeat behavior

These are profoundly different states of affairs. Indeed, as Morse and Lorsch suggest, the managers' morale would probably plummet if they were thrust into jobs that were characteristic of White's model. It is not a random occurrence that the managers of these managers, who also held the same view of competence, fought the introduction of new organizational designs that would move their work world toward White's meaning of competence. Initially they lost the fight, and the corporation became a world leader in experimenting with new ways to enhance the quality of life in, and the efficiency of, their plants. Some 5 years later, we have learned that these managers are still fighting the innovations but are now somewhat more successful. Their morale is now ascending, and the morale of those who are interested in enhancing the quality of life is descending (Walton, 1976).

It is possible, therefore, to have high morale, great satisfaction, and poor double-loop learning capacity. Attempts by people to increase morale and satisfaction not only may be incomplete strategies but also may, if successful, hide some deeper organizational learning problems. It is when practitioners sense this that they tend to conclude that their task is not to make people happy and satisfied but to create an efficient organization. The polarization between happiness and efficiency, under these conditions, makes sense *and* is counterproductive. It is counterproductive because ignoring morale and satisfaction can also lead to negative consequences. What is needed is a conception of satisfaction and morale that is different from the existing ideas of equilibrium or fit between people's needs and the organization's demands. For example, it is possible to have a state of affairs where people prefer to be dependent and submissive *and* where they are very satisfied. This state of affairs may appear satisfactory to some practitioners. But it should be the task of social science to make explicit the pitfalls of this condition. These pitfalls will not be made explicit until social scientists develop models of human nature other than Model I and models of organizations other than Model O-I. Without such models, it is not likely that we will discover the inner contradictions of the Model I and O-I world.

Summary

The examples of rigorous research described in this chapter indicate that they not only describe the world as it is but also help to reinforce it. The reason is that if citizens turn to social science for help to increase their effectiveness, they are limited largely to propositions about effectiveness within a Model I and O-I world. Some social scientists appear not to be aware that the descriptions they have asserted to be of new worlds (e.g., organic systems and beyond theory Y) actually tend to be, at the theory-in-use level, more subtle Model I and O-I propositions. Hence, the citizens who wish to apply these results may unknowingly reproduce subtle manipulative conditions in the name of emancipatory conditions.

CHAPTER 5

Normal Science and Advice

In Chapter 4 we saw that the Model I methodology of rigorous research can lead to generalizations that are limited to the status quo. This limitation is rarely voiced openly. Indeed, many social scientists have written books and articles to show the public how the results of rigorous research may be used to create a new and better world.

In this chapter I should like to examine in some detail the world that would be created if people took the advice given by some of the leading social scientists as to how to create a better quality of life. I should like to begin by noting that some social scientists hesitate to give advice derived from research because they believe that the research is too primitive.

State of Basic Research and Its Usefulness

A frequent response to the request for advice on a new or perennial problem is to assert that basic research on the subject is meager and primitive and that little advice can be given that stems directly from the research. For example, a group of executives asked a leading authority for advice that could be derived from his and others' theories about effective leadership. The scholar responded that research on leadership was too primitive and incomplete to derive practical advice. However, he would be glad to offer what he admitted were ambiguous and imprecise generalizations in the form of maxims or guideposts.

There are four aspects of that response that are intriguing. First, there have been decades of research on leadership, yet, as a recent reviewer suggests, little of it is additive and much that is known does not deal with the complexity in which leaders find themselves in everyday life (Stogdill, 1974). Second, the scholar seemed to be unaware of the possibility that the generalizations produced by normal science may not be usable in an on-line model. Under on-line conditions, human beings use propositions in the form of maxims and guideposts. Third, there is an assumption that the piling up of knowledge utilizing normal science criteria for rigorous research will lead to useful and directly applicable knowledge. I believe that this assumption is problematic for reasons already described. Additional reasons will be presented in the next chapter after we are able to document the discontinuity between the form of knowledge produced by normal science and that which is produced by action science. Fourth, because the social universe is an artifact, every delay in informing citizens about leadership (or whatever other phenomenon) serves to reinforce the present state of the world. The researcher who aspires to be descriptive is actually maintaining a normative position of conservatism.

An assertion made with increasing frequency (because social scientists and the citizenry are increasingly concerned about applicability) is that basic research is generating useful and applicable generalization. The author subscribes to this assertion but would add that the overwhelming number of these generalizations about practice are limited to a Model I theory-in-use and to O-I learning systems. To illustrate, I should like to draw upon examples from the systematic and creative empirical research of scholars who are leaders in their respective fields.

Aronson: The Social Animal[1]

Elliot Aronson (1972) has recently written a well-argued book about the applicability of experimental social psychological studies. Of the eight major topics listed in the contents of the book, all but two are topics that are central to Model I. We learn that:

1. The people most liked in groups are those who conform to group norms. The people least liked in groups are those who deviate from group norms (p. 15). Implication: If you wish to be liked, conform to group norms.
2. Pressure to conform to the judgments of others is effective if personal judgments have to be made publicly even though

1. This section draws heavily from Chris Argyris, "Dangers in applying results from experimental social psychology," *American Psychologist, 30* (4), 1975, 469-485.

there are not explicit constraints against individuality (pp. 19-20). Implication: Requiring people to make public their personal judgments will help to make them conform to group judgments.

3. Pressures to conform to others' judgments have little (if any) effect on the *private* judgments (pp. 19-20). Implication: Maintaining individuality may be best accomplished by keeping your judgments private.

4. It is possible to increase group conformity: (*a*) if members are seen as experts; (*b*) if members are friends; (*c*) if relationships with friends are insecure; and (*d*) if acceptance by the group is moderate (p. 21).

5. It is possible to decrease the conformity to other's views by: (*a*) having allies; (*b*) having high self-esteem; (*c*) having prior success in achieving tasks; (*d*) having secure relationships with friends; and (*e*) having total acceptance by the group (p. 21).

The pressure to conform may be decreased by becoming dependent on allies, by having success in tasks, and by having total acceptance in the group. But if the group tends to value those people who conform to its norms, then acceptance may mean high conformity. Also, having allies may require being dependent on or beholden to them. Succeeding in tasks focuses on the importance of productivity and assumes the acceptance of group goals. All of these conditions are congruent with Model I.

These illustrations could be expanded to show that research also suggests that someone can gain credibility by using people such as famous athletes or physically attractive women to propound his or her views (select allies in order to win), by acting as if he or she has something to lose (deception), and by getting a message to individuals in a way that they cannot sense others are trying to influence them. For example, A can speak to B about a "hot tip" loudly enough so that C can hear it, and then C may be influenced (pp. 61-64) by the statement (deviousness in order to control others unilaterally).

Zimbardo and Ebbesen: Influencing Attitudes and Changing Behavior

Zimbardo and Ebbesen (1969) also focused on showing readers how research results may be used to influence others unilaterally, mostly in a covert manner. For example, they advised that persuasion will work if the persuader is seen as an expert; as having good intentions; as being dynamic, sociable, and attractive; and as having an authoritative manner. They also provide interesting insights into how to design the communications (e.g., the order of presentation). The research in the field has focused on the following five questions that have relevance to practice and action: (*a*) Should the strongest arguments come last or first? (*b*) In a two-sided debate, should you present your case first or last? (*c*) Should you present only your position, or your opponent's position as well and then refute his? (*d*) Should the communicator draw the conclusions explicitly or allow the audience to do so from the arguments presented? (*e*) Should one use rational or emotional appeals with fear-stimulating properties? (Zimbardo & Ebbesen, 1969, p. 17.) All of the questions are phrased to provide assistance to a communicator who wishes to influence others unilaterally. The action strategies, therefore, are aimed at controlling and winning over others.

If one examines Zimbardo and Ebbesen's comprehensive list of findings as well as their implications for practice, it is not possible, I suggest, to find any principles that are not within the Model I paradigm. For example, they advised the following (as did Aronson, 1972): (*a*) Present one side of the argument when the audience is generally friendly or when your position is the only one that will be presented; (*b*) Present both sides of the argument when the audience starts out disagreeing with you; (*c*) There will probably be more opinion change in the direction you want if you explicitly state your conclusions than if you let the audience draw their own, except when they are rather intelligent (Aronson, 1972, pp. 20-22).

The first thrust of these results is to provide the actor with insight into how to get others to do what the actor wants them to do. This thrust is related to the Model I governing variables of achieving the actor's purposes. The second thrust is to advise the reader to be an expert, which implies using knowledge to influence others, again Model I governing variables. Third, the advice to persuade others by acting as if the actor is willing to lose or not seeking to win is based on the assumption that the governing variable is win, not lose. All of the recommended behaviors are congruent with controlling others unilaterally and doing so, at times, by devious procedures.

McGuire (1964) explored the experimental literature and identified the major approaches to the problem of inducing resistance to persuasion. They are as follows:

1. *Behavioral commitment*: The believer takes some more or less irrevocable step on the basis of his belief, thereby committing himself to it. Commitment is presumed to make changing

one's beliefs dangerous and costly (p. 194). This strategy relies on the Model I value of win, do not lose.

2. *Anchoring the belief to other cognitions*: Linking the belief in question to other cognitions may make it more difficult for the person to change his belief because such a change would require his changing all of the linked beliefs (p. 196). This strategy appears to focus on immunizing the person to double-loop learning and keeping him focused on single-loop learning.

3. *Inducing resistant cognitive states*: Inducing anxiety about the issue thereby induces aggressiveness and ideological preconditioning (p. 197). The strategy appears to maximize winning and to discourage double-loop learning.

4. *Prior training in resisting persuasive attempts*: Individuals are trained for selective avoidance or perceptual distortion of information that is at variance with one's beliefs (p. 199). Again, this strategy educates individuals to resist persuasion in a way that may reduce their predisposition for double-loop learning.

5. *Inoculation*: The person is typically made resistant to some attacking virus by preexposure to a weakened dose of the virus. This mild dose stimulates his defenses so that he will be better able to overcome any massive attack to which he is later exposed (p. 200).

All of these strategies assume that the way to deal with persuasion is to "plug into" the potential recipients of persuasion some skill and capacity to resist these persuasion attempts so that the recipients may remain effective at winning (i.e., maintaining their beliefs). Also, all of the strategies are covert. They do not recommend skills and capacities to openly confront the persuader with his attempts to induce change, nor do they provide insights into how the parties involved can create a relationship in which double-loop learning may occur (e.g., Why does the persuader strive to persuade through covert methods?). Finally, the resistance strategies are designed to be covert in order to reduce the probability of bringing to the surface negative feelings between the parties involved.

Rubin: Liking and Loving

Rubin (1973) has written a systematic, thoughtful, and carefully argued book about the research findings related to liking and loving. What is the reader told about the nature of liking, love, and interpersonal life? People spend energy seeking social approval. Individuals, if they are aware of social exchange theory and the experimental evidence, can shape and manipulate the behavior of others by saying "Mm . . . hm" or "Yeah" or by making approving sounds every time the other person states an opinion (p. 75). However, that should not be continued for too long because the other person can become satiated and stop being influenceable. Perhaps the best power leverage in personal relationships is to set the terms of the relationship by being the partner who is minimally involved. But there is a caveat: This principle may work best in unstable marriages. Stable marriages have equal partners, but exchange theory has little to say about equal partnerships (except how influence can be designed unilaterally by any given partner). Again, the use of power, the striving to control others, is central.

More results congruent with Model I principles are described in sections on how to gain social approval. The greatest success in getting social approval is to deny it to another person. For example, have him or her rejected by someone else and then come along and be accepting of the person (Rubin, 1973, p. 76). Another principle is: Express dislike for the individual first and then express approval.

The readers are informed that if they want to use social-psychological knowledge to become liked by another, they should reject the other person and then become more positive toward him or her. If the reader wants to reject someone, then he should say negative things about the other person after he is certain that the other person thinks the reader likes him or her (Rubin, 1973, pp. 77-78).

We like people who agree with us. Why is this so? Agreement provides a basis for engaging in pleasurable activities and reduces the probability of feeling uneasy, of having to express hostility toward another, or of dealing with negative feelings. Also, "people have the egocentric habit of assuming that anyone who shares their views must be a sensible and praiseworthy individual, while anyone who differs with them must be doing so because of some basic incapacity or perversity [Rubin, 1973, p. 140]." Furthermore, agreement tends to keep bickering and argument and other such unpleasantries, to a minimum (p. 141). Thus, we learn that we can be liked if we agree with others (conformity), if we provide a basis for pleasurable activities and reduce uneasy, negative feelings (suppressing negative feelings), and if we acquiesce in people's egocentric habits of sharing their view (again, conformity).

Varela: Psychological Solutions to Social Problems

Next, let us consider several examples of applied social psychology in the "real" world. The first is the work of Jacobo Varela. He is an engineer by background who has studied social psychology thoroughly. The rigor and carefulness of his efforts are attested to by the fact that George Miller (1969), in a presidential address to the American Psychological Association, described him as an excellent example of the valid and judicious application of social-psychological research.

Zimbardo and Ebbesen (1969) described a case in which Varela, using social science knowledge, was able to (a) increase the sales of ready-made curtains to retailers in Uruguay (even though many windows in Uruguay are of different sizes); (b) induce retailers to buy for inventory (a practice rarely followed); and (c) accomplish these and other goals under conditions of spiraling inflation when the government froze all prices and wages, devalued the currency, and established severe penalties for infringement that resulted in the virtual halt of all nonessential consumer buying and therefore all buying from wholesalers by retailers.

Varela developed two persuasion programs. The first program was designed on the basis of experimental research on commitment. In the first step, the salesperson skillfully piqued the storekeeper's interest and in the second step induced him into the wholesale showroom. The showroom, unknown to the storekeeper, was an experimental laboratory where even facial expressions were systematically observed. The sales strategy was designed on the basis of what experimenters had done to subjects in order to produce commitment. For example, whenever the shopkeeper responded that he was favorably impressed, he was asked to give his opinion about that product. To commit him further, he was encouraged to elaborate the reasons why he liked the sample.

Moreover, uncut yard goods were sold by indirectly influencing the shopkeeper to compare the new designs with the older ones. When the shopkeeper asked about the fabric, the salesperson hesitated but eventually agreed to show him bolts of the fabric: "Once the retailer made this verbal commitment to see the material, and in addition put the salesperson through the work of presenting it, he had to justify his behavior. In such ways he very neatly set *himself up* [italics in original] for placing a big order [Zimbardo & Ebbesen, 1969, p. 116]." The sales results were excellent. The wholesalers then trained the retailers to adapt these techniques to use in persuading their customers, the unsuspecting housewives with irregularly shaped windows.

The entire strategy was congruent with Model I governing variables to achieve purposes as Varela perceived them, win-do not lose, and remain away from negative options. The behavioral strategies were also consistent with Model I. The salesperson manipulated and controlled the environment; whatever testing was done was covert; and no double-loop learning occurred.

Notice also that the entire strategy was kept secret *and* necessarily so. It is doubtful that the strategy selected by Varela would work if the unsuspecting retailers and later the housewives were told about what they were to be exposed to in the selling relationship. Because Varela followed faithfully the dictates of the experimental treatment, he naturally treated the retailers as "subjects." He therefore kept the experimental manipulation (sales strategy) secret from the subjects (retailers and housewives).

Some readers may believe that such a manipulation could not be repeated. After all, the retailers would not be unsuspecting. Varela was aware that the retailers may have immunized their clients against further manipulation. He developed a second-phase sales strategy based on reactance theory that was even more manipulative and secret than the previous one. Reactance theory states that if a subject perceives that a communication is attempting to influence him, he will tend to view it as a threat to his freedom to decide for himself. Varela educated salespeople to chat with retailers, to engage them in small talk, but to covertly obtain attitudes about business conditions. These data were then given to a different set of salespeople who used them when they visited the unsuspecting retailers. For example, because most retailers felt (given the inflation) that times were bad, the salespeople were instructed to say, "Times are really bad, and I don't think it even pays to try to see what the new style trends are" in a way that implied sincerity. In order to maintain his freedom of choice, according to reactance theory, the retailer had to at least look at the materials. With carefully designed statements, the salesperson was able to influence retailers to disagree with him, but in disagreeing with the salesperson's statements, the retailer was forcing himself to buy (p. 188).

The sales techniques were effective with the retailers. The second phase, utilizing the showroom as an experimental laboratory, was also replicated with great ingenuity. The strategy included making buyers "yield," which involved bringing them into an unfamiliar environment under the control of the salesperson. The salesperson had been taught to scan expressions and ask questions only of buyers who possibly would be favorable, systematically rewarding the favorable comments and developing group pressure to persuade those customers who were not favorable into buying. The strategies were even differentiated to deal with highly authoritarian customers as well as customers who required "immunity against counterpersuasion."

In a systematic book, Varela (1971) continues his application of psychological research. He cites how psychological research results can be used in organizations, in families, and with close friends. In one case, a friend was covertly manipulated into going to a doctor for professional help. In another case, a son manipulated his mother into accepting a needed operation. The cases can be continued, but the exercise would produce the same unilaterally controlling Model I, coupled with secret use of behavioral science principles.

Varela includes a discussion in his book about ethical issues. He realizes that his work raises questions about the ethics of people producing change in others, of invasion of privacy, of unilateral control by the powerful over the less powerful (p. 139). Varela's response to these questions may raise even more concerns. First, he correctly notes that all new methods have been feared and resisted. Next, he notes that the principles that he suggests need not be limited to despots. The ideas that Varela has published are available to the poor; indeed, suggests Varela, the ideas could bring more power to the poor. This would be true *if* the poor had enough power to be in a position to manipulate others.

Moreover, what are the ethics of implying that it is good for the poor to manipulate the rich or for the less powerful to manipulate the powerful (which is a contradiction in terms)? Wherever this has happened, be it at the community level (participation of the poor in community government) or the social level (socialist-communist countries), all that has been generated is a society of oscillating Model I relationships.

Varela warns his readers against the misuse of his principles. There have been cases in which salespeople have sold much more than the buyer needed, producing a boomerang effect. Varela (1971) then advises: "Size up your client, decide what is best for him, make a survey of his needs and possibilities and then design a persuasion to sell him those requirements. If he buys the amount and finds that he can sell it, then he will feel grateful, because at all times he will have the correct sensation that it was he himself who made the decision to buy [pp. 140-141]." And so we find that Model I advice tends to continue a Model I world in a way that the client genuinely believes that he is making decisions when, in reality, it has all been managed by the persuader armed with results from experimental social psychology.

Abelson and Zimbardo: Canvassing for Peace

The application of social-psychological findings to politics has been presented by Abelson and Zimbardo (1970). The pamphlet tells the canvassers, "We advise you on skills of interpersonal contact in order to reach people successfully [success was defined as supporting the peace candidate, p. 8]." The advice given was designed to help them win, to advocate effectively, and to minimize client resistance. The possibility of a joint dialogue, with a result that the canvassers might have had their views altered, is not included. "Set firmly in mind exactly what you will want to obtain during your contact," advise the authors, "and look to your organization to tell you what the purpose should be [p. 8]." The pamphlet advises the canvasser to be well informed (in order to be viewed as an expert), to role-play a call ahead of time, and especially to practice being "the target person . . . experiencing the pressure to comply with your request [p. 10]." You must be confident and "you must be dedicated to winning, to making the 'sale' [p. 10]."

Sometimes the advice seems to place the canvasser in a dilemma that is neither acknowledged nor discussed. For example, the person must perceive that the canvasser cares about the person's views and about his reaction as a person. Yet the canvasser is admonished to win and not to lose; he is told that attentive listening establishes him as an open person, yet his goal is to make the sale. Finally, there is the advice that no matter what happens one should strive to help the person feel that his self-esteem is greater because of the session with the canvasser. So we have a world in which the client is genuinely to feel better about himself as a human being because he has had an encounter with a canvasser who was schooled in winning and in controlling others.

Zimbardo: The Tactics and Ethics of Persuasion

Two years later a chapter was written by Zimbardo (1972) that elaborated and went beyond the material in Abelson and Zimbardo (1970). For example, he recommends that those promoting an antiwar cause: (a) impress the audience with their expertise (but in not too overbearing a manner); (b) make points against their interest; (c) have someone who may be respected by the "target" introduce them; (d) agree with what the audience wants to hear or with whatever they say first; and (e) minimize the manipulative intent until commitment is requested *and* keep the strategy covert. Zimbardo

(1972) continues his advice to the student by suggesting the student "individuate" the target person and "make the person feel you are reacting to his uniqueness and individuality—*which you should be* [italics in original, p. 87]" and are not reacting in a programmed way to your stereotype of a housewife, blue-collar worker, etc.

How can a process of persuasion that is identified as "tactical guidance" in a how-to-do-it manual individuate a person except in a somewhat perfunctory sense (e.g., Zimbardo suggests calling a person Mr. or Mrs.)? What is the meaning of individuation if the influence processes are kept secret and deliberate? How is it possible for the actor not to react in a programmed way if his or her behavior is guided by a program? How can the actor "individuate" another human being or "make the person feel you are reacting to his uniqueness" when the purpose is to win and sell (p. 85)?

That Zimbardo is aware that all of this may be an act on the part of the student is acknowledged a few lines later when he states, "Plan the organization of your approach well enough so that it seems natural and unplanned [p. 88]." Zimbardo also recommends that the student be flexible enough to modify his or her approach, yet he provides no insights or generalizations on this issue nor any explanation of how an individual can be programmed with this advice and still remain flexible. Perhaps such advice is not included because social psychologists have yet to study such problems.

Zimbardo is aware that there are ethical issues involved. He asks: Is it right to deceive someone, "hit him below his unconscious, . . . arouse [in another] strong feelings of guilt, shame, or even positive feelings of false pride? [p. 91]." Zimbardo responds that only each individual can answer that for himself or herself. Then Zimbardo tells the reader that, when deception techniques are employed by a sophisticated practitioner, the "victim" (his word) does not realize that he has been conned: "But you always know what your intention was and that you 'broke a man' thus. What effect does such knowledge have upon you? Do you respect yourself more because of it . . . ? If you are so ideologically committed to your cause or goal that any ends justify the means, then ethical issues will get a zero weighting coefficient. But that alone should give you pause [p. 91]."

I interpret Zimbardo as asking readers to think twice before they use manipulative techniques. But how about those who are so committed that they want to go ahead? Zimbardo continues: If after a thorough search of one's self, "you still want to go for broke, then the time has come to go Machiavellian [p. 92]." Then he presents several pages of research evidence and experience (especially of cases of police interrogators) that show the reader how to be an effective Machiavelli. Apparently Zimbardo is willing to recommend all these Machiavellian tactics because there are times when the poor, the subordinate, and the disadvantaged have to find ways to overcome those who maintain the status quo.

But will the advice work? I doubt it, because in order for the advice to work, the other person must be unaware of the principles and unaware of the fact that the actor is using the principles. If Zimbardo grants that his material should be available to all citizens, then the powerful people vis-a-vis the poor, or the lower class vis-a-vis the students, will be immunized against the principles. The result of Zimbardo's recommendations may add up to a strategy of Model I persuasion processes oscillating between the sides involved. In practice, the argument is weak because powerful people are much more likely to learn these principles than are poor people and by perpetuating Model I we perpetuate qualities that people tend to dislike in their lives.

Langer and Dweck: Personal Politics

Langer and Dweck (1973) have shown that it is possible to learn principles about how to create happiness that are derived from psychological research. Their purpose was to help increase readers' level of self and situational awareness by making them skillful in obtaining and using information and "by emphasizing the *control* [italics in original] you have over yourself and your environment [p. 2]." Their focus is less on providing insight into possible causes of problems (a strategy they do not condemn) and more on dealing effectively with situations and people. The basic underlying concept is control over the situation. For example: "a firm understanding of the principles of reinforcement and a few other behavioral laws to be explained in a moment will equip you with the knowledge to give you the powers you desire [p. 20]. . . . Direct thinking allows you to systematically exert your control over important situations [p. 66]. . . . (The goal is to help the individuals develop competences that place them) in the driver's seat, determining and planning the route [p. 167]."

Langer and Dweck (1973) cited an example in which Stu was unable to persuade Phil to stop eating fruit crunchies. Stu told Phil of an article that stated that fruit crunchies contain chemicals that may cause cancer. Phil responded that it was a lot of political bull.

The authors advise that Stu should have known that Phil would have responded the way he did. Stu should have disclaimed Phil's objections in advance. For example, "Phil, I know everyday they say that another one of our favorite foods is no good, but this time it is not a lot of political bull." The strategy is how to win over Phil. What research is available to indicate that Phil will not soon learn that Stu uses disclaimers as a way to win him over?

The book is full of similar covert strategies with larger groups. For example, there are direct and indirect disclaimers. If you think the audience is actually thinking that you are trying for personal gain, then disclaim openly that you are arguing the side you have chosen for personal gain (p. 67). If you are not sure about the audience, be quiet; otherwise you may be putting ideas in their heads that were not there (pp. 68-70). One example of an indirect disclaimer is *initial agreement*. Letting people know you agree with them from the very start is effective even if you later contradict yourself. This is true because it ensures that your message will be heard.

Concern for the other human being is developed in one of the last chapters. First, the reader is reminded that others may also have this knowledge. However, no advice is given as to what to do, for example, when both parties are using disclaimers to win, both are using the yes-but strategy, and each mistrusts the other. The authors also suggest that we should reward persons' actions that fulfill goals they have established for themselves. Again, they provide no discussion as to what we should do if the others' goals were to shape our behavior.

The model the authors present is that effectiveness increases in proportion to the individual's control of the situation. The diagnoses of other people are conducted privately; the strategies are designed to achieve the actor's purposes, to win in spite of resistance, to be in the driver's seat while others are following his or her leadership and are under his or her control.

Mayer: Social Planning and Social Change

Robert Mayer (1972) has developed a framework for macroplanning that is based substantially on the research from experimental social psychology. For example, if the reader is interested in planning community units where prejudice can be reduced, Mayer suggests that the experimental work of Deutsch and Collins (1965) on prejudice can be very helpful. Deutsch and Collins, as a result of careful empirical research, concluded that prejudice was partially a function of contacts among individuals. More frequent contacts helped whites to see that blacks are as human as whites, that they have the same problems and the same potentialities.

It follows, for Mayer, that housing units should be planned to have a certain proportion of blacks and whites and also to situate black and white families near each other to foster contacts. How may this be accomplished? Mayer suggests inducing governing boards in housing units to require certain proportions of blacks to whites in every housing unit. The governing boards could also do their best to locate black and white families in such a way as to increase the probabilities for interracial contacts.

Mayer does not state whether the policy of selecting certain proportions of whites to blacks and the policy for location should be made public. Making public the motivations for the proportions and locations may be counterproductive. Residents may be willing to accept a rule that requires that blacks get their fair share of available housing units. Residents may even be willing to accept a mixing of families in terms of location. What would happen, however, if the residents were told that these policies were defined in order to decrease their prejudice? It seems likely that such openness could lead to defensiveness. The defensiveness, in turn, could immunize blacks and whites against reducing prejudice.

Thus, we see again that the results from experimental research may have to be kept secret, just as the experimental treatments were kept secret by Deutsch and Collins (1965). If the residents knew why the study was being conducted, the results might have been different, and Mayer's suggestions would not be valid.

Another problem with applying the results of the study is that the operational measures used to measure prejudice reduction were responses to questions asked in questionnaires or in interviews. All such questions produced data at the espoused level. If whites say that they now understand blacks better and vice versa, such answers do not give us any insight into the theory-in-use. The credibility of the finding of reduced prejudice depends on the respondents' respective theories-in-use and not on their espoused theories; it is the latter that are tapped when one uses questionnaires and interviews.

If the data on espoused theories and theories-in-use collected to date are validated with larger and more comprehensive samples, then the Mayer policy may be questioned at another level. Our data show that at the level of theory-in-use, the black-white dichotomy is less pervasive a problem because few blacks or whites deal with members of their own race on other than Model I terms. In other words, if blacks and whites were to become "fully integrated," they would still have problems of conformity, mistrust, and antagonism that would *not* be based on color. Thus, integration represents progress, but our research would suggest an additional set of variables that would continue in effect to reduce the quality of life after integration is achieved.

A third problem with the application of the Deutsch and Collins findings is related to the fact that the original research did not consider the families as systems of human relationships. Many of the husbands were not included in the sample. Nor were discrepancies between husband and wife regarding prejudice explored. It may be possible, for example, that the action recommendations suggested by Mayer are more validly applicable to the black and white housewives than to the husbands, who may have significantly less contact with the male or female members of a different race *and* who may be influenced by norms in the work place that are biased against blacks.

A fourth problem with the application of the findings is that it may inhibit the need for double-loop learning. One might argue, for example, that whites and blacks, if they are to be coerced, should be coerced into exploring the reasons why they do not contact each other to explore their misconceptions of each other, etc.

In another study quoted by Mayer (1972), he notes that "since the aged suffer from 'lower status' in the larger society . . . placing them in the position of neighbors with young people would inhibit the development of friendship [p. 57]." Another alternative is for young and old to be exposed to how their respective theories-in-use make life difficult for each other. If the problems could be overcome at the theory-in-use level, then there probably would be little need to make unilateral housing policies and to do so secretly.

As far as I can surmise, all of Mayer's suggested interventions are of the Model I variety. Someone in some centralized bureau is given the responsibility to change unilaterally the living patterns of people, to do it secretly, and to keep the motivation secret, which means that the controlling agency may have to lie if asked about its motivation.

Inevitability of Model I Advice

When asked for advice, some social scientists respond that because the world is not about to change, the most useful advice is on how to be effective in the world as it presently exists. Cohen and March (1974) illustrate this position when they state, "First we do not believe that any major new cleverness that would conspicuously alter the prevailing limits in our ability to change the course of history [in organizational theory and practice] will be discovered [p. 205]." This statement does not appear to be based on the whims of the authors. The models used by Cohen and March to develop their position require such an assumption.

Let us consider the paper by Wildavsky (1972). Wildavsky wonders whether organizations can ever be self-evaluating or, in our terms, double-loop learners. He considers different options available. First, one could decentralize organization and give people at the local level more autonomy. But he documents the games played between headquarters and the field that raise serious questions about the efficacy of decentralization. Then he makes assertions about human beings that are predictable in an O-I world, for example, that most people are too unskilled to help organizations evaluate and learn. Or, "the self-evaluating organization will have to convince its own members to live with constant change. They may think they love constant upset when they first join the organization, but experience is likely to teach them otherwise. Man's appetite for rapid change is strictly limited [p. 513]." Next he describes most attempts to change as sweeping away the old routines but replacing them with new ones and as pressuring and overselling, which leads to the condition in which last year's goods are now seen to be hopelessly shoddy. Next, one could assign double-loop learning to teams. But teams would become elites that also would seek to survive and also would become non-self-evaluating. "The self-evaluating organization, it turns out, would be susceptible to much the same kinds of anti-evaluative tendencies as are existing organizations [p. 517]."

Wildavsky, in our language, is illustrating the consequence of O-I learning systems. But, having no model of how it might be possible to move away from Models I and O-I, he concludes that self-evaluating would be costly as well as counterproductive, and besides, it would require an experimental society. The point being made is that all these statements are propositions about the unchangeability of Models I and O-I. But they are made on the basis of observing their existence and not on the basis of research that tests their unalterability. To show, for example, that organizations may develop Models II and O-II (in addition to Models I and O-I) would require that Wildavsky present other models, for otherwise there is no comparison; no dialectic is possible.

McClelland's (1978) recent analysis of successful and unsuccessful social science programs points up the importance of connecting action with theory (a connection with which I heartily agree). However, because McClelland does not differentiate between espoused theory and theory-in-use and because he has not been concerned with developing alternative theories-in-use, he provides generalizations and advice that are not accurate.

As to the connection between theory and practice, McClelland (1978) notes that the characteristics of the successful change programs included, "training [that] was more specific and appropriate than other aid programs that made vague appeals to people to improve their lot [p. 205]." When one examines where the specificity came from, one finds that it was "lifted" from the theory and the instruments used to test the theory during the basic research phases. For example, people could have their *n* Achievement diagnosed with the same instruments that were used by McClelland and his co-workers to develop the concept. The same experimental games used on "subjects" could be directly transferable to executives who wanted to have their *n* Achievement diagnosed and increased (McClelland & Winter, 1971). It was possible to teach people how to think, talk, and act like a person with high *n* Achievement as that behavior had been worked out by years of empirical research in the laboratory and in the field (p. 205). The point is that McClelland, being a clinician and empirical researcher, kept implementation in mind while he was carrying out the basic research on *n* Achievement and the power syndrome.

The stage can be set to illustrate the second problem by noting first that, if one examines the McClelland and Winter (1971) experiments as well as many of the behavioral modification experiments (Bandura, 1977), the subjects had the skills to learn the new competences being taught. For example, in educating people for *n* Achievement, the individuals are helped to develop a clear concept of the requirements of the motive. The requirements are taken directly from the measures used in the original research to differentiate between low and high achievers. Next, the individuals are helped to design specific goals to begin to implement these requirements. Finally, they keep records of their actions that can serve as feedback to correct error and as rewards to reinforce the success (McClelland & Winter, 1971, pp. 61ff.).

The implicit logic is (1) if people have clear maps of *n* Achievement; (2) if these maps range from the general to the specific; (3) if people design specific learning tasks and goals to achieve; and (4) if these goals are congruent with prevailing cultural values and norms, then there is a very good chance for success. To have these conditions hold, people must have the skills necessary to understand and implement the general and specific maps that social scientists produce, and the societal norms must sanction and reward the education. These are the conditions for single-loop learning within a Model I world.

However, McClelland writes as if his research, if applied correctly, can be used to overcome problems in a Model I world which, we suggest, requires a different theory-in-use. For example, McClelland indicates that executives who score high on need for power but who use power nonneurotically are more effective in the present world. McClelland and Burnham (1976) then state that the people who use power nonneurotically are those who do not dominate others but who free other people to generate their own self-confidence. These consequences appear to describe emancipatory Model II-type options.

However, when McClelland specifies in scenario form what the "mature" user of power would do, he comes very close to describing subtle manipulative Model I actions. For example, the mature user of power does not dominate but says to his subordinates, "Here are the goals which are true and right and which we share. Here is how we can reach them. You are strong and capable. You can accomplish these goals [McClelland, 1975, p. 260]." If that leader considered his subordinates as strong and capable, then what is the purpose of telling them so? Also, would strong subordinates need to be told their goals were true and right? Would they need to be told how to reach them? "His [the leader's] role is to make clear which are the goals the group should achieve and then to create confidence in its members that they can achieve them [p. 260]. . . . [The leader] gives group members the feelings of competence they need to work hard [for the goals, p. 263].

It appears to me that "creating" confidence in others or "giving" subordinates feelings of confidence illustrates what March once called mini-Machiavellian style of leadership (Argyris, 1976c). March recommended such a style because he, like McClelland, was conducting research to remain within Model I constraints.

Our research suggests when one is trying to help people make double-loop changes in their theories-in-use, it is possible to fulfill all the conditions stipulated by McClelland and yet not be assured of success. First, people do not have the skills to double-loop learn or to behave according to Model II, and they are unaware of this fact. Second, their present Model I behavior is highly skilled and hence automatic. Third, the internal cues that people may use to sense when they are not producing Model II behavior do not exist. The external cues that must come from others are not typically available, because most people do not have a Model II theory-in-use and to give such cues would violate Model I governing variables. Fourth, the prevailing espoused cultural values and norms may be consistent with Model II but not at the theory-in-use level. Thus, there is at the societal level a discrepancy between espoused theory and theory-in-use. Given the fact that social systems are typically of the Model I kind, this discrepancy is not likely to be resolved. Hence, not only are Models II and O-II *not* congruent with prevailing norms and values, but they also exist under conditions where to make explicit the incongruity would be seen by most as a hopeless and socially risky task.

Consider a concrete example. It is not difficult for people to understand the following rule: If you make an attribution, provide the directly observable data to illustrate your inference process. Yet people have great difficulty in using that rule even in a learning environment. Rules that require more complicated new behavior are even more difficult to produce. Although people understand the rule, advocate combined with inquiry, it takes months of practice to begin to behave according to the rule. This means that action science research is faced with an unusually difficult challenge if it is to take implementation seriously. It will typically be faced with subjects who do not have the skills to produce the rules that they well understand, who will have (defensive) skills to keep themselves unaware of this fact, and who consequently will feel embarrassed, frustrated, and bewildered, reinforcing their defensiveness. This will simultaneously assure the creation of an O-I learning system that will make the inhibitory behavior the natural behavior to use and that will evaluate the behavior that facilitates Model II learning as deviant and inappropriate.

The McClelland work and that referred to by Bandura (1977) does not face these levels of difficulty. They are relatively certain that their subjects have the capacity to produce the skills required, that feedback can be given to correct error and reinforce success (match), and that once learned, the behavior will lead to success, and hence the environment will act to reinforce and strengthen it.

Some researchers hold to the position that the Model I nature of the world is not changeable (Dubin, 1976). The evidence for that unchangeability is said to be the fact that experiments to help people move from Model I toward Model II show modest success. The argument appears strange for two reasons. In the case cited by Dubin (1976), the interventionists were able to help the participants achieve something that, at the outset of the project, they (the participants) stated was unlikely if not impossible. For example, the editor of the editorial page, the managing editor, and the publisher held several meetings and began to solve several deep-seated organizational issues that had been, up to that point, undiscussable. Also, a project that everyone predicted was dead was revived and authorized within one meeting.

The second reason why it seems strange for social scientists to use the argument is that the history of science is replete with researchers who have persevered after many failures or small successes until a major breakthrough was achieved. Surely the decision to stop a line of research should be made upon empirical evidence of continued failure with concomitant increase in the sophistication of the theories and the rigor of the methods used.

Taking a more extreme position, Feyerabend (1975) has been able to document the hypothesis that science moves, at times, through the emotional commitment of researchers. He documents in painstaking fashion that Galileo was able to get certain ideas tested by himself and others by preaching, cajoling, persuading, tricking, and even manipulating scientists. Although I am not recommending such behavior, it is instructive to see that even in the hard physical sciences emotion plays a role (Mitroff, 1974).

The key issue should not be the distinction between models that appear real and directly connected to present reality versus those that appear romantic and ideal. The key issue should be whether the work on the latter models is following the criteria for public disconfirmability. If the empirical work is being done, then the slowness of positive findings should not be a sign to stop the research program.

Some social scientists (Stephenson, 1975) argue that we should not conduct such studies because if people are not choosing to make such changes by themselves, then they do not wish these changes to occur. For example, he suggests that changing factors such as those included in Model I and O-I implies the rejection of existing social structures and values (Stephenson, 1975, p. 251). Stephenson implies that if people overwhelmingly prefer Model I and O-I, then other alternatives are unnecessary. But how will people make informed changes if they do not have other options to compare to and from which to choose? Moreover, if Models I and O-I inhibit double-loop learning, how will human beings make themselves and their societies self-corrective?

Advice about Model II Options

There is a small number of scholars who, if one may judge from their empirical work, remain dedicated to the study of the world as it is but who are interested in developing new alternatives. The researchers seek clues in existing research that suggest hypotheses about how to move from the world the way it is to a new and rare state of affairs. Presented earlier was an example from the work of Donald Schön and myself of a model that was naive and simplistic. The naiveté was due to the fact that we had not, at that point, conducted adequate interventions to illuminate the limits of the model. Moreover, I tried to show that this gap was not simply one of needing further research. The results that we obtained could only be obtained where an intervention was being attempted to help people move from Model I toward Model II.

Weick's (1977) recent perceptive article on how one can help organizations to become better single- *and* double-loop learners may also contain traps and gaps that are not discussed because interventions were not carried out. He cites the examples of the astronauts who conducted a strike because, in effect, mission control dealt with them in a highly Model I fashion. They controlled every movement of the astronauts under the assumption that they could not learn to detect and correct many of their own errors. The result was a control system that was efficient enough to produce solutions to problems but that could not take into account the conditions under which the astronauts had to try and solve the problems. Ground controllers were the planners and the astronauts the implementers.

In order to create a more self-designing organization, the participants must revise many existing patterns, reexamine everything, value features of the organization that they used to disparage. "The essential problem in self-design is to make a teacher out of the learner—that is, to have the same people performing both functions [Weick, 1977, p. 37]." In order to accomplish this change, the participants must:

1. Prime themselves with images and problems so that when they examine their organization, they can diagnose opportunities for self-design.
2. Realize that design is an ongoing process, recipes rather than blueprints, recipes that may require varying amounts cf improvision.

3. Arrange patterns in ways that change consequences from those currently occurring.
4. Evaluate continually the performance of their design.

How are criteria such as these to be fulfilled? First, the participants could act as if they are someone else. This would give them a different perspective. This rule, it seems, will be helpful in any situation where the new behavior required is not Model II. People who are programmed to behave according to Model I cannot act Model II even if they have clear maps of how the other behaves. For example, people trying to move toward Model II frequently use this rule and observe the faculty member. Even if the faculty member models the behavior, the students are not able to reproduce it (Argyris, 1976b, 1976c).

Another rule is that, in order to change, it may be necessary to freeze other aspects. The dilemma is to design systems that are frozen and whose frozenness is continually confrontable because people are taught a respect and an irreverence for structure. This requirement captures one of the most difficult design problems faced by people trying to move individuals from Model I to II. What it does not include is the prediction that this optimal irreverence (or the more radical state of enjoying a chronically unfrozen system) requires a high degree of Model II behavior. It is not possible for people to advocate and to be confrontable, or for organizational learning systems to be substantially altered, by people who use only Model I. Indeed, if people with a Model I theory-in-use are given an accurate and detailed map of how to behave, it is unlikely that they can use it; it is more likely that it will immobilize them (Argyris, 1976b, 1976c; Argyris & Schön, 1978).

Weick correctly points out that too often managers believe that problems can be resolved by redoubling their efforts. This is an error, he notes, because increased quantities do not change patterns; all they do is to help discover the pattern that already exists (p. 41). What is necessary is that organizations have the ability to doubt what they know for certain and to treat as certain the very things they doubt (p. 42). The first proposition describes the impact of Model I. The second proposition describes competences related to Models II and O-II. If most managers use quantities in the way that Weick suggests, then most are Model I. They can be Model I and understand the second proposition, but they will also be unaware that they cannot produce what they understand (assuming they wish to do so). In other words, the article indicates the complexities and manner of self-designing systems but does not do the same for the requirements and competences necessary to carry out Weick's suggestion.

Kohlberg and his associates are experimenting with the creation of genuinely new worlds in order to raise the level of moral reasoning, hopefully to levels hitherto not common in our society. In order to accomplish this objective, they create "just communities." The purpose of the just community is to create an environment where moral reasoning and action can be enhanced. Experiments have been conducted in schools and in prisons. The discussion will be based primarily on the work conducted in an alternative high school called the Cluster School.

Characteristics of a Just Community

The characteristics of a just community include (Kohlberg *et al.*, 1974) a democracy in which: (1) the rules and decisions are made by staff and inmates together; (2) the decisions are fair and just, which means that each person gives, and is given, his or her due through the impartial assessment of the rights of all; (3) the faculty relinquish traditional authority so that they are freer to participate in "more human interaction" with the other members of the group; and (4) the maintenance of a moral atmosphere through the emphasis upon group solidarity is considered a critical responsibility for all the participants. The norms of the just community are stressed through the working out of real-life problems in the school—issues such as use of drugs, further integration, and the de facto social desegregation that is present in the school.

The community meetings are a place where all 75 students and staff gather to discuss a previously assigned issue. Each large meeting is preceded by meetings of smaller groups (of approximately 12 each). This combination leads to widely discussed and carefully thought out decisions in the community meeting (Wasserman, 1976) as well as to the establishment of the norms of the just community—such as justice, equality, fairness, and a high level of morality.

In order to illustrate the issues, we examined two transcripts of two community meetings and one small group meeting in the Cluster School (Argyris & Argyris, 1979). Meeting A (held in October) and Meeting B (held in April) dealt with the question the students faced in admitting black students who were not on the waiting list in order to facilitate better integration at the expense of fairness to the white students who were on the waiting list.

Seven categories were utilized in this analysis. They were: advocacy without inquiry, attribution and evaluations without testing or data, task control, controlling inquiry, advocacy or inquiry coupled with punishment, attribution with data but without testing, and inquiry with no advocacy. We counted the number of units for staff and students separately. One unit equaled one person speaking. Sentences within speeches or comments were not counted individually as long as what was said did not change the score. If the speaker began a new thought in the middle of a paragraph, it was counted as a new unit. Less than 2% of the total number of units could not be scored for one of three reasons: a comment was unfinished, a comment was not decipherable, or a comment was executing rules of order, a pure formality (see Appendix).

In Meeting A, 95% of the meanings created by the faculty were congruent with Model I. Fifty-eight percent were attempts by the staff to control the task being performed. Nineteen percent were staff attempts to advocate their view without encouraging inquiry, and 15% were the staff making unilateral attributions. Turning to the students, 79% of their scorable units were Model I. Thirty-four represented advocacy with no inquiry, and 26% unilateral attributions. The remainder were unilaterally controlling inquiry (8%), coupling advocacy with punishment (7%), and controlling the task (5%).

One reason for the relatively high degree of unilateral control by the faculty over the task activities could be that the total community was present during the meeting. A large group may increase the difficulties of effective problem solving. We excluded the units called task-control on the grounds that such behavior may have been forced by the large group meeting. Staff advocacy without encouraging inquiry becomes 45%, unilateral attributions 35%, and controlling inquiry 8%. Thus, the Model I pattern is not altered significantly.

Meeting B, which was less volatile (but concerned a similar topic), also produced a Model I pattern. There were several units that were not purely Model I. The first was inquiry without advocacy (e.g., asking questions); the second, attribution with data but without testing. The staff made 31% attributions without testing, whereas the students made 20%. These units indicate that individuals made unilateral attributions, included the date upon which the attributions were made, but did not encourage inquiry into their attributions. It appeared that they included the data to "nail down" their attribution.

We asked and received from the staff the transcript of a small group meeting that they considered one of their better ones. We scored this meeting and found that the faculty were even more controlling rather than less.

A second-order analysis was also developed from the foregoing.

1. *Interpersonal level*: A high degree of advocacy coupled with unilateral control over others in order to win and not lose; unilateral, covert attributions and evaluations of others; attempts to impose one's own meanings on others.

2. *Group level*: A high degree of competitive win-lose dynamics where people appear to be talking at or past each other; where helping other people is almost nonexistent or, when helping others is observed, it appears as a move to win a point or to gain the floor; where taking risks in ways that encourage trust are rarely observed; and where conformity and compliance are significantly more powerful as norms than individuality and constructive confrontation.

Under these conditions, we find that the dialogue among participants tends to deteriorate. For example, whenever categories of advocacy are combined with unilateral attempts to control others and whenever attributions are made unilaterally with no encouragement for inquiry, it is not possible to disconfirm the statements made. Under these conditions, the speakers will be experienced as uninfluenceable in their thoughts, and all participants will come to expect to be persuaded and sold or even to be pushed to accept the other's ideas. The sense of uninfluenceability of others, coupled with the expected unilateral persuasion by others, may lead people to protect themselves by making "safe" statements—statements that cannot be disconfirmed.

Under the conditions described earlier, we have found that few people trust each other or the effectiveness of the group's problem-solving capacity. This lack of trust reinforces the individual, competitive, noncooperative, nonrisking orientation. It also makes it highly unlikely that people will share uncertain thoughts that may be highly relevant but threatening or that they will feel they are being heard. Solutions to problems occur because some subgroup controls and dominates the debate or because the staff is wielding their traditional authority. Under these conditions, single-loop learning is inhibited and double-loop learning is completely blocked.

We have found in studies of other groups over a period of several years that, under high-stress conditions, group maintenance through subgroup action does not work and the formal leaders (in this case, the staff) are usually forced back into their unilaterally controlling work. This appears to have been illustrated by a recent meeting where one of the staff members asked for more guaranties from the members that when they attended a weekend retreat they would not use drugs or get drunk. Apparently the majority of the students became angry at the staff member and accused him of not trusting them. He pointed out that the previous year's weekend was a bust. Instead of attempting to problem solve, the discussion was aimed at attacking the staff member who was trying to raise the level of group cohesiveness and the quality of life within the community. Finally, the members voted not to permit the use of drugs and other such disruptive actions during the weekend. The results were apparently disheartening because the norms were violated by many participants.

Models I and O-I and a Just Community

Next we describe the conditions required for a just community and compare them with results of our analysis.

1. *Fairness and democracy*: In a just community, conflicts between staff and student, and between students themselves, are treated as issues of justice between equal individuals and of fairness between the individuals and the group.

If fairness is based on equality and if equality means that people have an opportunity to speak and a sense that they are being heard, then fairness and equality were lacking in the examples we studied. Students in the large and small group meetings struggled to obtain air time. Only a few received acknowledgment that they were being heard; most of the acknowledgments were designed to advocate a view and were coupled with unilateral control over others or were unilateral attributions and evaluations. Without encouraging recognition that the processes of inference be made explicit and discussable, the freedom of the members to respond to each other in a meaningful way was low.

2. *Extending responsibility to the students*: Students develop a greater stake in the rules if they are responsible for making them.

If the group members are unaware of their theories-in-use, then if they are to make rules to govern themselves, they should be able to produce only Model I rules. Individuals may espouse, but cannot produce, rules that are beyond their theories-in-use. These Model I rules will reinforce Model I actions by members, Model I dynamics, *and* the members' unawareness that they are acting in Model I ways and that there may exist a different way to act.

It is not surprising, therefore, to note that rules for governance used by the staff and the students were Robert's Rules of Order, which formalize Model I action, or rules developed spontaneously that were congruent with Model I.

3. *Encouraging collective responsibility*: The individual is responsible for the welfare of the group. The group is also responsible to and for the individual, to give support and constructive criticism if necessary and to recognize when the group has failed that individual.

It was hard for us to find evidence that the members were concerned about group or individual welfare. If group welfare meant trying to preserve the sense that everyone was equal, we have already seen that the sense of equality was reduced considerably through the high percentage of Model I communication that took place in Meetings A and B.

Finally, it should be noted that in both meetings the group arrived at a conclusion only when a staff member made a proposal and called for a vote without first asking for a consensus from the group on whether they felt it was time for a final proposal to be voted on.

4. *Creating a climate of trust*: This involves bringing all matters to the group and avoiding concealment of relevant feelings and information by either staff or students. It depends on willingness of staff members to support community decisions even when they are in disagreement with them.

We have seen on the part of the staff and students a high degree of competition. Neither the competition nor the attempt at unilateral control over others were discussed by the group. Not surprisingly, the style of communication did not substantially change over time; 7 months later the staff and the students were still behaving in accordance with Model I and were creating O-I learning system conditions.

5. *Raising the level of the group as a group*: If a group is organized on the basis of fairness and if reasoning at higher stages is listened to and supported by staff members and students, the group will naturally move in a more moral direction.

It is difficult for us to judge whether the moral level of the group as a whole was raised. We would point out, however, that if raising the moral level depends on "fairness," "listening," and "support," we might conclude that it was not raised, as we saw no significant sign of these characteristics.

But we can examine the question in a different way. We see the raising of the level of moral reasoning as a path toward freedom to practice justice in the just community. If we assume that the level of moral reasoning was raised, did we see (springing from that) a greater degree of freedom in the environment that the staff and students at Cluster School created for themselves? From our analysis of the five conditions, we think not. We arrived at the same conclusion regarding equality.

We do not necessarily contend that the level of moral reasoning was not raised; it very well might have been. But whether it was or was not, there still were factors present that were blocking the achievement of a just community.

How Just Communities Arise

If we understand the theory correctly, Kohlberg and his associates recognize that just communities in this world are rare events. There is a developmental process that must occur if they are to come into being. The first necessary condition is that someone who understands the requirements of a community *and* is able to verbalize and defend them against attack must be implanted in the context. At the outset, the faculty take on the role of persuasion and defending. The theory is that as they model the behavior, others will realize that it is important for the development of a just community and will emulate the staff actions.

The difficulty with the proposed mechanism is not that it will not occur. The difficulty lies in the way it occurs. It may be, for example, that the students become committed to the requirements of a just community because they have learned the interpersonal skills required, because they are internally committed to it, and because the internalization is a personal choice and not an imposition. It may also be the case that the internalization is not accompanied by skills or does not represent an internal commitment. Under these conditions, some people may defend the just community through compliance and external commitment. No doubt these two conditions need not be completely independent of one another. However, our reading of the reports suggests that Kohlberg and his associates have a theory of community development that is consonant with external commitment and compliance. For example, Power and Reimer (in press) assert that in order to create a just community it is necessary for the staff and (eventually) the students to start with the assumption that the school is supposed to be a just community and that people are supposed to trust each other.

Let us explore what Power and Reimer consider an incident that is central to a shift in collective normative values. There was a theft in the Cluster School, and during the community meeting in which it was being discussed, a student named Phyllis raised the idea that, if Cluster School is in fact a community, it should be the entire community's responsibility to return the money. Power and Reimer assert that the group became more of a community when Phyllis stated

that if they were to become a community, they would have to respect and trust each other. The question arises, how do Power and
Reimer know that the Cluster School had progressed toward becoming a just community with that statement? In effect, they are suggesting that when Phyllis behaved the way their theory suggested
people ought to behave, she was not acting as an individual but was
speaking for the entire group. "Phyllis does not simply speak for herself . . . rather she speaks for the whole school, exhorting the other
members to live up to the normative values of caring and trust
[p. 10]."

If one examines the transcript, Phyllis was explicit that she was
speaking for herself. How do the authors infer that she hit the group
conscience of the members? Moreover, even if this did occur, why
would they see this as a sign of progression toward a just community?
If equality and personal responsibility are to be enhanced, why
would not Power and Reimer have wished that after Phyllis made her
statement, either she, the staff, or some student had attempted to
test publicly that what she had assumed, others assumed? Why would
they not have wished that someone had taken the opportunity to
generate an informed and explicit choice about Phyllis's suggestion?

Without any overt discussion during the meeting of Phyllis's views
and values, the authors tell us that Phyllis's values were shared by the
others. Phyllis's individual values had been transformed from individual values into "collective moral judgments [p. 10]." It is difficult
to see how they arrived at the conclusion that this crucial transformation occurred. It is even more difficult to find any data predicting
the mechanisms that underlie the transformation. According to
Power and Reimer, what gives force to Phyllis's values was that they
were perceived by the others as necessary for creating a just community. Once the students decided their class was to be a "real" community, then Phyllis's requirements followed (p. 10). But previously
the authors told us that it was Phyllis's statements that marked the
beginning of an explicit statement that the school should become a
community. As evidence of the group's having become more of a just
community, Power and Reimer point to the participants' assigning
any failures to the group and not to individuals. For example, if there
is stealing, the group must pay. The community should "put pressure
on the guilty party to return the money." In the case discussed, a
motion was actually adopted that "if the money is not returned
anonymously by a certain date, everyone will be assessed fifteen
cents [p. 9]." The person who stole owned up to it, and was ejected
by the community. No thefts have occurred since then. According to

Power and Reimer, we now have the signs of a just community. But if a just community emphasizes the responsibility of the group, then why eject the student who admitted the theft? Is not the implicit assumption of this policy that the causality of the theft can be assigned fully to the individual?

Moreover, there are no data presented nor any speculations made as to how an individualistically centered, win-lose oriented aggregate of individuals suddenly switched their values to become concerned for the community once Phyllis spoke. Nor do the authors explain why the Model I patterns mentioned earlier continued with the same frequency and intensity after Phyllis spoke. But even if they were correct, the only way one could account for the transformation is that the students became committed through some sort of covert process (e.g., Phyllis's logic and/or emotional commitment) to the idea of a community. If such a process occurred, the students' commitment would have been external. External commitment can lead to a sense of community, but the responsibility for such feelings would be attributed to Phyllis and to the staff who supported her. Such conditions do not encourage equality, nor do they enhance the personal responsibility of the members to build a community.

So far we see little evidence of moral action. Some may interpret the decision itself (to accept six black students who were not on the waiting list) to be the action element that should be evaluated because it was apparently based on a norm of fairness. We have two responses to that interpretation. First, it is difficult to trust decisions that have been reached without benefit of concrete data and exposure to reasoning. Without being able to identify the data that led to the reasoning behind the decision, it is impossible to tell whether the group may have felt "railroaded" into a decision. It may have been that they felt, for instance, that if they opposed the vote, they would be seen as coming out against the community.

In accepting more blacks to make present blacks more comfortable, the community (staff and students) glossed over and buried the chance to look into the issue of why the blacks felt uncomfortable in the first place. It could be that it was not a question of simple numbers—some of the white students may have been purposely making the blacks uncomfortable. Another possibility is that some of the blacks at Cluster School may be insecure and brittle. They may have been trying to satisfy their own personal needs, and not the needs of their race, by raising the number of blacks in Cluster School. The neglecting of this issue may be related to a problem the Cluster School is having at the moment. The school finds itself split into "cliques" that are based heavily on race. Black students interact with blacks; whites with whites. It is a difficult issue because it is a volatile one (judging from a videotape of a community meeting on the subject the writer has seen) and because it is very hard to visualize an intervention for problems in social choices that do not infringe on students' privacy to choose their friends.

Potential Danger of the Theoretical Perspective

We suggest that one reason for these inconsistencies is the theoretical perspective selected by Power and Reimer. It views the creation of communities as a result of such processes as compliance and loyalty. It is not accidental, we suggest, that the authors depend on Durkheim's analysis of how moral character develops.

Durkheim, according to the authors, saw a profound harmony between the good of the individual and the group. "He asserted that true happiness could *only* [italics are mine] be found in self-sacrifice for the group [Power & Reimer, in press, p. 11]." Self-sacrifice is an accurate description of the processes required in an O-I world if people are to follow the "collective normative values." Power and Reimer state that moral character did develop in the group by the students' limiting their behavior for the sake of the community. "The norms and rules of the community made compelling by the authority of the group help students to learn that they must live up to certain social obligations [p. 11]." This factor is reinforced by the attraction to remain within the group. "The individual experiences personal fulfillment in accepting the discipline of the group because in doing one's duty one becomes more intimately involved in community life [p. 11]."

These speculations appear to us to be valid if people are programmed with Model I theories-in-use and if they create O-I learning systems in their communities. Our perspective suggests that there is no way that Model I unilaterally controlling and competition-oriented dynamics can lead to a sense of cohesion and community unless the individuals choose to ignore the counterproductive aspects of Model I action through an extremely high sense of loyalty and sacrifice to the group.

There are several difficulties with such loyalty and sacrifice to the group. First, they may reduce the striving of individuals to find new theories-in-use where they may be more proactive without inhibiting the community. Second, they may place a limit on individual moral development and the just community. If our research is correct, any strategy that works within, or limits itself to, Models I and O-I also reduces the probabilities that the individuals and the community can reach for Levels 5 and 6 in moral judgment and action. The reason is that Levels 5 and 6 are postconventional; postconventional judgment and action require a paradigmatic shift. Such shifts require double-loop learning, and double-loop learning cannot occur under Models I and O-I conditions. Third, if the Durkheim emphasis on sacrifice and loyalty requires the maintenance of Models I and O-I, then at the individual level the defenses that protect one from having to face the dysfunctionalism of Model I will be strengthened. It will also serve to reinforce the camouflage that is necessary to an O-I system if it is to function. Under these conditions, there is the possibility that the community can facilitate group think (Janis, 1972). Group think is a subtle process that goes beyond overt compliance. It is a complex process by which people become skillful at not recognizing error in the underlying assumptions and values embedded in the substantive issues and in the error-enhancing equality of their group dynamics. These consequences, we have seen, are predictable under Model I and O-I conditions.

Under these conditions, group effectiveness is related to group co-ercion of a subtle and (individually) unintended kind. It is subtle and unintended because the Model I actions are tacit and automatic. People are unable to see how any other way is feasible. It is unin-tended, therefore, because lack of competence for other alternatives, coupled with unawareness, leads to automatic responses where conse-quences therefore may be unintended.

But if the norms for self-sacrifice and adherence to what the faculty and some students point out is necessary for group survival, if those consequences are contradictory to the espoused theory of the just community, if the members can see how others violate the espoused theory but do not see how they themselves violate the espoused theory, and if there do not exist skills to produce genuinely differ-ent states, then one has powerful forces in action for group think. Kohlberg and his colleagues, we suggest, should be at least as con-cerned about this "hidden curriculum" as the one they have ques-tioned in most schools.

It is not accidental, we believe, that the direction of Kohlberg's group thinking is toward adopting a sociological analysis of the group as a whole which cannot be reduced to the sum of the individuals who comprise it. Such sociological approaches may unintendedly lead to analysis of groups as if they had no parts or, more accurately, to the ignoring of very complex interpersonal processes that go to make up the group dynamics (Argyris, 1972a). For example, exactly what was going on that made it possible for Phyllis's privately held, publicly untested assumptions to become group properties? How do highly win-lose, self-oriented, unilaterally controlling faculty and students create a group atmosphere of group wholeness and individual sacrifice?

It may not be accidental that the highest stage of collective values and sense of community identified so far by the moral development scholars is one where the emphasis is on obligations of the individual members of the group to the group as a whole, on members' obligation to act out of concern for the welfare and harmony of the group, and on resolution of conflicts by appeal to one's role within the group or to the established rules and procedures of the group. These requirements focus on individual compliance and appear to leave room for a sense of community only when the appeal is to group roles and group procedures, never when the individuals may be challenging the group as a whole nor when they may be questioning the obligation to be primarily concerned for group welfare and harmony.

This emphasis is congruent with a perspective that is limited to Models I and O-I. The dilemma arises because, under such conditions, moral reasoning at Levels 5 and 6 will not be possible because that requires Model II theories-in-use and Model II learning systems. If our perspective is valid, we would predict that: (a) the members will not be aware of such requirements (although they may be aware of injustices within the community); (b) the members will be unable to change the community to learn and to maintain Levels 5 and 6 of moral development; and (c) the members will protect themselves as individuals and as a group primarily through the mechanisms of compliance and sacrifice, a set of conditions that are self-sealing to moral reasoning Levels 1 through 4, group stages 2 through 4, and Models I and O-I.

Creating a Model II World

There are social scientists who believe that the world would be better off if people were given greater political and economic control over their destiny. They look at organizational life, for example, and see the negative consequences it can have upon its members. The purpose of this analysis is *not* to question their political aspirations, nor is it to juxtapose my position as a more correct normative one. Nor is it to disagree with the assumption that organizations can have negative consequences upon human beings; indeed, I believe that I have published similar views. The purpose of this analysis is to show that whatever the political persuasion, if the goal is to provide citizens with greater power and control to make decisions, the results will be as counterproductive as is presently the case because of the Models I and O-I conditions that exist in all organizations. Workers, for example, have the same theories-in-use and would create the same O-I learning systems as have bureaucrats administering a socialistic system. The assumption, for example, that the pyramidal structure is basically a capitalistic power strategy to keep workers in line (Hymar, 1972; Marglin, 1974, 1975; Sweezy, 1972) is simplistic.

According to the theory of action being proposed here, the pyramidal structure is the embodiment of a power strategy that has four features that would hold for *any* political system. The first root is related to the nature of skillful behavior. Employees who behave skillfully do so by not concentrating on their actions. Indeed, concentrating on their actions could cause them to lose their effectiveness (Argyris & Schön, 1978). Consequently, skilled individuals are poor detectors of incipient error in their performance. Someone else is needed to observe and manage the activities of employees. The role is that of superior.

But superiors (as well as subordinates) are finite in their information-processing capacities. As the organization grows larger, more superiors will be needed as well as superiors to the superiors. Coordination becomes a key activity. Here we have the second root of a pyramidal structure (Argyris, 1977).

The third root is that people are programmed with Model I. If this is the case, then no matter if they are young or old, wealthy or poor, white or black, male or female, they will produce Model I unilaterally controlling actions.

The fourth root is that Model I people tend to create O-I learning systems. This, as we have seen, leads to ineffective organizational double-loop learning, double-bind games, and withdrawal from taking risks. This, in turn, leads to increasing organizational ineffectiveness. Those responsible will react in the only way that Model I people in an O-I system can react. They will attempt to tighten controls, which in turn reinforces the pyramidal power strategy. Thus, the prediction is that the Chinese and the Yugoslavs (to use two examples frequently cited in the literature) may espouse values different from those of the capitalist industrialized nations, but they should not differ in terms of their theories-in-use. For example, Schumann

(1968) quotes Liu Che: "Modern large-scale industry and dispersed management are incompatible. . . . The plant manager has the authority within the framework of presently constituted law, to decide on all matters . . . for fulfilling and over-fulfilling state plans. . . .The plant manager is the fully authorized representative of the state, and is the one who assumes full and complete responsibility for all work in the plant [p. 258]." Schurmann concludes that Chinese plant managers may have more unilateral authority for final decisions than do their American counterparts, for at times they have the right to act in technically illegal ways in order to achieve supreme goal fulfillment of the plant.

A more recent description of Chinese policies and practices suggests that Chinese and Western theorists on participation may be converging (Whyte, 1973). Whyte notes, for example, the deep mistrust of the Chinese of bureaucracy and elitism. The Chinese not only emphasize employee participation but also do their best to de-emphasize specialization and professionalism, especially at the managerial levels. They prefer managers who are more general and politically pure to specialists who become distanced from, and tend to dominate, the employees (Oh, 1977).

But as one examines Whyte's descriptions of the quality of the participation that these generalists produce, one wonders if this is not a new form of unilateral manipulation. For example, although decisions originate from above, they are not supposed to be simply announced and obeyed. Yet there are elaborate procedures for mobilizing support "for decisions made at higher levels [Whyte, 1973, p. 152]." Whenever a new policy is announced, subordinates break into regular discussion groups to go over each point in detail. "In these groups, efforts are made [by the people just mentioned] to convince everyone of the need for a change in the routine, to elicit suggestions and ideas, and to get 'activists' to encourage their co-workers to support the change [p. 152]." Who are the activists? Whyte notes: "The group leader will cultivate within the group certain 'activists' whom he can count on to help him steer discussion and criticism meetings along proper channels [p. 153]." Finally, individuals are not to let personal emotions interfere with their performance. Unemotionality, however, is not an overarching goal because passion and zeal are expected even for the most mundane tasks as long as it is in the interests of the goals established by the superiors (p. 155).

Whyte concludes that Chinese participation may be characterized as top-down and in practice may stifle many of the subordinates' views (p. 161). Brugger's (1976) analysis makes it clear that the Chinese and the Russians believe in the importance of centralized power but differ in how to achieve it. The Soviets expect the individual to be loyal to, and controlled by, a complex administration hierarchy that begins within the firm and extends beyond it. The Chinese strategy is to politicize small, informal work groups, and to connect them with the hierarchy of the party organization that espouses participation as long as the participants do not question the underlying policies and assumptions of the Party.

Some economists and behavioral scientists cite Yugoslavia as a better example of the world they are proposing. The Yugoslavs believe that Russia and the United States are similar in that both systems give to an elite group power to confiscate the profits (surplus capital) generated by individual plants to accomplish the purposes of the centralized elite (Vanek, 1977). Genuine self-management, the Yugoslavs maintain, does not require that the employees own the plant. Ownership is counterproductive to self-management because it hampers the mobility of labor and capital. The key to genuine changes are to be found, according to the Yugoslavs, in the use of a competitive market coupled with "genuine channels of decision-making which enable all members to feel that they are contributing and that they can effectively master their immediate environment [Adizes & Borgese, 1975, p. 28]."

The Yugoslavs point out that the external environment in the United States and Russia has the same impact upon the internal management of enterprises. However, the Yugoslavs do not explain why their internal management of enterprises appears to be the same as those in the United States and Russia. The Yugoslavs may deny this assertion and maintain that they are different. However, the differences may be more at the level of the espoused theory than differences of practice. For example, their prescription for effective leadership includes: The manager "instills confidence in the constituents that the manager is not only in control of the situation but that he adequately expresses and implements the community's desires and aspirations [Adizes & Borgese, 1975, p. 31]. . . . [He] must be an entrepreneur, educate and lead the group into risk-taking [p. 32]. . . . The central figure in participation is the plant manager [p. 91]. . . . Without a manager who has the entrepreneurial spirit and directive leadership traits, the plant will probably fail and the workers will become depressed [p. 33]."

True, the workers can replace their manager. But what are the probabilities that this will happen if the workers become as dependent upon their manager as the foregoing quotations imply? Moreover, to have the power to dismiss the manager unilaterally is to give the workers the same top-down management that self-management is supposed to reject. It appears that self-management in reality may be top-down management by a few who live under the continual threat that their power can be taken away from them (Lammers, 1974). One can predict that the managers still strive to assure their survival by maintaining, and perhaps magnifying, the workers' dependence upon them. In a recent observational study of a workers' council in Yugoslavia, Obradovic (1975) found that the managers and the technocrats did dominate the interactions and the conversation. The empirical research on employee control and influence suggests that the slopes of these curves do not differ markedly from those found in the West (Tannenbaum *et al.*, 1974).

A theory of action perspective provides an explanation for the apparent gap between the espoused theory and actual behavior. If people do not know the skills of effective participation, if they are predisposed to repeat error, to camouflage the noncorrection of error, and to feel dependent and submissive, then it is understandable that pyramidal structures, specialization of work, and top-down management are in use. Indeed, it is predictable that they will be used in all industrialized nations with complex systems to produce products and services. Hence, the conclusion that the features of organization that some scholars attribute to capitalism are endemic in all organizations.

Apparently Marx was not unaware of this possibility. He realized that the problems would not be solved simply by turning over the ownership to employees or by giving them higher wages. He apparently believed (Nord, 1974), as the Chinese still believe (Whyte, 1973), that the mundane can be overcome by the worker identifying with higher socialist goals. For example, "Involvement tends to be developed through relating the individual mundane work to its impact on the future of socialism and communism [Nord, 1974, p. 575]." This may offer a partial explanation of why the socialist-communist countries have not been leaders in such changes as job enrichment and autonomous groups.

There are some scholars who maintain that job enrichment and the development of autonomous groups are simply tinkering with the system. It is my thesis that basic changes must begin with the Model I theories-in-use and the O-I learning system. The socialist-communist societies may not wish to alter these factors because they foster double-loop learning. People who master such learning are prone to question underlying assumptions, goals, and plans. The quotations cited earlier clearly indicate that such questioning is not permissible in the socialist-communist nations. To express this another way, changing ownership is trivial compared to changing people's capacities to learn. The former can be accomplished without necessarily threatening those in power. The latter is a recipe for reflection and confrontation that can lead to the questioning of underlying assumptions. Such questioning is feared by those in power, no matter what political philosophy they practice.

There is growing evidence that in some job enrichment and autonomous group experiments in the United States, middle and lower management are beginning to resist because the very success of the programs threatens the traditional functions of lower and middle management. Moreover, employees can also resist the same type of program when they face a new set of challenges. For example, Walton (1976) revisited the General Foods plant that was one of the first to install job enrichment and autonomous groups. He found that work performance and commitment were still very high. However, he also found that management and workers had difficulty in dealing with what appeared to be double-loop type problems. For example, workers were having difficulty in reducing wages of the poor performers. Although some employees felt abandoned by others who had left to go to new plants, they did not discuss these feelings before the transfers occurred. Middle managers resisted further expansion of the concepts in other parts of the company because of the threat that it posed to their role.

When scholars support Marxist theory by stating that "human development requires man to exercise control over his actions, but achievement of that condition requires that control be shared by everyone [Nord, 1974, p. 482]," it is important for them to develop a map of how to get from here to there. When Marx states, "The only way for individuals to control modern universal interaction is to make it subject to the control of all [Easton & Guddar, 1967, pp. 467-468]," then what is needed is a map of how everybody is to be able to control the activities of everyone else. It is these maps that will transform the espoused theory into a theory-in-use.

Nord (1977) criticizes social science for not viewing the existing set of political, economic, and social structures as variables and for not considering structures where employees can have power through ownership (pp. 1027-1033). Nord suggests that the socialist experiments in other countries may make a difference. But as we have seen, quality of life issues in those nations do not appear to be ameliorated; indeed, there is evidence that even such simple notions as job enrichment are resisted. Nord also recommends exploring the ideas that economic competition and growth should be reduced, that work not be a central life interest, and that the maintenance of the existing power structure be challenged. These suggestions would be resisted as much in the socialist nations as in the capitalistic ones.

We can continue these illustrations with examples from the Great Society programs within the United States during the past decade. I know of no evidence that where the poor and minorities were given power to rule, their rule became more humane and effective. This statement is not meant to denigrate the idea. It is to say that reformers are operating at the level of espoused theory. Advice, if it is to be useful, must inform the theory-in-use. When such information is obtained, the promises made by politicians and reformers tend to be questioned. Genuine citizen participation will require first that they be educated in Model II theories-in-use so that they can create O-II learning systems.

Summary

Normal science research results tend to support the normative position that the status quo should be illuminated. Emancipatory research that seeks new alternatives is discouraged. Results are pessimistic about the potential of individuals and organizations for creating double-loop learning and changing in substantial ways. The creation of rare events is highly unlikely and not seen as the basis for a profitable research program. Also, normal science results ignore the inner contradictions of the Model I and O-I world that are not illuminable without interrupting the flow of everyday life (in order, for example, to create new states of the world).

Moreover, many normal science research results are nondisconfirmable in the action or local context. Advice can range from being overly pessimistic about change to being overly optimistic (e.g., organic systems will lead to openness, trust, and double-loop learning; hiring new professionals will change an organization; or shifting leaders around can solve leadership effectiveness issues more effectively than can reeducating individuals).

Conventional research also tends to support the present biases and defenses that researchers must have if they are to maintain their present programs. Hence, if a research program assumes that organizations are anti-double-loop learning, then statements will be made to that effect even though no empirical research has been conducted to illustrate the assumption.

The advice that social scientists may give, derived from rigorous research to create a world with a better quality of life, is largely limited to a Model I and O-I world. Apparently many social scientists are not aware of this limitation. One reason may be that they neither strive to create models of alternative worlds in order to create a dialectic nor do they tend to conduct normative empirical research. Some social scientists go further and assert that alternative worlds do not and cannot exist. This assertion about the potentialities of human nature is made with almost no empirical research evidence. The same social scientists would become quite upset if someone with so little data made equally strong statements about the world as it is.

Finally, there is a small group of social scientists interested in new alternatives. Unfortunately, most of these remain at the espoused level of analysis and do not conduct actual empirical research. Hence, the data base that is so urgently needed remains lacking.

As social scientists, we are fond of saying that the truth will make us free. If this analysis is valid, the truth emanating from rigorous research may make us free, but the freedom will be limited by the constraints of the existing universe.

CHAPTER 6

Action Science: A Perspective

In this chapter, I explore one perspective for an action science. Before describing the differences between this perspective and normal science, I should like to remind the reader of the underlying similarities of the two perspectives.

The major similarity between normal science and action science of the kind that I will describe is that both highly value public disconfirmability, order, causality, and elegance. Knowledge should be produced in a form that allows it to be disconfirmed. An underlying order in the universe is assumed to exist (or more accurately, to be enactable), and so causality is a central feature to be understood. These three features being dealt with equally, the theory that contains the minimum number of concepts and untested assumptions or axioms is the one to be preferred.

Central Purpose of Implementation

There are several major differences in perspective between normal science and action science. The first of these is that the technology of action science created to obtain disconfirmability, to describe order, to identify causal relations, and to develop elegant knowledge has as its primary purpose the production of knowledge that can be implemented. Understanding, or explanation plus prediction, are in the service of implementation and are not ends in themselves.

As we have seen, understanding or explanation of a particular phenomenon obtained when the purpose is discovery can be different from the understanding or explanation of the same phenomenon obtained when the purpose is to take some action related to that phenomenon. The reason that it is different is that taking action always requires working within on-line constraints. This, in turn, means that whatever knowledge is produced must take into account the finite information-processing capacities of human beings and the scarcity of time to make precise analyses, the lack of power to control the ongoing world to our design, and the difficulties for iterative learning embedded in a Models I and O-I world.

Creation of Alternative Universes

The second major difference is that action science takes as a central concern the building of universes alternative to those presently existing. Because action science values valid information, then it will always limit itself to those alternative universes that do not increase the threats of validity. Action science, therefore, cannot be used to explore any alternative universe.

There are two purposes of exploring alternative universes. The first is to discover and create worlds that enhance, more than is at present the case, the production of valid information and its concomitant requirements such as informed choice, personal causality, and ongoing commitment to the detection and correction of error. The second purpose is to create conditions that interrupt the automatic responses that people have acquired through socialization. Automatic responses are interrupted when existing theories-in-use and skills are to be found to be ineffective. When these factors are experienced as ineffective, a host of defenses organized around the sense of competence and the feelings of self-esteem are mobilized. When these defenses are mobilized, actions are executed that, when examined, lead the actors to become aware of a second layer of defenses that keep them unaware of what would happen if their learned skills were to be interrupted. Recognition of these unawarenesses brings to the surface tacit causal mechanisms that are at the heart of understanding the deeper structure of the present universe. Hence, creating alternative worlds is necessary to get at the operative but tacit structures of individuals and systems of the existing universe.

Integration of Research and Education

The third major difference between action science and normal science is the intimate connection for the client between learning and the production of knowledge. In most of the research reviewed, the subjects' skills were not interrupted; indeed, the research instruments were designed to remain within the subjects' present abilities in order to ensure high reliability and validity.

If one asks people to involve themselves in research where they will be exposed to the experiences of bewilderment, frustration, and failure, it is necessary to connect these consequences with the development of new and additional skills. This is necessary because it is unethical to upset people, leaving them with, at best, a thorough debriefing and counseling. It is necessary to connect research with the provision of education for the subject, because this very connection will influence the way the subjects will frame their participation and the degree to which they will not knowingly distort data or, if necessary, the degree to which they will strive to monitor and make public when they may be producing distorted data.

Closely associated with this reason for an intimate connection between research and learning is the objective to produce, as much as possible, knowledge of the world of action. This means that the researcher must observe and develop inferences about the world in which the subjects are embedded. I believe it is now quite well accepted that the nonparticipant observer is rarely being nonparticipant (Argyris, 1968). All observers are participating to some degree or other. If subjects experience social scientists as meddling in their world, then they will have explicit or tacit reactions. If they do not communicate the former and because they are unaware of the latter, we run the risk of not being aware of important threats to validity. We reduce this risk if the subjects know that their reports and actions will serve as bases for educational programs that may alter the social universe in which they are embedded. Although this awareness may act to enhance their vigilance for unrealized distortion, it does not guarantee the elimination of such distortion. Education based upon data collected from the subjects helps to increase the probability that they will bring to the surface the distortions made unrealizingly during the diagnostic activities. People are rarely interested in redesigning their universe in ways that are congruent with tacit distortions.

Low a priori Precision with High Accuracy

Under On-Line Conditions

The fourth major difference from normal science is the emphasis in action science upon generalizations that can lead to a high degree of accuracy under on-line conditions and that are achievable under those conditions. The generalizations, therefore, must not only show respect for on-line constraints but also must be usable under these conditions. Such generalizations will tend to have a low degree of precision yet a high degree of accuracy.

Accuracy may be defined in terms of the degree to which the actors (or social unity) achieve their intended objectives without unrecognized, unintended consequences. Accuracy is consonant with effectiveness as defined in Chapter 2. Problem solving is effective to the extent that it solves problems so that they remain solved and in a way that does not reduce future problem-solving effectiveness. Accuracy, therefore, includes predictability and validity but goes beyond to include applicability. The thrust of the argument about rigorous research has been that the technology of normal science focuses primarily upon prediction and validity.

Normal science also emphasizes precision. Precision exists to the extent one can define quantitatively the relationship among variables under varying states. It is a sign of precision to state that a stipulated variation in X leads to (or is associated with) a stipulated variation in Y. This precision is valued because it leads to greater confidence in the inferred causal relationships if one can vary X systematically and see what happens to Y.

The difficulty with the technology presently used to gain such precision is that it creates concepts that may not be applicable in the action context, as well as introduces conditions such as unilateral control over subjects and minimal interest in new universes, all of which increase the likelihood of producing unrecognizable threats to validity. These conditions combine to make it unlikely that knowledge will be additive in the sense that it will eventually yield a significant reduction in the applicability gap. It appears difficult to take rigorous knowledge with high precision and low predictive validity (low, from the actors' view) and combine it to produce low precision and high accuracy. The high precision that may lead to whatever accuracy a proposition contains, requires, if it is to be emulated by an actor under on-line conditions, a set of constraints that act to reduce the accuracy when it is being used in real life. To put it in our terms, the theory-in-use that leads to high precision necessarily leads to conditions that produce unrecognizable errors and low accuracy.

Zadek (1972) correctly points out that the relationship between precision and validity is complex. He suggests a "principle of incompatibility" that states that as system complexity increases, our ability to make precise and valid statements is maintained until a threshold is reached. Beyond that threshold, precision and significance are probably mutually exclusive. The closer one looks at the real world, the fuzzier it appears and the fuzzier will be useful solutions.

An Illustration

What are some of the features of research that produce knowledge containing low precision and high accuracy *and* that can be used under on-line conditions to produce accuracy with low precision? This is an extremely difficult question to answer. Nevertheless, we must begin, even if the ideas are primitive.

Fortunately, there exists one model of research produced by Kurt Lewin and his associates, illustrated through their studies on the climates of children's groups. In these experiments, low precision was coupled with high accuracy and produced generalizations that were highly implementable by leaders in everyday life. Indeed, I hope to show that when some of Lewin's associates continued the leadership research by using the normal science view of rigor and precision, they may have produced knowledge that was less applicable and, if used, knowledge with a lower probability of on-line accuracy.

First, let us show how the early Lewin, Lippitt, and White (1939) experiments contained many of the features that are central to action science. The authors began with a commitment to study action contexts (authoritarian, democratic, laissez-faire group atmosphere) by creating a social order. The social order had to have important social value. Lewin, having narrowly escaped Hitler's Germany, was committed to show the advantages of democracy over autocracy or laissez-faire societies. Next, the experiment had to involve the participants. They had to profit from it while they were participating. Their payoff was not limited to the debriefing period.

In creating three different social orders, the researchers acted as all human beings do in everyday life. They became designers and implementers of several different theories of action; they had to design meanings for each type of leader. The instructions for each leader were lengthy, detailed, and multifaceted. They described the behavioral, as well as the governing, variables for each leadership style.

The research began with an a priori design but not specific and precise hypotheses about the interrelationships among the variables. Indeed, if one examines the many different levels of variables used, one could produce a map of empirical relationships that would make the Mann, Indik, and Vroom (1963) map presented previously look like a simple network. But, as we shall see, they found powerful conceptual maps to organize the information in ways that could be easily stored, retrieved, and used by actors.

The authors designed a series of situations, provided evidence that their designs "took effect," and then observed the consequence. It is important to note that the group tasks selected were complex and allowed plenty of "freedom and variation to bring to the foreground the essential characteristics of group life" (Lippitt, 1940, pp. 56ff.). The objective was to maximize the personal causality of the participants in the behavior that they were producing.

The major data-gathering technique was the observation of behavior. There were stenographic notes; minute by minute observations of many psychological, social, and physical variables, and tapes and films of later experiments. The basic objective was to strive to study the totality of co-existing parts (Lewin, 1940, p. 33). The social space should include the psychological past, present, and future that exists in the present (Lewin, 1940. p. 36).

How did they analyze the data? The most important criterion appeared to be to try to capture the meanings that existed in the action or local context, even if this meant that units of analysis would not be equal or that observers would have to make subjective inference. Thus:

> It was not our main purpose to make the techniques and data independent from the observers as has often been the aim. We wanted reliable, valid data, but were not willing to sacrifice the skillful interpretive abilities of four graduate students of child psychology for complete reliability of observation or insignificant items/behavior [Lippitt, 1940, p. 36].

Turning to the definition of units, Lippitt quotes Dorothy Swaine Thomas approvingly:

> Our attempts to record more complicated situations (e.g., aggressive acts, resistant acts) have led to claims of a qualitative similarity (as indicated by relatively high reliability on simultaneous observations) but no quantitative equivalence. . . . These units of resistance are not interchangeable or additive. An attempt has been made to make one unit "mean" the same as another, but in form they differ greatly from one another. For statistical analyses of observational materials, equality of form is more important than equality of meaning [Thomas, 1933, pp. 436-467].

If rigor means a faithful systematic representation of reality, and if reality includes the action context, then equality of meaning is more rigorous in the sense that it describes the action context with abstractions of the type used by actors who are embedded in that context. These units of meaning are not equivalent in size or form and hence are not subject to the quantification to which scientists aspire. But the rigor obtainable with normal science may not be usable by human beings in the world of action. And if they cannot operationalize that rigor in the action context, then they cannot apply the ideas systematically. The key to the mathematics of everyday life may be equivalence of meaning.

Meaning of action must be inferred by observing the action. The latter can be tape- or videotape-recorded. All modes are incomplete, and all provide an overabundance of information. It is possible to spend a lifetime analyzing movies of group behavior, yet, they are incomplete because it would require a battery of cameras to record everything. But everything does not need to be recorded; the world of action is full of redundancy and behavior that is overdetermined. It is possible to observe only a part and yet make valid inferences from that partial segment. Human beings also face the same constraints. They cannot observe everything.

The original monograph presents many pages of conversations. To the right of the conversation, the meanings inferred from it are given. In our language, the researchers presented the (relatively) directly observable data and the meanings inferred from them. It is possible then for the readers to judge for themselves the validity of the inference process. The data are presented, in other words, in ways that make it possible for the readers to conduct their own interobserver reliability test.

Examples of meanings inferred were "hostility toward Tom," "Tom is defensive," "work-minded behavior," "blaming behavior toward S," "leader controls decision." Each meaning was inferred from different size units (of sentences). At times, one sentence could have several meanings. At other times, one meaning was inferred from several paragraphs of conversation and observations of physical behavior (e.g., Tom leaves the group, children cleanup). The next step was to categorize the meanings and then provide overall data for each category. The quantification used was basic addition and percentages. This led to summaries of the actions of the leaders and the members.

Next, the data were formed into patterns. For example, the findings that the autocratic leaders dictated most of the activities (e.g., choice of tasks, materials, companions, the time perspective) were organized around the concept of space of free movement. The authoritarian leader was shown to decrease the space of free movement.

He did not permit the children to locomote freely in these activity regions in the social space.

From the concept of space of free movement, it was possible "to derive" consequences. For example, as the space of free movement decreases, individuals become frustrated, de-differentiated and more primitivized. These predictions came from the psychomathematical properties of the topological space and from generalizations developed through experimental research, in this case experiments on frustration (Barker, Dembo, & Lewin, 1941). The concepts were defined in ways that led to predictions under a given set of conditions. This is the key to Lewin's concept of lawfulness. He states, "determinism [lawfulness]. . . means that the same conditions always lead to the same effects. . . . [Lewin, 1940, p. 16]." In this case, a decrease in space of free movement causes frustrations, shorter time perspective, etc., no matter in what action setting.

Another important concept was the gatekeeper. Whenever a gatekeeper controls who shall enter the region of achieving their goals, it is possible to predict that the people striving to achieve their goals will become dependent upon the leader, competitive among each other, etc.

Lewin would claim that the predictions are logically or mathematically derived from topological and vector concepts. Many scholars doubted this claim. They saw the maps depicting psychological space of free movement or the gatekeeper as informative graphics. I, too, doubt the case for the logical derivation. However, I believe that Lewin's models were more than graphics. They could serve as efficient ways to store complex sets of relationships, as ways to easily retrieve the knowledge, and hence as techniques for on-line design and action. Lewin's topological drawings may have been effective innovations to be used to facilitate and expand human information-processing capacity; in other words, they were excellent external memories.

To summarize so far, an attempt was made through complex interventions to create social order. Three theories of action were designed that led to different group climates. Initially, a priori hypotheses were tested. However, careful and systematic notes were obtained. The most important criterion was not to sacrifice the manings that existed in the action context. The quantitative techniques used were of the most simple kind (counting, percentages, etc.). The ultimate goal was to create complex patterns of concepts that validly explained the bahvior observed and could act as efficient information-processing aids (e.g., space of free movement and gatekeeper).

These studies illustrate, I suggest, Von Neumann's (1958) argument that human action may gain accuracy by using a sloppy calculus that is not easily distorted by noise. Yet, Lewin's students believed (and Lewin himself appeared to agree) that these early experiments were too sloppy and that they should eventually become more precise. They believed that the next step would be to decompose the many variables in the original experiments so that one or two of them could be studied much more thoroughly. Thus, one may read in later articles by Lewin's colleagues of the "pioneering studies" by Lewin, Lippitt, and White but a few lines later be told that these studies dealt with democratic procedures in a global way and used preliminary concepts that lacked clear and precise conceptual definitions (French, Israel, & As, 1960).

It is my belief that we will learn more about precision and accuracy required in the action context by remaining with that philosophy of experimentation and quantification illustrated in the earlier studies. For example, in the later, allegedly more rigorous, series of studies, participation (by A) was defined as "the amount of A's influence on the decisions and plans agreed upon, or equivalently the amount of influence that B, C . . . accept during the joint decision-making process [French, Israel, & As, 1960, p. 314]." How can any A determine (in an on-line manner) the amount of his or her psychological and objective participation as well as the amount of influence that B, C . . . have? We are back, I suggest, to the same problem described in the discussion of Fiedler's work.

French raises the level of abstraction further, and in an even more systematic and rigorous paper, develops a formal theory of social power that I believe disconnects his thinking further from the action context. For example, "For any given discrepancy of opinion between A and B, the strength of the resultant force which an inducer A can exert on an inducee B, in the direction of agreeing with A's opinion, is proportional to the strength of the bases of power of A over B [French, 1956, p. 184]." If any A's were to take this statement as a basis to inform their on-line designs and implementations, either they would be immobilized or the world would have to slow down dramatically and give A all the time and power he or she needs to obtain measures of these relationships. If that were to happen, then the measures would be of a world that would soon speed up again to its normal pace, and hence their external validity would be questionable.

I believe that French would argue that the postulates and theorems that he defines rigorously are meant to be related to the distant context and not to the action context. If so, the problem now is that the gap between the two contexts is so great that the knowledge is only minimally useful for the purposes of design. Indeed, I believe that the "sloppy" predictions that came from the early studies, especially from such concepts as "space of free movement" and "gate-keeper," provide a better base for designing and executing leadership styles vis-à-vis members than does much of the leadership research that followed, not only at Michigan but at many other locations (Argyris, 1978).

Cartwright (1959) writes that, during the initial stages of research, "a general map is needed to show the full array of interdependence before undertaking a precise quantitative determination of the relations among a limited number of properties. Research should proceed by a series of successive approximations, beginning with a gross determination of what goes with what, and moving progressively to an exact specification of the form of the functional relations [p. 56]." I agree with the importance of presenting the full array of interdependencies. Whereas Cartwright sees that as the first step to more precise quantification, I see it as the issue to resolve if we are to understand rigorously what goes on in the action context (not merely in the distant context). In the action context, actors are always trying to make gross determinations of what goes with what. The successive approximations that I envision are studies to understand more clearly the processes of "what goes with what."

Cartwright also states that the wholeness of the first approximation is not destroyed by the succeeding approximations; the first approximation is simply more articulated in the succeeding ones. When I examine the line of inquiry by French and his colleagues cited earlier, I have difficulty in seeing the features that characterize the first approximation, and my belief is that the French studies are much closer to the original approximation than is the case for much of the leadership research conducted elsewhere. Are not concepts such as gatekeeper and space of free movement more informative to a leader who wishes to design his or her behavior in a given local context than French's proposition about participation and influence? Perhaps French would add that his studies could be quite informative about probable consequences of participation when it is considered legitimate and when it is not. The study could be used to map policies. I would agree with that addition but point out that such knowledge is being used to inform the probable espoused theories (policies) of the organization.

Features that Combine Low a priori Precision with High Accuracy

The following features appear critical if the propositions produced are to combine relatively low precision and high accuracy in ways that potential users can produce high accuracy under on-line conditions.

1. The models of individual or systemic actions developed to organize aspects of the action context are relatively easily validatable by the actor. Such models contain meanings directly connectable to the action context. This means that the concepts are developed from a data base of relatively directly observable data and not from espoused-theory data such as the types of questionnaires described in Chapter 3. Moreover, the data base is deepened to obtain tacitly held knowledge by creating research tasks that interrupt presently held skills and question the effectiveness of existing learning systems.

2. The models produced attempt to specify what Lewin called the wholeness of the problem. It is difficult to operationalize wholeness in the terms that will be necessary if we are to put it to tough tests of validity and reliability. In the Lewin studies, specifying wholeness appeared to mean striving to focus on the patterns of variables that subjects might experience and not on the precise quantitative relationships of the variables within the patterns.

Attention to wholeness also appeared to mean creating models that attempt to account for a meaningful macro-unit of everyday life. For example, the concept of gatekeeper contained within it a model of cooperation and competition among peers, a model of dependence upon a gatekeeper, a model of relationships of peer needs and gatekeeper's objectives, etc. The early studies did not break out of these models because the pattern that the subjects experienced in the action context included all of them. Later some researchers, for example, decomposed the issues of cooperation and competition by separating them from many of the other contextual issues in order to study these factors more rigorously. These studies produced at best a string of generalizations that, even if additive, ignored the remaining context. The generalizations could have high accuracy in a world where the other models were not operating, in our terms, the distant context. The moment one takes the wholeness issue seriously (because leaders under on-line conditions may subdivide at their peril) the research results become too numerous to organize and use.

Wholeness somehow captures a pattern of variables whose validity is tested by seeing the degree to which actors can use the model to produce accuracy (or to be effective) under on-line constraints. Much research is needed to specify the "somehow."

3. In order to retain the concept of wholeness, one must also hold the idea that the universe is composed of a set of interrelated patterns of variables. The action science perspective is that human beings create the patterns at all levels of reality. The task is to discover the theory of design in the heads of actors, or those that exist in systems, that can inform us of the probable meanings that people will create and in what pattern they will appear. The theories of design at the individual or systemic level are what we have called theories-in-use (not the espoused theories). It is the theories-in-use that define the genotypic meanings that individuals will produce. If we know the genotypic meanings, then we do not need to know a priori all the possible phenotypic meanings or relationships. Implicit in action science, therefore, is the assumption that individuals and social systems (of various sizes) design their actions.

4. Because the propositions are not highly precise, the requirements for public disconfirmability in action science must be very high. As Lewin pointed out, the criterion is that even one instance that did not conform to the prediction could disconfirm an hypothesis. The test in action science therefore requires neither "residual" categories nor a high degree of ignorance about the whole situation, so that it is acceptable to account for low amounts of the nonrandom variance. If an exception is observed, it should be used to test the hypothesis. The researcher could show, for example, that the exception occurred under a different set of conditions and that the occurrence was predictable by the theory. Implicit in this assumption is that individuals or systems will not design meanings that are not embedded in their presently held theory of design. Implicit in that assumption, in turn, is the assumption that people choose to create their universe, even the one that may dominate them.

Our position combines the perspectives that philosophers of science have called realism and idealism. The realists claim: "The world of perception and cognition has an immutable existence all its own; entirely independent of the perceiver. Man looks out onto a world that has an independent existence [Rychlak, 1968, p. 17]." The idealists claim "there is no external world of reality apart from or having an existence independent of the perception and cognition of the perceiver. . . . Man looks out on a world of his own making [p. 17]."

Closely related to these two perspectives are two others: objectivity and subjectivity. The objective perspective maintains that "abstractions, and hence the relationships between abstractions transcend the individual abstractor and may be grasped or understood by all individuals in a specified class [p. 22]." The subjective perspective maintains that "our abstractions and the relations between them are somehow private, and difficult or impossible to circumscribe, much less to generalize beyond the behavior of the abstractor in question [p. 27]."

Idealism and subjectivity perspectives are at the forefront when we are studying how theories-in-use and learning systems arise and how they can be altered. For example, individual theories-in-use create the reality for individuals. Understanding how they arise will help to explain why man looks out on a world of his own making. Realism and objectivity come to the forefront when we are studying how theories-in-use and learning systems contain imperatives that channel human action in predictable ways. A learning system is an abstraction that can be grasped by all individuals. Learning systems exist even though different people move in and out. One of the interesting puzzles in the perspective that we are propounding is that individual theories-in-use also manifest coercive channelizing properties to their designers and holders. As we stated in Chapter 2, people can use theories-in-use that inhibit their personal causation and proactivity. The action scientists sees these perspectives as describing different aspects of a circular process. The idealist-subjective perspectives focus on the processes by which the "out there" external world is created. The realist-objective perspective focuses on the demands the outside world makes upon individuals and systems.

As we shall see, it is possible to define patterns of self-maintaining relationships at various levels of complexity that are identifiable by the actors. They exist not only for the present set of actors but also for future actors as they take on roles within these patterns. For example, we will describe in Chapter 7 the pattern of relationships among the partners of a professional firm. We will see how the partners created these patterns and then how the patterns served to keep behavior consistent with their requirements for survival or, more accurately, how the partners chose to remain within the constraints of these patterns in order to make their world more manageable.

In action science, these perspectives are not juxtaposed against each other with pressures to select sides. The moment one takes applicability seriously, the question of design of human action becomes central. Design is the plan or organization of behavior to accomplish intended consequences. In order to accomplish intended consequences, one must be able to predict accurately. In order to predict accurately, one must focus on creating constancy and manageability in an environment that is continually changing and so complex that it often appears unmanageable. Hence, constancy requires that the environment be enacted. Once the environment is enacted, it must be able to coerce specific human actions; otherwise the intended consequences will not be realized. Thus, human beings must design their environments and then permit the environments to coerce their behavior. This is comparable to people creating streets and sidewalks and then choosing to let these constrain their behavior.

The interplay between realism and idealism and between objectivity and subjectivity may be experienced especially vividly when one is conducting intervention experiments to help individuals move from Models I and O-I to Models II and O-II. During the stages where the individuals were diagosing and describing the world in which they were embedded, they created a realistic perspective whose existence was dependent upon the assumption of objectivity. The individual theories-in-use and those interaction patterns that they had created, and that were counterproductive to double-loop learning, were seen by all as existing "out there," independent of themselves. Indeed one of the major learnings was that not only did these theories-in-use and counterproductive cycles exist "out there," but the individuals and systems appeared helpless to change them.

However, during the stage when the actors were striving to redesign their world and create new patterns, the idealistic and subjective perspectives dominated. The participants, for example, froze and learned at a different pace. The realities that they were attempting to alter were highly subjective ones. The realities that they were trying to create were even more ambiguous; so much so that they were often unable to describe them to themselves.

Another intriguing finding was that others tended to understand the theories-in-use better than did the actors who utilized them. What appeared to be variables that were likely to be most subjective (i.e., one's theory-in-use) were actually more illustrative of the realistic-objective dimensions: "My theory-in-use is apparently out there for others to see more clearly than I see it; I have created a map to manage my life that I then cannot fully manage." The first part of the puzzle is partially resolved when we recall that a theory-in-use is constructed from behavior. The actors must reflect on their behavior before they can construct their theory-in-use. But to do so they require feedback from others. The second part of the puzzle cannot be resolved unless people learn Model II skills and are able to live in O-II learning systems.

The point is that, from an action frame of reference, human beings create a universe that they can follow, thereby making their action design and implementation activities more manageable. People create the world to which they will become pawns. In this sense, the realistic perspective is valid. But the state of being a pawn is, or should be, continually subject to inquiry and redesign. Under these conditions, the idealistic-subjective qualities play a very important role.

To test hypotheses that may be imprecisely stated requires a strategy that overcomes the imprecision but that is not itself invalidated by the procedures used. Human beings will have generalizations made available to them by action science that will have gaps. These gaps may be due to the fact that the models used may not include all the genotypic meanings and may lack the phenotypic meanings required to cope with a particular situation. People must therefore accompany the use of any generalization with an on-line testing of its gaps and of its effectiveness.

Human beings are forever applying propositions and inquiring continuously about the accuracy and effectiveness with which they are operating. Human beings are always intervenors and experimenters, testing the effectiveness of their interventions. In order to conduct on-line tests of the effectiveness with which they implement a particular set of generalizations, individuals must collect relatively directly observable data, must make explicit the inferences made from the data, must eventually make explicit the theory that they used to recognize data, and then, organizing it into patterns, they must package it in ways that others are able *and* willing to disconfirm. All these conditions are conditions of what Lewin called the good experiment. Hence, individuals are experimenters. They need the knowledge base and skills to conduct genuine on-line experiments.

Willems (1969) has suggested that a fruitful way to characterize research activities is to think of a two-dimensional descriptive space. One dimension is the degree of the investigator's influence upon, or manipulation of, the antecedent conditions of the behavior studied. The second dimension is the degree to which units are imposed by the investigator upon the behavior studied (pp. 46-47). The latter dimension is related to the degree of a priori precision. Normal science aspires toward increasing precision which, it has been shown, tends to be accomplished through restrictions or limitations on the range of data and meanings to be collected. The former dimension is akin to the quality of unilateral control. Normal science experimental and correlational methods aspire toward the highest possible unilateral control.

Describing the space of research activities in this manner permits one to plot many different possibilities of research. Some of these are identified in Figure 6.1. An example of a high-high research activity would be an experiment where the units are highly restricted (eyelid movement) and the control over triggering their movement is very high. An example of a high-low investigation would be an experiment having a high degree of control over the situation but utilizing rich, open-ended, descriptive records of behavior such as the Lewin, Lippitt, and White (1939) studies previously described. The French studies would be closer to a high-medium moving toward high-high. An example of low-low would be the naturalistic studies of Roger Barker and his students (Barker & Wright, 1955) where the natural conditions studied were, relatively speaking, "investigator-free" (Barker, 1965). Finally, an example of low-high would be an unobtrusive counter that recorded the number of people entering different rooms in an art gallery.

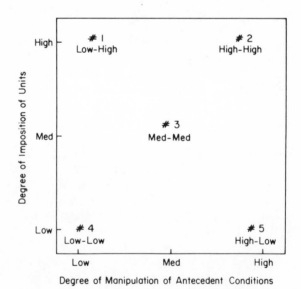

FIGURE 6.1. *A space for describing research activities. [From Willems and Raush (Eds.),* Naturalistic viewpoints in psychological research, *p. 47. Copyright © 1969 by Holt, Rinehart & Winston. Reprinted by permission.]*

Action science may also be mapped upon this space. The research that I will describe in the next chapter always contains two phases. The first is low-low. This is usually the diagnostic phase where it is necessary to document what people do in their everyday lives and the distribution of these activities, and to develop a taxonomy of behavioral repertoires in a favorable ratio of expenditure to yield under conditions where there is minimal chance for being accused of being manipulative and coercive. As Willems (1969) points out, naturalistic low-low methods are suited to these conditions.

The second phase of action science is intervention of the low-high variety. The objective there is to assist the clients (subjects) to redesign their universe. This will require that *they* manifest a high degree of control over the antecedent conditions for every experiment they design and execute as they attempt to move from Models I and O-I toward (in our case) Models II and O-II. The unit imposition is low because, whatever methods of inquiry are used, they should provide the clients with maximum control over what and how much they choose to reveal, over the depth of their revelations as well as the timing, and over the freedom to "erase" something they have said.

Action science requires a diagnostic phase of low-low so that the clients cannot explain away the findings as induced by the methodology of intervention. The corollary of this is that the subjects' responsibility for the data produced should be high because it is, as Barker notes, relatively observer-free. Both of these conditions are required if the clients are voluntarily to choose to enter the second phase. However, the interpretation of the data is another matter. Once the interventionists organize the data into patterns or maps, they are imposing their meanings. These meanings must be subject to public disconfirmability just as are any other research models (Argyris & Schön, 1978, pp. 167-206).

Another reason for the two-phase model is that the interventionists and the clients require the best possible assurances that the experimental treatment (the change program) is the cause of the results. Control groups would help to increase confidence in the findings, but strict control group procedures are unfortunately not likely in action science. Even if one could find a group that matched the experimental group perfectly, one would have to treat them as an entity that would not experience the second phase and keep that information secret from them.

If the purpose of a control group is to help assess the choice among possible interpretations of the findings, then a low-low phase makes it possible to compare the experimental group against itself at an earlier stage, a procedure recommended by Campbell and Stanley (1963) when quasi-experimental technology is used. In order to use such control groups, it would be important to show that going through the diagnostic phase did not educate the clients toward the results or that being picked as an experimental group did not have the famous Hawthorne effect. When one is conducting research that is the equivalent of moving from Model I toward Model II, this is not a difficult task. As has been noted, it is possible to educate people about Model II, to create an internal commitment to the Model, to have people design actions in accordance with Model II, and yet find that they are not able to produce Model II behavior. The reasons are (1) they do not have the new skills that they require; (2) their old skills lead them automatically to create Model I actions; and (3) the old skills plus the O-I world they create lead them to be unaware of the first two until after they have produced the actions. But by then we have taped the behavior. Indeed, we will also have tape recordings of the frustrations, bewilderments, and confusions that the people experience. It is data like these that make it highly unlikely that any of the threats to internal validity mentioned by Campbell and Stanley (1963) are operative.

As long as action science combines low-low with low-high designs of the kind summarized in Figure 6.1, and as long as the study includes double-loop changes, then the results should be replicable in every experiment. Hence, one does not need to depend on previous research to provide control groups.

Summary and Conclusions

The analysis to date suggests that normal science approaches will have difficulty in achieving the objective of informing individual and system actions to the extent that they utilize the present concepts of rigorous research. The causes of the difficulties include (1) the distancing from the action context usually required for precise formulations about invariant relationships among an unnaturally coupled or uncoupled set of variables; (2) the unilaterally controlling methodology of rigorous research (high-high in Figure 6.1) that creates situations that may attract particular attitudes and actions that in turn affect how people may respond knowingly or unknowingly to the experimental manipulation or questionnaire and hence affect internal and external validity; and (3) the constraints placed by on-line (everyday life) encounters, such as (a) the fact that the world is more complicated than the information-processing capacities of human beings; (b) the low probability that people can have all the information that they require in any given situation; (c) the low probability that people will have the time required to conduct on-line rigorous diagnoses; (d) the low probability that the world will remain benign while individuals diagnose or take action; and (e) the likelihood that as the completeness of the information increases, the probability of the actor being immobilized and acting in an authoritarian manner also increases.

The objective of action science is to design a research methodology that takes these constraints seriously while not sacrificing the criteria of public disconfirmability in order to produce knowledge that comprehends increasingly larger domains while using decreasingly complex models with fewer unconfrontable assumptions and to create knowledge that illuminates the status quo but also provides liberating alternatives. The point of view that action science aspires to inform is that of a person or of an organization trying to comprehend reality in order to take action. Action science seeks more to inform individual or system theories-in-use rather than espoused theories.

Focusing for the moment on the individuals, they are pictured first as trying to comprehend the relevant variables of a given problem, to decide which of the variables they wish or they are able to control (or they do not wish or are unable to control). There is a dilemma built into this early diagnostic phase. On the one hand, to decide what are the relevant variables, to identify which to control, and to do this in an on-line manner requires that the individuals have models in their heads to help them organize the world. Models are simplified pictures of the world that have some of the characteristics of the real world but not all of them. Models are a set of interrelated guesses about the world. In addition to being central to science, models are a part of normal existence. People may not label their guesses as models, but they are; this is why all human beings are always theorists of human behavior (Love & March, 1975).

Models act in ways to exclude or to couple variables that may represent the individuals' idiosyncratic views. Hence, those models that are used to diagnose reality may also sustain it. Individuals are forever in the situation where the reality that they are enacting may or may not make sense to others in the same situation. Individuals must always test the extent to which they "perceive" reality correctly and the extent to which others wish to join them in turning their perceptions into propositions about reality.

The assumption made by action science is that the key to understanding individual or systemic actions is to understand their procedures for designing and implementing actions. Variance among variables in the world is interesting to the extent that it implies different meanings and different theories-in-use. Variance within theories-in-use is phenotypic. Detailed information about variables could in principle lead to understanding of human actions; the difficulty is that the number of variables studied and the potential number of propositions are enormous. As we have seen, this normal science strategy can lead to volumes of propositions that have minimal additivity and applicability.

CHAPTER 7

Illustrations of Action Science Models[1]

In this chapter, I would like to present examples of some of the models that I have found useful in trying to develop an action science. The presentation is intended, as the title of the chapter indicates, to be illustrative and not definitive or complete. The models represent my primitive attempts at conceptualizing one approach to action science. It may be helpful to begin by illustrating the inference and reasoning processes used to select data, create meanings, and organize them into various levels of abstractions in order to design and act in the context of action. The levels are summarized in Figure 7.1. I will quote from an actual case of Mr. Y dealing with Mr. X.

The Case of Mr. Y

Y had the difficult task of informing X (his subordinate) that his performance was below standard, that the firm could not continue to condone the low level of performance, that they were going to give X one more chance, and that they hoped that X would react constructively.

First Level: The Relatively Observable Data

The first-level data may come from tape recordings, observations, or scenarios written by the actors. Strictly speaking, all these involve selections and hence do not represent directly observable data. In

1. Recent descriptions of other possible perspectives include Dobyns, Doughty, and Lasswell, 1971; Levinson, 1972; Normann, 1977; Reason, 1978; and Rowbottom, 1977.

141

conducting the empirical research, steps would have to be taken to
establish the validity of these first-level inferences. For the purpose
of this illustration, let us assume that Y actually said the following
sentences:

1. *Your [X's] performance during the past several years has been,
   and continues to be, unacceptable.*
2. *I want to give you one more chance. One action I will take is
   to transfer you to a new location in order that you can start
   with a clean slate and a superior who wants to be of help.*
3. *The other action is to discuss your attitude. You seem to be
   carrying a chip on your shoulder. I've heard words like "leth-
   argy," "uncommitted," and "disinterested" used in describing
   your recent performance.*
4. *Our supervisors cannot have those characteristics.*
5. *Let's discuss your feelings about your performance.*

Second Level: Meanings Inferred from the Directly Observable Data

The next step is to infer the meanings embedded in these sentences.
The meanings should be those that an actor who lives in a similar
social-cultural context would infer. The meanings should represent,
therefore, the understandings that people would have learned through
socialization and acculturation. To express it another way, the meanings should be found in the dictionary that is used by the population
or the informal dictionary used during socialization. The meanings
should not be those that are inferred from a specialized theory such
as the one presented in this book. Again, the meanings inferred should
be subjected to interobserver tests.

Conversation	Meaning
Your performance during the past several years has been, and continues to be, unacceptable.	Your performance is not adequate.
I want to give you one more chance.... I will transfer you to a new location... to start with a clean slate... and a superior who wishes to help.	I am trying to be fair, which means I will trans- fer you to a new location with a new superior.

I want to discuss your attitude. You seem to be carrying a chip on your shoulder. I've heard words like "lethargy," "uncommitted," and "disinterested" used in describing your recent performance.	Your attitudes appear to be lethargy, uncommittedness, and disinterest.
Our supervisors cannot have these characteristics.	These characteristics are unacceptable.
Let's discuss your feelings about your performance.	Talk about your feelings.

Third Level: Implications of the Second-Level Meanings

Up to this point, the data collected and the meanings inferred are not influenced by the theory of action that informs the perspective of this action science approach. The next step is to raise the order of abstraction and introduce our special meanings to the second-level meanings that we have just suggested were embedded in the sentences.

Meaning (second level)	Theory-of-action meaning (third level)
Your performance is not adequate.	Unillustrated evaluation
I am trying to be fair, which means I will transfer you to a new location with a new superior.	Unilateral action
Your attitude appears to be lethargy, uncommittedness, and disinterest.	Unillustrated attribution
These characteristics are unacceptable.	Unilateral evaluation
Talk about your feelings.	Advocacy

The moment we have "scored" the societally acknowledged meanings with the use of our theory of action perspective:

1. We have chosen to examine the impact the meanings have upon learning and upon effective action.

2. We have organized conversation into a smaller number of categories; hence, we have begun to be economical. When we are scoring hundreds of scenarios, it is necessary to reduce the variance of the second-level meanings to a smaller number.

3. The categories are part of a theory that can be used to predict the probable consequences of these categories upon learning and action. The theory tells us, for example, of the impact that unillustrated attributions and evaluations have as well as of how they relate to other categories such as advocacy. This makes it possible to begin to state predictions about what will happen in the future under defined conditions.

Fourth Level: Behavioral Strategies and Theories-in-Use

All the foregoing third-level meanings may be subsumed under the category of advocacy of a position combined with unilateral control in order to minimize losing and maximize winning (i.e., advocacy-unilateral control). If we had "scored" the entire case, we would have presented meanings related to unilateral and covert face-saving of Y and of X by Y. Advocacy-unilateral control and face-saving are the two major behavioral strategies of Model I. Hence, we have now gone from several pages of conversation to two categories. As we climb up the ladder of abstraction and create new patterns, we are able to comprehend more of the directly observable data and make more powerful predictions without losing contact with the levels below.

Fifth Level: Counterproductive Learning Processes (Living System)

Model I predicts that the foregoing conditions will always lead to a behavioral environment that is defensive and counterproductive to the detection and correction of error, especially of double-loop or single-loop error that cannot be discussed without threat. For example, self-sealing processes, misunderstandings, and inconsistencies should occur. The people involved should act as if they are unaware of their own contributions but be aware of the others' contributions to escalating error. In order to illustrate the kinds of inferences at this level, I will return to Y but draw upon data in the original case that have not been presented. (Examples have been published elsewhere, e.g., Argyris & Schön, 1974, 1978; Argyris, 1976a.)

As we saw earlier, X was unilaterally evaluated and diagnosed. Neither the evaluations nor the attributions were illustrated. Nor did

Y invite inquiry into them. Y also made several covert evaluations (in thoughts not expressed but written in the case) about X that he did not raise because he believed that the ideas might upset X and not lead to problem solving. Therefore, Y also made an untested attribution that X cannot deal effectively with questions that place his competency in doubt.

When X attempted to discuss his view of the past, Y ruled such a discussion out of order. He was told that people right up to the top saw him as underutilizing his capacities and as having little motivation to better himself. When X responded, he learned from Y that he had selected a response that Y believed was counterproductive to making progress. ("No sense in talking about the past. It is the future that counts.") From this sentence, X may have concluded that Y evaluated him not only as an ineffective subordinate but also as one who did not know how to carry on a profitable discussion.

Y then told X the responsibilities of people in his job. If X knew these in the first place, then he must have wondered if Y didn't realize that he (X) knew what Y was saying. If he did not, would this not be adequate evidence that he was not competent? So we have Y telling X that his performance was below standard, that his motivation was below standard, that his capacities were adequate or above standard, and that he was deliberately performing below standard.

Once having built a case "against" X, Y then announced that a decision had been made to place X in a new location. However, X must promise to alter his attitudes and commitments. He must become more enthusiastic. X's response was to ask for alternatives—here and now evidence that he had difficulty in becoming enthusiastic. He also asked for higher compensation which in Y's view was further evidence that X did not understand the seriousness of the negative evaluations made of him by his superiors.

X reported that he had been experiencing in this situation conditions that he described as having been unfairly created for him by the organization. For example, X said:

I have not been treated fairly.
I have been kicked in the teeth.
I am underutilized.
I am judged unfairly.
There is not much that I can do.

Such feeling may make it easier for an individual to see the organization as the culprit and to blame it for his poor performance. If X saw these conditions as simultaneously unjust and uninfluenceable, it would make sense, from his perspective, to withdraw his energies and commitment. On the one hand, X can be unproductive, have low commitment, and feel mistreated, and on the other, morally justified in having a low performance.

So we have Y believing that he and the organization were being forthright and fair, X feeling mistreated and misjudged and believing that Y and the organization were unaware of their impact and of their uninfluenceability, Y concluding that X was blind to the seriousness of the situation and uninfluenceable, and neither side discussing these conclusions. These are illustrations of games and self-sealing processes that will tend to escalate error.

To summarize:

1. Y produced some of the consequences that he intended. He communicated to X "the current evaluation of his performance" and that the transfer would be made only if X were committed to making a success of it. He did not, I believe, create the conditions for X to discuss his "lack of desire."

2. Y's behavioral strategies were (a) making unilateral and unillustrated evaluations and attributions of X's actions; (b) barring discussion that X felt was important; (c) controlling the purpose of the meeting and the tasks that were to be accomplished; or (d) coupling these behavioral strategies with action that directly or indirectly informed X that he (Y) was not open to inquiry and confrontation of his position.

3. Behavioral strategies such as these made it likely that (a) X would feel that Y had his mind made up and was uninfluenceable; (b) Y's actions would reinforce X's views that the organization was not giving him a chance; (c) X would conceive of these actions as injustices that were not discussable, which was an added injustice; (d) X would understandably generate feelings ranging from anger (which could be surpressed) to withdrawal; (e) X's feelings of suppressed anger, injustice, and withdrawal would make it possible for X simultaneously to blame the organization and to remain minimally motivated to look at his responsibility in creating poor performance and low commitment; and (f) X would not discuss his feelings and reactions nor would he say that this was the case.

Hence, Y may have created the conditions that reinforced X's blindness to his own responsibility (for his low performance), his sense of withdrawal, and his rationalizations that the fault lies outside himself. Simultaneously Y made it clear that he wanted a promise from X that he would change his performance and his commitment by altering his attitudes of withdrawal and bitterness, the very attitudes X used to protect himself and which Y reinforced during the session.

In order to make the fifth-level inferences, we needed the patterns developed at the third and fourth levels. These patterns, in turn, required the meanings of the second level and the relatively directly observable data of level one. Second, we needed a theory that could organize these patterns into a causal sequence. By organizing relatively directly observable data into behavioral strategies and relating them to governing values, we created a causal sequence; that is, given a particular pattern of Model I governing values and behavioral strategies, the counterproductive cycles should occur. This prediction, in turn, hinged on the necessary connection between Model I actions and counterproductive learning which, in turn, could not be established unless there was a theory of skill with its consequences of automatic responses and unawareness (Chapter 2).

With this theory in place, then the prediction would be that individuals such as X and Y should never knowingly design and produce actions that would be congruent with Model II. X and Y should be able to design and produce actions that are congruent with Model I, the opposite of I, and with oscillating Model I. These predictions should hold in all contexts for as long as the actors have only Model I theories-in-use.

Sixth Level: Learning Systems

Once the living systems are inferred, it is possible to translate them into a more abstract social system concept, namely, the learning system. It is then possible to take many different living system maps and coordinate them with maps of O-I or O-II learning systems. The six levels of this hierarchy of inference are illustrated in Figure 7.1.

Sixth level	Effects of living systems upon learning and effectiveness for social units being studied (learning systems)
Fifth level	Effects of interacting theories-in-use on learning and effectiveness (living systems)
Fourth level	Meanings created by combining meanings from lower order (Largest combination is a theory-in-use.)
Third level	Meanings assigned by references to a specific theory
Second level	Meanings from everyday language
First level	Relatively directly observable data

FIGURE 7.1. *The hierarchy of inference.*

We have experimented with several simple procedures for scoring the transcription. For example, every time a different individual speaks, it is considered to be one unit, no matter how much he or she has said, unless the third-level meanings change. It has not been difficult to obtain a minimum of 75% agreement among experienced observers. The purpose of the quantitative picture would be to obtain a more differentiated view of Y's theory-in-use. The picture could be used by the researcher or by Y to learn such information as: (1) what proportion of his behavior is represented; in this case by categories such as advocacy-no inquiry, unillustrated evaluation, and unillustrated attributions; (2) the variance of these proportions in different situations and/or over time; and (3) the variance in these proportions in different situations and/or over time; and (3) the variance in these proportions if Y were in a learning environment in order to learn Model II. These variances, it should be pointed out, represent differences "within" the same theory-in-use; for example, in scoring the sentences in Y's case, we find:

Meanings	Number
Advocacy-no inquiry	7
Unillustrated evaluation	4
Unillustrated attribution	6
Covertly withholding information	5
Total	22

There are some interesting issues involved with these quantitative pictures. If our purpose is to assess whether individuals are using Model I or Model II, then they provide us more information than we need. If the number of Model I units varies among individuals or with a given individual under different conditions, the variance is not significant if all we are trying to establish is the degree to which actors are Model I or II. The quantitative picture is more useful to the actors who are interested in learning about their behavior. They can see, for example, if they favor the use of unillustrated attributions or evaluations or face-saving actions, etc. But even this information is less appealing because we find that those who wish to learn Model II are interested in any units of behavior that they produce that are Model I.

Early in our work, we felt that the quantitative scores would be especially useful in establishing movement from Model I toward Model II. Indeed, the scores were useful but not as meaningful as we had thought. For example, the production of the first Model II unit was such a rare event that its potency was extremely high to all the actors.

They had just produced a rare event, one which in many cases they had doubted was producible (Argyris, 1976a). As people became more skilled, the rarity of Model II units decreased and so did their potency. But soon we found that people began to try to produce Model II units under conditions that they had previously thought were out of reach. Again, these personally novel units had greater psychological meaning. In Case A (p. 164), we find that a valid picture of Model II attainment is more a function of the discussability of Model I units than of their quantity.

The theory predicts that the variance within each category should not make a difference in the effectiveness of learning and problem solving (the key criteria in a theory-of-action perspective). Any combination of the scores should lead to a defensive behavioral environment (fifth level) which in turn should lead to O-I learning systems (sixth level). From a theory-of-action perspective, therefore, what is more important than this simple quantitative picture is to organize these aggregate scores into a pattern that mirrors how Y behaved in this episode and that illustrates how the pattern would lead to the observed consequences in terms of learning and problem solving. In order to organize quantified descriptive material into a pattern, one must use some concepts. In our case, these include Model I and 0-I. Once we organize the categories above into a pattern called Model I and O-I, we can then explain the dysfunctional learning and problem-solving consequences described in our earlier analyses.

But this explanation is weak because it is ad hoc. The explanation will have more credibility as we test it under different conditions. For example, we can make predictions of how Y will behave in other such situations over time and in different settings (e.g., business, home, church, learning seminar). We can predict how X would react if he were interviewed by someone who was unaware of the episode we have examined. We can also predict how Y will behave in other types of situation (where we would be able to observe his behavior) in which the learning and problem solving are related to double-loop issues. For example, other predictions would be as follows:

1. Y will utter conversation whose meanings are Model I behavioral strategies.
2. This will lead Y to behave in ways that illustrate unilateral face-saving and advocacy coupled with unilateral control in order to win, not lose.
3. The others in the episode (also programmed with Model I) will experience Y as: (*a*) unable to detect and correct error that de-

pends upon feedback from others; and (*b*) uninfluenceable and unaware that he is being experienced as uninfluenceable.

4. The others will not discuss or test these views publicly. If they attempt to test the consequences, they will do so covertly.
5. If Y senses covert meanings, he, too, will not test his influences. Hence, interpersonal games and camouflage will develop.
6. The potential for escalating error will increase because the foregoing conditions will make it highly likely that ambiguity, lack of clarity, inconsistency, and incongruity embedded in the information will be reinforced.

This model of the development of counterproductive learning cycles should hold for Y under any condition as long as the problems are double-loop and/or threatening. The model is based upon the assumption that Y has a theory-in-use, that he uses it to design and implement his actions, that it is Model I, and that he will be embedded in O-I learning systems. If Y is placed in an O-II learning environment (e.g., a seminar designed to learn Model II), Y should behave at the outset in accordance with Model I.

Theories-in-Use

The development of one's theory-in-use is not a particularly difficult task. However, like the development of any theory, it requires much data collection and hence time. People who wish to develop a model of their theory-in-use must obtain relatively directly observable data from tape recordings, observations of conversations by others, recollected scenarios, etc. The next step is to listen to or read this material and analyze it just as we analyzed Mr. Y's case earlier. It is important for the actors to obtain as wide a range of data as possible. It is also necessary that they subject the validity of their inferences to test by such actions as asking others to make independent inferences but also stipulating a priori predictions and noting if they are not disconfirmed, etc. In other words, the actors take on the role of creating and testing the validity of their inferred theories-in-use. (For examples of tests made by actors, see Argyris, 1976a.)

Following are three examples of theories-in-use developed by three executives who were members of a learning environment designed to teach Model II.

Theory-in-Use I

GOVERNING VARIABLES

1. Consider people to be more important than things.
2. Treat the company as a proprietorship and use it consciously as a vehicle to pursue social objectives.
3. Hide feelings that may give others equal control and influence.
4. Assume very high levels of aspiration for individual and organizational effectiveness.

BEHAVIORAL STRATEGIES

1. I develop high control over the high-risk decisions, most of which happen to be mine.
2. I withhold telling others how risky decisions may be (for fear they might not consider them).
3. I retain control over corporate policies.
4. I screen all my strategies unilaterally for their impact upon people. (I describe or hide strategies depending upon what I believe their impact on others may be. I also hide this fact.)
5. I conceal personal feelings except when asked. I can become open at the initiation of others (not by myself).
6. I seek information from others by asking indirect questions (because I do not trust answers given to me by direct questions).
7. I monitor the behavior of others continually and excessively.
8. I am flexible in positions that do not threaten the governing variables.

CONSEQUENCES ON SELF AND ENVIRONMENT

1. Associates are used primarily as information producers. They are rarely used as providers of feedback to me.
2. Associates become dependents: (*a*) Every key issue is thought of and controlled by me; (*b*) they seek cues to feel out my position; and (*c*) they continually check to reaffirm my strategies (everybody seems to be monitoring).
3. Associates hesitate and resist probing important areas that they believe I am concealing.
4. Dissent by subordinates on major risky issues is difficult.
5. I am seen as uncompromising of my personal goals (which are listed here as the governing variables).
6. I am blind to people's rights when they interfere in reaching corporate objectives.

CONSEQUENCES ON LEARNING

1. Associates give very little help to me on risky issues.
2. There is little double-loop learning.
3. High on self-sealing processes.
4. There is public testing of others' job satisfaction. Low public testing of self and others' personal feelings as well as basic company policies (the latter are closely tied to my personal feelings).
5. Nondirective questions become covertly directive.

Theory-in-Use II

GOVERNING VARIABLES

1. Win; do not lose.
2. Maximize the intellectual aspects and minimize the emotional.
3. Maximize positive feelings and evaluations. Hide negative feelings and evaluations.
4. Define my goals and achieve them as I define them.

BEHAVIORAL STRATEGIES

1. I avoid confrontations on business and interpersonal issues if they could surface negative feelings.
2. When others resist my views, I manipulate them more to get them to agree with me.
3. My behavior vacillates from dominance to withdrawal. (I dominate when I want to control and withdraw when there is little need for me to control or where feelings are becoming strong.)
4. I sell people my views and say dishonest things (if I think that this will win them over).
5. I am a perfectionist. I set very high standards.
6. I withhold ideas and feelings (until I think they will be accepted).
7. I reject people whom I do not value (but I do it diplomatically; i.e., I suppress negative feelings and lie about rejection).
8. I continually categorize people and ideas.
9. I "sell" conclusions without directly observable data.
10. I exhibit high attribution and evaluation.

CONSEQUENCES ON SELF AND ENVIRONMENT

1. Others withdraw from taking initiative.

2. Others see me as defensive and manipulating, but they hide these views.
3. Others become cautious and try to psych me out before they act.
4. There is mutual mistrust.
5. Others depend on me for the major decisions.
6. There is low internal commitment to the major decisions (because they are my decisions).
7. There is distorted communication.
8. There is rivalry and intergroup conflict.
9. I do not invite feedback that could level peaks and valleys of enthusiasm.
10. I am indiscriminately receptive but covertly discriminating.
11. I am angry toward others.
12. Others withdraw.
13. An "inner" and an "outer" group are developed.

CONSEQUENCES ON LEARNING

1. Defensive processes are self-sealing.
2. Others withhold valid information when they do not believe that I want to hear it. (They also keep this fact secret.)
3. There is public testing of only those issues that I consider important.
4. There is private testing of issues that involve emotional components.

Theory-in-Use III

GOVERNING VARIABLES

1. Achieve purposes as I perceive them.
2. Value innovation highly.
3. Value professionalism very highly.
4. Emphasize intellectual issues, de-emphasize emotional issues.
5. Win; never lose.

BEHAVIORAL STRATEGIES

1. I exhibit a high competitiveness to win (keep selling, be enthusiastic, listen to others in order to win them over and change their minds).
2. I structure all situations in a way that positions myself to win.
3. I design the environment and manage it.

4. I share ideas as a way of achieving interpersonal consequences.
5. I control through teaching.
6. I assume a high level of aspiration for effective problem solving.

CONSEQUENCES ON SELF AND ENVIRONMENT

1. I am willing to share other people's problems but only when I am controlling others or when others need me.
2. I am uncomfortable with confirmation of my own innovation.
3. I do not encourage others to describe their enthusiasm.
4. I excite others with my own ideas; describe them with the apparent expectation of approval; am open to confirmation and not open to disconfirmation.
5. Others do not know what and when to believe.
6. It is difficult for others to know when I have been reached.
7. Others depend on me for definition of key issue.

CONSEQUENCES ON LEARNING

1. High double-loop learning on technical-issues (constrained by those technical issues that are threatening to me).
2. No double-loop learning on self and interpersonal issues.

Validity of These Theories-in-Use

How do we know that these theories-in-use exist and that they operate to make behavior consistent with their requirements? In developing an answer, we must keep in mind that it will be valid only to the extent that individuals are free to actualize their theories-in-use. In the next section, we will present models of what happens when several theories-in-use interact.

The first answer, and the weakest, is that the individuals in fact were able to create these maps of their theories-in-use. The task of mapmaking was not a simple one. They had spent 10 days (over a period of 2 years) working together to generate data from which they could infer their theories-in-use. They had written and examined several dozen cases, a like number of transcripts of tapes, plus a larger number of microcases that they produced by observing and reflecting on their own behavior during the approximately 155 hours together. (None of these figures includes the time spent in private reflection between sessions.)

There are several reasons why it takes time to construct a theory-in-use. Most people studied so far have difficulty conceiving of a theory-in-use. Many have even more difficulty in believing that they are Model I (but almost no difficulty in thinking that others are Model I). Developing a theory-in-use appears to many as "reducing their life" to a cognitive map. Some wonder if the map is not an over-simplification; others wonder about the possible loss of their free will; and a few have seen the act of developing a map as an examination that they might "fail."

There is a puzzle related to mapmaking. On the one hand, people seek ways to make their behavior more understandable and manage-able. They seek patterns or maps of aspects of themselves that they can store in their heads and retrieve whenever they design and take action. They seek, some to the point of pleading, ways to organize and manage the buzzing, blooming complexity of life. Yet they ap-pear to us as resisting the making of a map. Initially, the resistance was explained as related to competitiveness. Mapmaking was a task and most subjects saw it as an exam that they wanted to pass with high grades. But resistance was also found among the less competitive. Moreover, after people had developed their maps, they resisted refer-ring to them. Some have not resisted, and their progress appears much greater and faster. They are continually reexamining and up-dating their maps. This suggests that the resistance cannot be because the creation of a map is not a helpful process.

I am bewildered by the emotionality and sense of trepidation that I have observed around mapmaking. It is as if people resist when they begin to realize that mapmaking can work. It is as if they feel that having a relatively valid map of their theory-in-use opens them up to being held responsible for behaving responsibly. The existence of a valid map makes it less likely that they can hold others responsible for their lack of effectiveness. It is almost as if they tacitly sense that mapmaking is a first step toward becoming origins and not pawns, and the potentiality is frightening. All these are speculations, and much research is needed into this puzzling phenomena.

Nevertheless, all subjects to date have generated maps of their re-spective theories-in-use. Once they have done so, most go through a stage of testing and correcting the map to be as certain as is possible that the map is relatively valid. They realize that it would be danger-ous and counterproductive to anchor one's understanding of one's self in a map that is invalid. Hence, creating a map of one's theory-in-use is associated with ongoing experiments to test its validity.

The second type of evidence that can be collected about the valid-ity of the map is the data developed when the mapmakers offer their maps to others for test through disconfirmation. Individuals spend many hours confronting errors and gaps in each other's maps. Each of these attempts has the characteristic of a miniexperiment. The individuals are asked to present the empirical data that they used as well as the reasoning that led to the inferences about their governing variables, behavioral strategies, and consequences. The inquiries rarely take less than a half hour, and many take several hours. The process is a microspecimen of the confrontations that occur among scholars with competing theories. As the questions are raised, they conduct experiments, reanalyze their data, and redesign their models in order to respond to them appropriately.

The third test is the most rigorous developed so far. It is composed of situations with which the actors may experiment to test their theories. Three illustrations may be considered:

1. The first opportunity is in the learning seminar. After individuals have created their maps, they can design experiments to alter their behavior. For example, the individuals may design ways to increase their capacity to combine advocacy with inquiry. They may then simulate (role-play) their inventions. These productions are then analyzed by the actor and the others to assess the degree to which they approximate Models I and II.

During the early phases, almost all the productions are judged by the actors and the observers as approximating the Model I theory-in-use the actors have developed. Hence, the original maps are typically not disconfirmed.

2. After people have learned Model II and after they have committed themselves to making Model II one of their theories-in-use, many are unable to redesign their old cases to include Model II scenarios. This often occurs even when they have insisted that they can include such scenarios. If individuals write a case whose scenario approximates Model II early in the learning process, it is highly likely that it is a random event or some kind of cheating. These hypotheses are themselves testable by observing how the individuals behave when their cases are being discussed or when they are trying to help others. If the Model II scenario is a genuine indication of a Model II theory-in-use, then the individuals should have little difficulty in behaving according to that model during the discussion.

3. Interviews, observations, and tape recordings have been made of the individuals behaving in situations other than the learning seminars. Again, the prediction is that we should observe only three conditions: Model I, the opposite to Model I, or an oscillating Model I. There should not be any behavior that can be "scored" as Model II.

Therefore, a theory-in-use appears to be a reliable and valid indicator of the genotypic aspects of action patterns that people will design in any situation where they have an adequate freedom to do so. So far, with some rare exceptions, we have not obtained any data that disconfirm these robust predictions. The findings are robust because the predictions are made with the knowledge of the actors under conditions where they wish to prove us wrong (i.e., when we say that they cannot produce Model II actions and they wish to do so). The rare exceptions to which I refer are a few (usually professionally trained) people who are able to behave in accordance with Model II. These exceptions prove the rule because they are found to exist under the conditions predicted by the theory: These people already have a Model II theory-in-use.

Living Systems and Learning Systems

As we have seen in Chapter 2, the learning system is a model that purports to depict the quality of the organizational learning that is probable in all organizations populated with individuals who use only Model I theory-in-use. The living system is a model of the actions that exist in a particular organization or in a category of organization. A living system map is more concrete. In Figure 7.2, I present a living system model that purports to describe the actions that exist in professional organizations such as law, accounting, and consulting organizations. The map may be divided into two parts. Columns 1, 2, and 3 describe the behavioral strategies, the interpersonal and group dynamics, and the consequences of the first two columns of factors on problem-solving and decision-making effectiveness. This part of the map appears to apply to many other organizations because it describes the consequences of Model I theories-in-use (Argyris, 1969). The second part of the map (Columns 4, 5, 6, and 7) attempts to plot the consequences of the previous columns for organizational integration, norms, dilemmas, and complexity. The consequences described in these columns are meant to apply largely to professional organizations.

Briefly, the model states that the more frequent behavioral activities are: articulating and selling ideas, evaluating others and agreeing or disagreeing, discouraging the expression of threatening issues, and experimenting with ideas in order to get the job done better without altering its basic requirements. Feedback about interpersonal impact upon others, expressing negative feelings, encouraging the expression

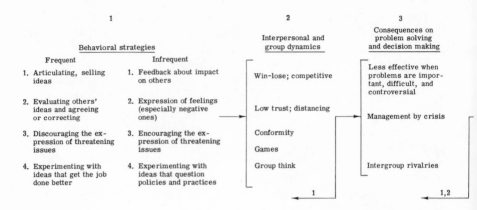

FIGURE 7.2. *Living system of a professional organization.*

of threatening issues, and experimenting with ideas that question existing underlying policies and practices are rarely observed. These behavioral strategies lead to certain group dynamics. They are: win-lose competition, low trust and high psychological distancing, conformity, political games, and group think (Janis, 1972). These group dynamics feed back to reinforce the behavioral strategies, feed forward to make problem solving difficult and controversial issues less effective, increase management by crisis, and increase intergroup rivalries. These consequences, in turn, feed back to reinforce the group dynamics and the behavioral strategies. Hence, we have a pattern of individual behavioral strategies, group and intergroup dynamics, and problem-solving actions that are interdependent, self-reinforcing, and not self-correcting. The feedback loops are positive, not negative. This model purports to describe crucial aspects of the world in which people live and work. Because the world is, in effect, a self-reinforcing pattern of variables, I call it the *living system*.

The model of the living system can be extended to show the consequences of these first three components (the first three columns) on other components of the living system. The model (Figure 7.2) is continued with the pattern of variables that we have found in professional organizations that service clients (primarily law, accounting,

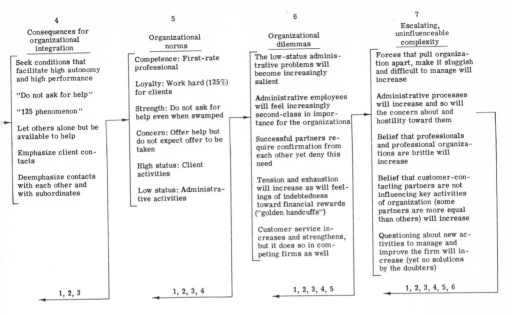

and consulting firms, and secondarily universities, hospitals, and other health-care delivery systems). The main point of the model is that the professionals (called partners) will be highly motivated to deal with clients, will de-emphasize problems of internal administration, and will create norms that reinforce these actions as well as the distancing among the partners. The result is the creation of dilemmas, such as that low-status administrative employees will feel second class yet important, and the increase of tension among the partners, despite which (particularly in those organizations where financial rewards are substantial) the partners will remain together. These consequences, in turn, lead to an increase in forces that create internal fractionalization and to the beliefs that professionals are brittle people, that the client-serving partners will have increasingly less influence over the organization than will the administrative partners, and that no solutions will seem practical. The organization will appear to be in a state of escalating dilemmas and dysfunctional activities. Again, each subsequent consequence feeds back to reinforce the previous ones and feeds through to create new ones.

The secondary consequences identified in Columns 4 to 7 may vary in content with different organizations. What should not vary are the escalating forces that fractionalize the organization, that escalate the dilemmas, and that make the living system complex and un-influenceable.

The question that arises is: Why do Columns 1, 2, and 3 hold for all systems studied so far (including families, schools, religious groups, and voluntary organizations) and Columns 4, 5, 6, and 7 hold at least for professional organizations? To put it more specifically: Why should people create these particular interpersonal and group dynamics? Why do we not observe cases where the proportions in Column 1 are reversed? Why have we not found systems with norms of high trust, individuality, and low frequency of political games and group think? Perhaps more importantly, why is it that so many systems appear to have self-reinforcing, noncorrecting feedback loops? Most of the people that we interviewed acknowledge that such loops are counterproductive, that they create a "can of worms," and that they lead to a sense of resignation about the level of organizational learning that is possible. Why do individuals design and/or maintain such counterproductive activities? Finally, how do we know that the factors in Column 1 lead to the factors in Column 2, etc.? Could they not lead to a different set of factors? Our position is that the meanings in Column 1 necessarily lead only to meanings such as those in Column 2, and both, in turn, necessarily lead only to those types of consequences identified in Column 3. These meanings appear rational but when one states, as we do, that they must necessarily be the way they are, more information is needed because we are implying causality.

In order to imply causality in normal science, one must be able to show that: (a) A must precede B in time; (b) variations in A must precede variations in B; and (c) there are no plausible alternative explanations of B other than A. According to our model, this is not possible. We are stipulating that the four frequent and the four infrequent behavioral strategies lead to the group dynamics, and the group dynamics feed back to reinforce the eight factors. Moreover, the factors in Columns 3 to 7 influence the causal connections between Columns 1 and 2. Hence, there are a lot of A's leading to a lot of B's leading to a lot of C's, etc., each of which feeds back to lead to whatever came before it.

In addition, the notion that Column 1 precedes Column 2, etc., is an hypothesis and one which can never be tested rigorously in the world as it exists. The reason is that in the present world all the 38 factors exist simultaneously, giving information to, and receiving information from, each factor. These factors are a pattern; the pattern is an entity; and it is the entity that the participants experience. Even if this were not the case, a study of these 38 factors and all their possible empirical relationships would lead to the complexity and overload of information noted earlier in leadership research; these, in turn, could lead to immobilization of action. If this is the case, then why arrange the factors in the columns as noted? Because underlying this model of the living system is a theory in the form of Model I theory-in-use and O-I learning system. The "causal" relationship, the escalating errors, the increased fractionalization do not become compelling unless we introduce the theory-of-action perspective.

Assumptions Embedded in a Theory-of-Action Perspective

I should like to review several underlying assumptions of this perspective. They are:

1. All human actions are based upon designs called theories-in-use. These designs define the genotypic meanings that are probable.
2. Human beings cannot knowingly produce meanings that are beyond, or incongruent to, their theories-in-use.
3. Behavior that is produced by applying a theory-in-use is usually internalized and skillful. Skillful behavior is usually tacit. It tends to blind people to incipient error that has not yet become large enough to be unignorable.
4. Individuals can be skillful at reflecting on those actions that are in keeping with their present governing variables and values. However, they are not skillful at reflecting on the effectiveness of their actions when such reflection requires that their governing variables be questioned. People in the environment will reinforce this "skilled incapacity" because they are programmed not to behave in ways that may threaten others.
5. Whenever two or more individuals programmed with (only) Model I interact to deal with important issues that are ambiguous, vague, inconsistent, and incongruent, they will create a condition of escalating error. Hence, the information around the issue will become more vague, ambiguous, inconsistent, and incongruent.
6. If people are not skillful at reflection on their (double-loop) errors and if others are programmed to reinforce this incompetence, then they will find themselves aware of escalating error, aware of the others' role in creating the error, and significantly less aware of their own role in creating the error.

7. People will tend to form more accurate and complete pictures
    of others' impact on reality than of their own. They will tend
    to be better at recognizing their own impacts after the fact
    than at anticipating them before the action is taken. They will
    find it difficult or impossible to detect in their inside, before-
    the-fact views of the situation the elements of error that out-
    siders or they themselves can recognize so easily after the fact.

The Causal Status of Models I and O-I

We can now return to the model of the living system. If we hypothesize that the behavioral strategies in Column 1 (of Figure 7.2) are
designed by individuals holding Model I theories-in-use, then it follows that the meanings designed are not simply empirical observations,
but theoretical imperatives. It is not possible for someone programmed with Model I to produce meanings other than those consonant
with Model I. Hence, the group dynamics must also be congruent
with Model I. In other words, the arrow from one column to another
indicates that the subsequent meanings must follow and that only
the subsequent meanings could follow, because people are programmed with Model I. Moreover, people programmed with Model I will
always create primary inhibiting loops to learning that will make it
likely that problem solving will actually reinforce vagueness, lack of
clarity, and inconsistency when the information on a difficult, threatening, double-loop issue is vague, inconsistent, etc.

The O-I learning systems reinforce these causal relationships in the
O-I learning systems. Recall that individuals programmed with Model
I will necessarily create a learning system, the result of which is a set
of secondary inhibiting loops that reinforce the primary inhibiting
loops and simultaneously create games, deception, camouflage, and
double binds—all factors that reinforce Model I and the resulting primary and secondary inhibiting loops.

Thus, the world may be biased against variance beyond Models I
and O-I. Whatever variance exists may be within Model I, making
Model I theories-in-use and O-I learning systems both highly functional and dysfunctional. They are functional in the world as it is, but
the world as it is has built into it escalating errors, uninfluenceability,
double binds, etc. They are dysfunctional because they inhibit the
learning required to overcome these problems. Hence, the inner contradictions of Models I and 0-I is: That which leads to success also
leads to failure.

But stacking the cards against variance other than that permitted by Model I and O-I also makes it possible for us to state robust predictions. For example, if people are programmed with Model I and if they create O-I learning systems, then we should never observe living systems that contain the factors in Column 1 of Figure 7.2 in reverse proportions. Nor should we find group dynamics where individuality is stronger than conformity, trust stronger than mistrust; where open, candid actions occur more than covert deception and camouflage; and where double-loop errors are corrected before they are escalated.

We are now in the position to explain the emphasis upon ideology embedded in the living system model. Although factors in the living and the learning systems coexist in patterned interdependence, and although this means that logically one could place any set of factors in the first, second, etc., columns, this is not the case when one attempts to change these systems. The theory of intervention associated with the present perspective is that first the focus must be on the theories-in-use and hence the primary loops and later on the O-I systems. It should never be possible to work the other way. One cannot first change the O-I system and have that lead to a change in the theories-in-use and hence in the living system. Recall that in the earlier example the presidents were placed in a learning environment where the educators espoused and practiced Models II and O-II. Yet for nearly 2 years that learning environment was dominated by Models I and O-I.

The explanation lies in the nature of skills. Recall that everyday actions are skilled, which means they are informed by a Model I theory-in-use. Recall also that individuals place into action their different mini-theories-in-use or subroutines of skillful behavior, depending on the external and internal cues. In the present world, the external cues come from the O-I learning system; the internal cues come from the theory-in-use; and neither set of cues violates the other. Hence, if we changed the system, the external cues would be different. However, because the theories-in-use have not changed, the internal cues will not recognize the external cues, or if they do, they will see them as threats. This is what tends to happen once people begin to experience Model II: They wonder if it is realistic and practical or if it could be a new insidious Model I. All these concerns are valid. Model II does appear difficult to use in a Model I world. Model I individuals will use Model II behaviors as a new Model I because that is the only theory-in-use they have. This is why learning Model II is a very complex learning experience.

If the presence of living systems models and the O-I learning system model within the present perspective indicate that, descriptively
speaking, the psychological- and sociological-level variables coexist
and are of equal importance, studies that focus on one or the other
miss important features of the world as it is. However, when one is
learning a new theory-in-use, then one must begin with individuals
because their theories-in-use control their internal cues *and* because
they are the agents for learning in all social systems. Experience to
date is overwhelming that the moment individuals begin to understand the requirements of Model II and the implication for changing
their internal cues, the living systems and their respective learning
systems immediately come to the forefront and remain so throughout the transition period.

Following are two examples that illustrate two questions central
to the type of action science being described. The first question is related to what a map of the living system in which individuals or systems are moving from Model I to Model II would look like. Case A
represents such a map of individual and group movement. This particular case has been included because it also illustrates that people
in transition continue to have difficulties but that these difficulties
become discussable and hence solvable. Case B has been included to
illustrate how a case study can be used to test aspects of a theory. If
this can be accomplished, then the use of stories and cases may become more frequent. This is considered to be a valuable trend because,
in intervention activity, cases and stories may provide an important
diagnostic base that is understandable by the client. Moreover, as we
have found, the cases and stories can become the leverage for change.

Case A

This is a case involving six presidents of private corporations and
two faculty members. When the episode occurred, the members were
participating in a seminar designed to help them develop Model II as
a theory-in-use. One of the presidents, D, began the episode by asserting that he could document that the group had behaved toward him
on previous occasions in a Model I fashion. He also asserted that he
was aware that he had difficulties with being in touch with his feelings,
with predicting accurately his impact upon others, and with remaining in touch with the group process if he felt that he had hurt someone. D also acknowledged that such behavior could lead him to be
seen as an ineffective group member. For example:

D: *I think that I can demonstrate that the group was acting toward me in a
Model I manner, the worst aspects of a Model I approach.*
[later]
*The other item that I would like to share with you is that I am still bewil-
dered as to why it is that I have suppressed feelings. I have great difficulty
in making my feelings available to myself. As I think about it, I see myself
as easily becoming emotionally constipated.*
[and later]

E: *What do you mean?*

D: *I withdraw. I can't really participate. I get hung up on thinking about one
thing and can't get off that. I also found out I can be a poor predictor of my
impact. For example, I felt badly about hurting B, yet I found out that neither B nor others felt that he had been hurt. So I don't know what to do. As
a result, I freeze. Then I become preoccupied with freezing.*
*Others see me as withdrawn or confused or constipated. That leads them to
behave in ways that confirm, in my eyes, that I am not doing well in the
group.*

D then added that he would become angry with himself because
he was not doing well. Then he would become angry at himself for
becoming angry at himself. The second anger would come from the
belief that the reason he blamed himself for not being effective was
that he aspired toward being a perfectionist.

D repeated that he felt later the group was not being candid with
him. The group members responded by giving examples of D's behavior that led them to withhold information from him. D acknowledged
that some of his behavior might have provided cues to the members
that he was "fragile." However, he added that C had not viewed him
as being as fragile, as most of them had. E reminded D that, every
time D talked about aspects of reality that were difficult, he withdrew. What else were the members to conclude except that D may be
fragile?

E: *I am in a bind. You ask for help, yet you withhold the data that is important. I don't want to pressure you.*

K: *Neither do I. If you do not wish to talk about the problem, that's fine. But
then you accuse us of withholding information from you.*

G: *It is difficult to deal with you. We do not wish to withhold information, but
on the other hand, we do not wish to hurt you.*

D returned to accusing the group members of "colluding to maintain my blindness." He added that he was also feeling that there was
a cliquishness in the group and that he was an outsider. E then re-

peated in scenario form an example of the previous meeting in which he and several others had decided to withhold information because D had said that he did not wish to discuss the issues. D responded that E and the others may have been making attributions about his fragility that they were not testing publicly.

E: *My point is completely different. And this is what happens to me all the time. I gave you a specific example of this group's attempts to confront you on fragility and related it to your assertion that the group had never attempted to confront you on the issue of fragility.*

D: *I hear your point. I just do not see that as a confrontation of attribution about my fragility.*

The discussion between D and E continued with the expression of different views of what had happened in the group. E then said with feelings of exasperation or frustration:

E: *D, let me take the ultimate risk, and that is—what I'm sitting here thinking is—"I don't want to go through this again. If this is the price I pay to come to another session, I'm not coming back." I don't know where it comes from, but that's what's here. That's what I'm feeling as I sit—*

D: *I think you can make a number of choices. I suggested putting this on the agenda. We could work on cases. This is something you don't want to deal with, and this disrupts the group.*

E: *That isn't what I said, not at all.*
   [jumbled]

D: *But I am, in effect, leaving the choice to you. I didn't force this discussion, at least I don't think I forced this discussion with the group. If it's something you don't want to deal with or you don't feel you should deal with—*

K: *That's not what he said—Yeah, not at all.*

D: *Okay, then I'm reading this—I heard E say, "If this is the price he has to pay"—but there again, I may have misunderstood you—the price of discussing these issues with me, my role in the group?*

E: *No.*

D: *Oh, then, I'm sorry—*

C: *The price is the way you discuss these issues. The issues are terribly important. The way you deal, the way you discuss them—*

E: *I had hoped that D would say, "E, if you feel that strongly about this, I'd like to examine it." What I hoped for didn't happen. You didn't hear me, or I am either incapable of phrasing the shout, or it wasn't loud enough. What I got in return was defense and some anger. That's what I feared.*

D responded that he did not interpret E's comments as an invitation for inquiry. "I experienced it as a threat, yet I am willing to explore it." C then suggested another way that E might have made his intervention.

C: *Could you have said to D, "I'm going to say something that I see as high risk. My intention is to see if I can get into a dialogue with you on my increasing feelings that I am unable to communicate with you and reach you...."*

E agreed that such an intervention would have been more effective. D added that the difficulty was not all E's responsibility. "I didn't handle my response well either." E and D reexamined several interchanges they had during the episode in order to make clear where each had miscommunicated or had been misheard by the other.

D admitted that he was having difficulty in being an effective member. But he insisted that he was taking the group seriously and asked others not to ask him to change immediately:

D: *It is not that I don't respect you or the other members of the group. I just can't do much better right now. I look at this as a process. It is frustrating to you, but it is also frustrating to me that it takes so long.*
I am surprised at your questioning my commitment. I didn't understand that you didn't think I was trying.

Let us recapitulate the episode by examining Figure 7.3. We note that when D realizes that he is not behaving effectively, he freezes, withdraws, and becomes preoccupied with his thoughts. He also becomes frustrated with himself and predicts that others will get frustrated and angry with him. He also predicts to himself that his future behavioral strategies will fail, which reinforces his freezing and withdrawal. The others see D as withdrawing, distancing himself, and as behaving in ways that make him appear confused. D sees other people as able to help him and that the others are low in taking risks to help each other.

The first consequence for learning is that D is experienced as being unable to detect and correct error as well as uninfluenceable. However, D is also seen as being aware that he is uninfluenceable. D sees himself as having difficulty in detecting and correcting error and as being difficult to influence. D sees others as able to detect and correct error. Thus, we have a situation where people are frustrated, bewildered, acting in ways that are attributive and coercive, yet behaving in ways that acknowledge the difficulties and the defensiveness.

But the struggle to be influenceable and to help others is accom-

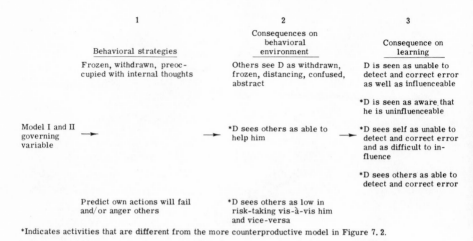

1	2	3
Behavioral strategies	Consequences on behavioral environment	Consequence on learning
Frozen, withdrawn, preoccupied with internal thoughts	Others see D as withdrawn, frozen, distancing, confused, abstract	D is seen as unable to detect and correct error as well as influenceable
		*D is seen as aware that he is uninfluenceable
Model I and II governing variable →	→ *D sees others as able to help him	→ *D sees self as unable to detect and correct error and as difficult to influence
		*D sees others as able to detect and correct error
Predict own actions will fail and/or anger others	*D sees others as low in risk-taking vis-à-vis him and vice-versa	

*Indicates activities that are different from the more counterproductive model in Figure 7.2.

FIGURE 7.3. *A model of a counterproductive cycle moving toward a productive cycle.*

panied by some strong defensive behavior. Indeed, perhaps the defensive behavior can surface precisely because the members have cues that they will not get into counterproductive cycles that will destroy the group. Hence D tells the group that they must help him. D also is disappointed by his own defensiveness and resentful for being rejected by others. The others admit to some games of deception and camouflage. However, unlike Case B, they are willing to discuss these games.

The strongest test of the group's cohesiveness occurs when E tells D that either he should change or E will not return. Once the frustration, anger, and the order are expressed, D responds immediately, with others following close behind. The others empathize with E's frustration but cannot agree that E's order will achieve its intended purpose to help D "open up." D confirms their diagnosis, and E does the same. Both explore the actions that have frustrated them.

The result is that attributions that are usually private and untestable become public and testable. The self-sealing processes are managed and eventually reduced. There is not the helpless spiraling toward increased counterproductive action as in the case of Y. The uninfluenceability of the participants is also reduced. Finally, there is an increase in the members' confidence that they can solve very difficult problems, problems that are usually suppressed in most groups or that, if brought to the surface, can cause the groups to fragment and in some cases even cease to exist as groups.

4	5	6

	Consequences on behavioral environment	Consequence on learning
D tells group it is their responsibility to help him but does so in a punishing manner	E's blow-up	*Private and untestable attributions become public and testable
D is aware that his behavior indicates that he is defensive; D is disappointed with own defensiveness and resentful for being rejected by others	*Blow-up is discussable by E, D, and all others	*Self-sealing processes are managed and reduced
*Others are playing games of deception but are willing to discuss them; others hold D primarily responsible for their game playing	*D and E own up to their errors and maintain those aspects that were not errors yet did produce defensiveness in others	*Double binds are reduced *Uninfluenceability of participants is reduced *Confidence in problem-solving process increased

Case B

Recently Neustadt and Fineberg (1978) published an insightful case study of the decision-making processes involved in the swine flu program from March 1976 to March 1977, a program designed to produce drugs to innoculate millions of Americans against influenza. The purpose of the case study was to provide practitioners and scholars an opportunity to reflect upon practice in order to generate intelligence about effective decision making for the future.

The goal of this analysis is to illustrate the difficulties that may arise when the theories implicit in the case analysis are not made explicit. I hope to show that, because of a lack of theory, Neustadt and Fineberg: (1) do not make as powerful claims for generality as their analysis deserves; (2) are not able to use the case study as a test for theory; and (3) provide recommendations that may be of limited value because they remain within the constraints of the causes of the problem that were correctly (I believe) identified by the authors. If these objectives can be achieved, then an illustration (albeit primitive) will be produced that provides insights into how case method, theory, and empirical generality can be combined in ways that protect the prima facie validity of case description yet produce advice and recommendations that are useful for practitioners.

Let us begin by summarizing the major causal factors of the problems identified by the authors regarding decision making in the swine flu program.

THE "CAUSES" OF INEFFECTIVENESS IN DECISION MAKING

Neustadt and Fineberg (1978) identified seven leading factors of ineffective decision making for the swine flu program. Six of them are relevant to this analysis. (The seventh is related to the media.)

1. Overconfidence by specialists in not fully validated theories about influenza and influenza epidemics.
2. Advocating ideas based upon personal agendas and acting as if this was not the case.
3. Subordinates manipulating superiors to perform in a manner the former believed to be correct.
4. Premature commitment to unnecessarily early decisions.
5. Addressing uncertainties in ways that made their reconsideration unlikely.
6. Insufficient questioning of implementation prospects.

Because these causes are interdependent, overconfident subordinates or superiors advocating personal agendas make it more likely that issues will be discussed in ways that make their confrontation and reconsideration less likely.

REEXAMINING THE DIAGNOSIS

The first feature of this list of factors is that it focuses on relatively directly observable data. This is a very important bias for several reasons. The concepts used are abstractions that maintain their connectedness with empirical reality. This makes the study more vulnerable to disconfirmation by the actors. It is easier for them to say, "No, it did not happen this way," than if the authors had used abstract theory that was significantly less connected to the action context. The choice also makes it more likely that the actors will use the lessons inferred to design their future actions.

The second feature of the causal factors is that they are behavioral. By "behavioral" I mean that such factors as overconfidence, conviction for personal agendas, zeal to manipulate superiors, and premature commitments belong to the domain of interpersonal relations, group and intergroup dynamics, and organizational norms. Such formal structural factors as the chain of command, the organization of groups, the policies regarding who should meet with whom, the financial rewards, and the formal evaluation schemes were not found to be key causal factors. These behavioral factors have structural fea-

tures in the sense that they represent patterns of interpersonal relations, group dynamics, and intergroup dynamics. They could not exist
in organizations over time without creating structures of relationships
and expectations that profoundly affect decision making.

The third feature of the list of causal factors is that they appear to
me to be valid beyond this particular case. The focus on such variables
as "overconfidence in undertested theories," "zeal...to make lay superiors do right," "premature commitment," the win-lose interpersonal relationships among the actors within groups and between
groups, and the political and administrative games people played that
were illustrated richly by Neustadt and Fineberg appear to exist in
many different kinds of organizations.

GENERALIZABILITY OF THE RESULTS

The authors underplay the generality of their conclusions. Playing
down one's conclusions may be as unhelpful a practice as playing
them up if it is true that the findings can be corroborated by other
experiences and research. If the authors mean to interpret the case
method in its most narrow construction—namely, that it accounts for
one and only one case—then why do they include lengthy recommendations? Surely they are assuming that the recommendations are valid
for future swine flu programs if not for other similar programs.

The difficulty lies, I suggest, in the separation of the case analysis
from the relevant behavioral theories. It is possible, I believe, by using
our theory-of-action perspective, to explain the authors' findings as
well as to reexamine the recommendations made by the authors. For
example, the concepts of Model I and O-I provide an explanation for
the individual maneuvering, defenses, actions, games, and camouflages
identified by the writers. The same concepts also provide an individual (Model I) and an organizational (Model O-I) explanation for why
the six causal factors identified by Neustadt and Fineberg were omnipresent yet undiscussable. It would have violated Model I governing
values to discuss these issues because they would have been seen as
personal attacks and, hence, as leading to emotionally and interpersonal rejection. It would have violated Model O-I because politicizing,
manipulation of superiors, covering one's ass, and so on, are played
in organizational contexts that are not discussable for the purpose of
correcting them.

Recall that the theory predicts, given that the conditions identified by the authors are created by conditions consonant with Models
I and O-I, there will always be a predisposition to enhance the condi-

tions for error when the problems or issues are serious and when there is a crisis. The reasoning underlying this prediction is that Model O-I shows that the probability for error enhancement increases as information about an issue takes on such features as being ambiguous, unclear, scattered, vague, inconsistent, and incongruent. Neustadt and Fineberg have documented how different memoranda were used to polarize the situation, how each actor chose to emphasize certain features when reporting to his or her superior, and how group members chose to ignore important admonitions and questions raised by a minority of their members. All these conditions increase the probability that actors will experience different aspects of the problem as vague, unclear, and so on.

When I say that the theory predicts the conclusions found by Neustadt and Fineberg, I mean to state the following: People utilizing Model I theories-in-use and embedded in O-I learning systems should never be observed dealing directly and openly (and I might add, competently) with the causal variables identified by Neustadt and Fineberg. I mean to hypothesize that, when the substantive problems are serious and when they exist under conditions of crisis, there should always be error escalation for the double-loop issues.

The logic of these predictions is relatively straightforward. Theories-in-use are the basis for the design and execution by individuals of all meanings, and O-I learning systems are the basis for the constraints placed on theories-in-use. The latter reinforce the former. And, as shown previously, people will not knowingly design and execute meanings that violate their theories-in-use and the O-I learning systems. Hence, the error-enhancing features identified by Neustadt and Fineberg are predictable and uncorrectable by the actors if left to their own devices.

There are two implicit assumptions embedded in this logic. The first is that the case method may now be translated into a vehicle for generalization and hypothesis disconfirmation. The features identified by Neustadt and Fineberg are predictable from Models I and O-I. Moreover, it is predicted that these features, plus their unintended consequences, are never publicly discussable in an on-line manner. Neustadt and Fineberg should not have found such features, or if they did, those people who created them, or thought of creating them, should have seen them as deviant activities. In other words, one or two instances of consciously planned and executed double-loop learning, under the conditions described by the authors would be adequate to disconfirm the theory.

But there is an even tougher test. Let us imagine that the actors in the drama had not changed. The theory would predict that they would not deal with threatening double-loop issues in ways that were incongruent with Models I and O-I. In other words, they should repeat these or similar errors. The hypothesis should not be disconfirmed even if the actors wished this to be the case. A second, and I believe equally tough, test is the following: If the new team that is in place is also programmed with Model I and embedded in an O-I learning system, they should have the same difficulties.

These hypotheses are empirically disconfirmable. The predictions are asserting that double-loop problems under crisis situations will be handled in ways that escalate the conditions for error. Does that mean that, in the future, people will behave in ways that manifest overconfidence in undertested theories, that conviction will be fueled by personal agendas, that subordinates will manipulate superiors, and that there will exist competitive win-lose groups and intergroup dynamics? The answer is yes.

Does this mean that the actors will continue to produce the same substantive errors? The answer is yes and no. Errors can be reduced if they are translated into single-loop problems. One way to do so is to make it mandatory for the actors to go through tougher reasoning processes. This is the thrust of the Neustadt and Fineberg recommendations. They want to institutionalize analytic toughness in the organization. In that spirit, they make specific recommendations about how people must be required to back up their generalizations with specific details, how groups should be required to explore the minority views, etc. For example:

1. A tracing out of relationships between deadlines and each decision.
2. An explicit statement of assumptions underlying each decision.
3. An awareness that an early memorandum, with its 2-week go or no go, actually obscured, not clarified, relationships between deadlines and individual decisions.
4. The decision to begin manufacturing and the decision to institute a mass immunization program should have been kept separate.
5. Explicit and detailed analyses of key action memoranda, either in probabilistic terms or in terms of what evidence would falsify the logic and actions planned.
6. A forced systematic and detailed airing of views on each question, one by one (pp. 87-89).

There are two problems with these recommendations. First, the relationship between the causal factors identified by the authors and their recommendations is complex. For example, most of the recommendations require actors to tighten up on their thinking, to make it more confrontable, and to explore perspectives that are counter to the trends they develop. But what is the probability that people will perform these requirements effectively if their purpose is to win and not lose, to manipulate superiors, to ride hobby horses, and to unilaterally control others?

The fundamental thrust of the recommendations is to control error by making the logic in peoples' heads more public and hopefully more influenceable. This thrust will work, especially if it is backed up by sanctions from a superior. But people will not forget their personal games, competitiveness, and so on. They will develop new ways to use them and to camouflage the fact that they are doing so.

To express it another way, the recommendations assume that truth is a good idea and that modes of logic and control can be defined to enhance the production of such knowledge. The difficulty is that, in a Model I world, truth is a good idea when it is not threatening. If truth is threatening, appropriate tactics and games will be deployed to reduce threat while covertly distorting the truth. Exercises in "tougher" decision-making processes will not erase these consequences.

In another set of recommendations, the authors state that the actors should do much more thinking about doing (before and after a decision is made). The difficulty with this set of recommendations is that it does not take into account that people who are overconfident, selling personal agendas, and manipulating people may unrealizingly subvert the recommendations. Certainly the actors should have thought further ahead and in more detail (p. 92), but even if they were to agree with these recommendations, the question arises as to how effective their thinking would be if they were also thinking about selling, manipulating, and winning.

In all these recommendations there is an implicit assumption that the causes for error identified by the authors are reducible by not discussing them and by laying on a template of rational decision-making. In my experience, most people are usually unaware of the extent to which they are producing conditions for error. They are unaware of it because: (1) the actions that produce the errors are skilled and tacit; (2) as the authors have shown, the causes for error are frequently undiscussable; and (3) they hold theories in their heads about effective action (Model I) that make them blind to what they are doing and blind to the fact that they are blind.

The recommendations made by the authors remain within and, therefore, unintentionally may reinforce the conditions that created the problems in the first place. They also may provide subordinates with a rationality as to why they must go even further underground with some of their tactics. Going even further underground means that they run a bigger risk if they are caught. This, in turn, may lead to more frequent "dry runs," just-in-case-I-am-caught memos to the file, and more layers of camouflage. These reactions, in turn, may lead actors to feel even less optimistic that governmental systems can initiate and sustain double-loop learning. Hence, there become established new, more hidden, self-sealing activities to inhibit double-loop learning.

Summary

Because implementation is the ultimate objective, theories-in-use are central to understanding. Hence, we begin by obtaining conversations or other relatively directly observable data. Next, inferences are made about the everyday meanings embedded in the relatively directly observable data. These first two levels of data are extracted from the action context but remain connected with the meanings typically used in that context.

We use a particular theory to organize the data on the first two levels in a way that will permit us to create an order that is economical yet comprehensive and that will permit us to make propositions that are disconfirmable. The first step is to identify the behavioral strategies embedded in the meanings identified at level two. These behavioral strategies are then organized into models of theory-in-use. The consequences of Model I theories-in-use upon the living system are then explored. Finally, we translate the features of living systems into a more abstract notion of learning system. This makes it possible to speak economically and comprehensively about living systems as well as to make predictions about behavior that are refutable.

This map of the six levels (see Figure 7.1) represents one way for scholars to distance themselves from the context of action yet be able to return to it. It is possible to make explicit the inferences involved in moving from one level to the other. Hence, we could show Mr. Y how his actions could be perceived as being consistent with Model I and how that in turn could lead to a counterproductive living system between X and himself that would have the features of a Model O-I learning system. The capacity to move up and down these levels not only is important in conducting research but is central in any intervention where the attempt is to help Y and X learn new actions and new theories-in-use in order to create new living systems whose components facilitate learning, especially of the double-loop variety.

Embedded in this approach is the view that human beings design their actions and the implementation of these actions. A design perspective, in turn, means that any consequences that are not consonant with the design (intentions) are errors (mismatches). Consequences that are consonant with the design are not errors. Individuals cannot knowingly design for error because any consequence that is consistent with their design cannot be a design error (although it could be a social error).

Once we accept that people cannot design meanings for which they have no theory-in-use, then we should be able to predict the meanings that they will define and produce. The theory can then be tested by identifying the meanings observed to be embedded in conversations. It is possible to predict, for example, that individuals with Model I theories-in-use will not produce behavior with Model II meanings in any situation. Hence, a recording of the conversation of individuals holding only Model I yet producing Model II meanings would disconfirm the theory.

This perspective makes it possible to use case material as a test of a theory as long as the case material includes relatively directly observable data plus the meanings embedded in that data. In the case of the swine flu affair, we could predict that the same actors, or a new set, would repeat many of the counterproductive thinking processes and actions as long as they held a Model I theory-in-use. A program that required them to be more analytical and that monitored their thinking probably would drive their Model I competitiveness and unilateral face-saving underground but would not eliminate them.

CHAPTER 8

Summary

Basic Research: The Study of Practice

The basic research activity of the action science that I have proposed is the study of our practical world. It is the study of the actions people take in the conduct of everyday life. "Practical life comprises the attempts we make to alter existence or to maintain it unaltered in the face of threatened change. It is both the production and the prevention of change, and in either case it is not merely a programme for action, but action itself [Oakeshott, 1966, p. 256]."

This book begins by taking the world of practice—the action context—as the focus of basic research. It asks how social scientists can produce knowledge that is usable by human beings in their everyday, face-to-face relationships when they are designing and taking action. How can we help people to maintain or alter their existence while at the same time producing knowledge that can be used under real time constraints?

To repeat again, there is a difference between a program for action and action itself; there is a big gap between, on the one hand, discovering problems and inventing solutions and, on the other hand, producing the solutions behaviorally. The purpose of basic research in action science is to produce knowledge that helps people in their face-to-face relationships to discover, invent, *and* produce actions under on-line conditions.

This is not to say that social science should not attempt to illuminate plans and policies (which, in our language, are espoused theories). The exact relationship between research to inform planning and that to inform action is not discussed in this book. Our perspective suggests that policy-oriented research may contain gaps that will be unrealized until there is an attempt to implement the policies. For example, a review of the literature on what happened to the Great Society social policies suggests, as is the case of the research reviewed in this book, that many of them waned when it came to the implementation processes (Bardach, 1977).

It is common for social scientists to maintain that policy-oriented and discipline-oriented research should be differentiated (Coleman, 1972; Cronback & Suppes, 1969). This view, we may now suggest, requires further inquiry because for some problems the differences identified may not be differences that should make a difference. Coleman (1972) correctly points out that the world of action involves real time, whereas disciplinary research does not; that the former involves language and concepts that are different from the latter; and that the former is less concerned with economy of information and more with redundancy. Coleman then goes on to accept these differences as given and unchangeable. Yet if the world of action involves real time, peculiar language and concepts, and redundancy and if research is to apply to this world, then these features should be taken seriously. Action science research should be designed to produce propositions that take these features into account. In other words, discipline-oriented research would include research on the properties of the world of action.

In arguing against such differentiation, I am not launching a polemic "against method" (Feyerabend, 1975) or suggesting that we abandon method (Phillips, 1973). Indeed, both of these authors are, as I understand them, asking for new alternatives rather than to ignore method. I hope that this book adds to the dialogue that will someday shape these methods.

I am in agreement with the social scientists in the recent volume by Brenner, Marsh, and Brenner (1978) who believe that the methodology of rigorous research does not "elaborate systematically and on the level of adequate social theorizing, the social processes that constitute the practice of method, . . ." and hence "the relationship between postulates of measurement, as conceptualized, adequately, in the science paradigm of methodology, and the actual social practices necessary and sufficient to realize social measurement, is under-identified [p. 10]." However, I do not agree with the emphasis of some of the contributors on not seeking causal laws nor with the implication that the carefully controlled traditional studies are inaccurate, whereas their less-controlled, more "humane" research activities are more accurate. I find myself more in agreement with Meltzer, Petras, and Reynolds (1975), who state that such new perspectives as symbolic interactionism have not been more clear about the nature of causality and prediction. Indeed, I would go further and add that most of the studies have provided insightful analyses that are after the fact. The researchers have not taken the next step of showing how their propositions may be used to take action in the world.

Features of Rigorous Research in Normal Science

There exist rules that guide researchers in designing and executing their empirical work. One of the most fundamental rules is that scientists should strive to describe the universe as it exists; scientists should refrain from conducting research about universes that do not exist presently. A second fundamental rule is that scientists should minimize threats to the validity of their results. This rule can be approximated by striving for a priori precision, by unilaterally controlling the conditions and meanings of the research activity, and by distancing the researcher from the action context.

Requirements such as these are consonant with Model I theories-in-use. The consequences for validity are not trivial when one is conducting research using human beings as subjects and where the research is intended to produce generalizations about face-to-face relationships in any context. The conditions of unilateral control and distancing create conditions where the subjects are dependent upon the researchers for the meanings embedded in the instruments, for the conditions that they will experience, and for the time perspective. These consequences are not neutral in that they may produce reactions on the part of the subjects that are invalid. These distortions are not random but systematic and tacit. Hence, they may not be overcome by appropriate sampling or pretest procedures.

Basic Features of Action Science

If practice is taken to be the beginning and the end point for research, then the first feature of action science is to produce knowledge that lends to understanding and prediction in order to design and take action in the action context. Although the methodology for producing this knowledge may turn out to be somewhat different from the ones presently in vogue, it will still have to meet at least three normal science criteria. All propositions produced should be subject to public disconfirmability, should contain some form of causality, and should be as elegant as possible.

Elegance is needed because, other features being equal, the simplest yet most comprehensive theories are the preferred ones. Some notion of causality is needed because actors (and systems through their agents) intend to make events come about. Such ideas as personal responsibility imply initiative or proactivity, which in turn imply some notion of causality. Public disconfirmability is necessary because social scientists should not unintentionally be in the position of misleading themselves or others.

In addition to satisfying the foregoing criteria, the propositions must also be stated in a form that people can use under real time constraints. First this requires that meanings embedded in the propositions be understandable by the actors. To return to our model of levels of meaning (see page 147), the propositions should be stated either with level-two meanings or meanings at higher levels that can be unambiguously connected to levels two and one. Second, the propositions must be producible in the form of action, in the context of action. This requires a great deal of empirical research because propositions that are producible in the context of action and under on-line constraints may be different from those presently encouraged by rigorous research methodologies. This leads to the third feature, namely, that the propositions may well be characterized as being of low precision coupled with high accuracy. Implicit in the requirement of accuracy is the requirement that the validity of propositions should always be tested. Implicit in on-line testing for accuracy is the concept of learning. Actors will always have to be alert to detecting and correcting error, especially of the double-loop variety.

At this time it appears that, along with propositions about human action, there is required a theory of on-line learning about how well the implementation process is going. An on-line learning capacity is needed because, as we have suggested: (1) it is rarely possible to have complete information ahead of time; (2) if we tried to obtain complete information, we would rarely be able to act; (3) if we had complete information and we tried to act upon it, we would probably have to be in complete control of the context of action; and (4) if we had such unilateral control, it would result in conditions (such as authoritarian relationships) that would inhibit the production of valid information. Action science, in short, will produce propositions that contain, by design, information gaps. Hence, action science requires the development of a set of propositions about the conduct of on-line gap filling.

Consonance between Science and Practice

Embedded in action science is the assumption that there is a high degree of consonance between the domain of practice and the domain of science. This assumption requires further testing. At the moment, the logic underlying the assumption includes:

1. The function and mode of theorizing for the development of action science and for taking action in everyday life are similar. The function of theory in action science and in practice is to enact an order and to comprehend that order. The scientist and the practitioner use theory to get their arms around the problem, to create some degree of stability, to diagnose the order created under on-line conditions, and to provide the basis for the design and implementation of action.

2. The mode of theorizing is to produce models (such as Models I and O-I) that extract from the action context those patterns required to operate effectively in that context and yet that can be generalized to many different domains. The scientist and the practitioner, therefore, seek those models that comprehend the action context in a way that allows the models to be used under on-line conditions.

3. Public disconfirmability plays a central role in the world of practice and in the world of science. Actors cannot make their intended consequences come true nor detect error without placing a high value on disconfirmability. Disconfirmability not only places a responsibility on the actors to behave in ways that encourage testing but also makes it more likely that others will come to trust the actors and their intentions. As trust and credibility increase, the probability that valid information will be produced for the difficult issues also increases.

4. The requirements for producing and using valid information are also consonant. The practitioner is more apt to use models that require or permit: (a) incomplete information; (b) low precision; coupled with (c) high accuracy.

5. The assumptions made by the action scientist and the practitioner about the nature of the universe are also consonant. Both assume that there is an order, that the order is enacted, that the order and the way that it is enacted are discoverable, and that both of these are alterable.

6. The practitioner and the action scientist also assume that some nontrivial concept of causality exists, otherwise public disconfirmability would be a meaningless game. Along with causality is the

assumption that elegance is desirable. Elegant explanations are those that comprehend more of the action context with the least number of concepts and untestable assumptions.

7. The assumptions that the universe is enacted, that causality exists, and yet that the order is alterable lead to yet another similarity. The order of the universe acts to constrain what actions are possible. If the order exists, it means that people use skills in ways that lead them to be effective and simultaneously maintain the order. This means that individuals' sense of competence is intimately related to the maintenance of some commonly accepted social order.

Under these conditions, skills used by individuals in everyday life, and the societal norms and values upon which they are based, become tacit. Once tacit, little thought is given to altering them, and much thought may be devoted to preventing them from being altered. But, as we have seen, the resulting overly determined stability acts to make people unaware of double-loop errors and inner contradictions. Therefore, both scientists and practitioners are concerned about generating new alternatives. New alternatives may be *discovered* and *invented* without changing theories-in-use or learning systems. New alternatives can be *produced* only by acquiring new skills and creating new learning systems. Hence, at the core of action science and of practice is the assumption that individuals are causally responsible for maintaining their world and for changing it.

Inner Contradictions

Present Conceptions of Rigorous Research

The dominant aspiration of present social science research is to state as precisely as possible the invariant relationships between, or among, a specified set of variables. Precision is to be achieved primarily through the use of quantitative methods. In many cases, the type of quantification used tends to distance the researcher and the subjects from the reality to which the propositions are supposed to apply. To be sure, all concepts are abstractions from, and hence distance individuals from, the context of action; indeed, that is their purpose. However, the distancing that results from the attempt to satisfy the requirements of precision through quantification frequently goes beyond abstracting from reality so that the concepts become disconnected from the context of action.

The requirement of aspiring to state as unambiguously as possible the invariant relationships among variables leads to two difficulties. First, researchers must unilaterally control the tasks, meanings, and time perspective of the subjects in order to rule out, as best they can, threats to validity. In order to generate the high degree of control over subjects that is required, the researchers create conditions that may briefly be described as authoritarian (Model I), and uninfluenceably so. Some subjects may not experience these conditions as neutral and may react against them by producing overtly or covertly, explicitly or tacitly, distorted responses.

A more profound difficulty is related to the possibility that the conditions that researchers create to generate control are basically no different from the conditions human beings create when they interact with others or when they create systems to organize human effort to achieve certain goals. But why should this be a difficulty? Would not such a congruence between the requirements of rigorous research and the requirements of everyday life act to enhance the generalizability or the external validity of the results? The answer is "not necessarily so." Most people, as we have seen, hold theories of action that they use to design and execute their everyday actions. These theories of action blind the actors to important distortions and errors that they create and to their unawareness of this fact. The distortions, errors, and blindness are especially strong when individuals are placed in authoritarian situations that permit a low degree of mutual influence. Moreover, the distortions, errors, and unawareness triggered by authoritarian conditions are learned early in our lives and are highly skilled responses. An important feature of skillful behavior is that the programs in our heads that we use to produce it are tacit. The programs must be tacit if the behavior is to be skillful. For example, people who can ride bicycles are, I am told, following a program that is over 400 pages long. The reason they can ride a bicycle is that they no longer attend consciously to the program; the program is tacit. Indeed, if we required them to pay attention to the program, they would be unable to ride the bicycle. Subjects who may wish to be cooperative and not to distort may do so and be unaware that this is the case because their distortions are skillful responses learned through acculturation to the kinds of situations that researchers use to produce rigor. Distortions and unawareness may also be related to psychological defenses (which are also skillful responses). For example, individuals who project fear and insecurity upon others when they are feeling insecure and fearful may not wish to explore the reasons for such defensive behavior.

The point being made is that behavior learned through acculturation contains many features about which we are unaware. The unawareness may be a result of the behavior's being skillful and/or the
behavior's being a defense. Reactions to authoritarian research conditions may trigger off precisely the everyday reactions that may
include unintended and unrecognized distortions on the part of the
subject. Given that researchers are also subject to these limitations
and given that all this occurs under research conditions where the
tacitness is reinforced (because of the congruence of the requirements of rigorous research and those of everyday life), then it appears
highly likely that these sources of invalidity may go unrecognized.

The Axiom That Social Science Research Should Be Descriptive

If people hold information about which they are unaware, and if
the reason they are unaware is that they are following an internalized
program whose effective implementation requires unawareness (because they are skilled), then normal research is unlikely to uncover
information that is limited to describing the social universe, using
procedures that are congruent with the social universe as it is. This is
the case because, as long as the research requirements remain within
the constraints of acculturation, the skillful behavior will be triggered
automatically, and the personal and societal information that under-
lies and maintains the skills will remain tacit and hence unrecognized.

If this argument is valid, there is a way to study the information
that is at present kept tacit through the use of skillful behavior. The
way to bring this information to the surface is to create conditions
where the skillful behavior is no longer skillful, where it no longer
appears to be effective. Under these conditions, the subjects will have
to examine their tacit programs and their tacit defenses. They will
not be able to examine them unless they become aware of them. If
they make them explicit, then the researcher can study the previously
tacit knowledge as well as the processes the subjects used to make
explicit what was tacit.

The only way to create conditions where present skillful behavior
is no longer skillful is to create conditions in which this is in fact the
case. But such a world will have to contain properties that are significantly different from the world as it is presently constructed. This is
not likely if social scientists remain merely descriptive and utilize
research conditions that are congruent with the present make-up of
the social universe.

Researchers, Intervention, and New Options

One way to deal with the problem is for social scientists to generate models of social universes that are different from the present models. But why would subjects desire to enter into research situations where they will find that some of their most cherished skills have become counterproductive and ineffective? Why go through the pain of learning about one's incompetence, especially if the world is not designed to reward genuinely different behavior?

One reason people may wish to join in this venture is their desire to better the quality of their life. In order to do so, they will have to unfreeze aspects of their theories-in-use and change aspects of their O-I learning systems. People learn, for example, to censor their feelings unilaterally and covertly lest they upset others. Yet time and again it can be shown that this action leads to even deeper pain (for both parties), compounded by the fact that the actions are not discussable. In organizations, we create pyramidal structures because of the finite information-processing capacities of human beings. The same pyramidal structures that grow out of a respect for important human cognitive qualities also may lead to less humane consequences where people at lower levels are placed in dependent, submissive situations and hence lack control over their immediate work life.

The point is that the motivation to cooperate with researchers to explore genuine changes in our behavior and in the make-up of our social systems is available and will probably increase. The question is whether researchers will be able to provide the help needed. If they cannot, they not only will let down the public that supports them, but they will have missed the opportunity to conduct research that describes existing features of the social universe that, up until now, have been unavailable for study.

I believe that the public will make at least two requirements of researchers if this cooperation is to occur. First, researchers must exhibit skills of intervention. They not only must know how to describe reality but also must have skills to intervene in it. This includes skills to generate maps of new options; skills to help subjects as they experience the bewilderment, frustration, and pain resulting from realizing the ineffectiveness of their hitherto cherished skillful behaviors; skills to help systems alter their make-up without, in the process, significantly reducing their effectiveness; and skills to design learning environments to accomplish these requirements.

The second requirement that will be made of researchers is to reorient their priorities to make them congruent with the features of everyday life. The present priorities of researchers call for the production of knowledge in order to understand and explain and to make predictions that can serve as tests of the understanding and explanations.

Finally, if there is to be a new cooperation between the public and the researcher, the public also must become more committed to learning and experimentation, especially in the difficult issues that raise questions about underlying societal assumptions, norms, and practices. I am more optimistic about this occurring because of the oppressive forces created by our inattention to societal inner contradictions. The public will be ready, I fear, before we are. I fear this alternative because change then may be left to the activitists who, at best, demand changes at the policy or espoused-theory levels. They rarely, if ever, help citizens to learn the new skills needed to transform an espoused theory into a theory-in-use. Too often activists have been for change but not for progress. I hope that I have shown that social scientists have an obligation to produce applicable knowledge about new alternatives because without such knowledge they cannot fulfill the presently accepted criteria for understanding the universe, and unless they become more concerned about the citizens who support them, the latter may turn against them, not only in funding research but in cooperating as willing subjects.

Appendix

TABLE A.1

Meeting A–Model I.

	Staff ($N = 95$)		Student ($N = 146$)		Total ($N = 241$)	
	N	%	N	%	N	%
Advocacy-no inquiry	18	19	49	34	66	28
Attribution with						
no data	14	15	39	27	52	22
no testing						
Task control	55	58	8	5	63	26
Controlling						
inquiry	3	3	11	8	14	6
Advocacy coupled						
with punishment	0	0	10	7	10	4
Total	90	95	117	79	205	85

TABLE A.2

Meeting A (without task control)–Model I.

	Staff ($N = 40$)		Student ($N = 146$)		Total ($N = 186$)	
	N	%	N	%	N	%
Advocacy-no inquiry	18	45	49	34	67	36
Attribution with						
no data and	14	35	38	26	52	28
no testing						
Task control	0	0	8	5	8	4
Controlling						
inquiry	3	8	11	8	14	6
Advocacy coupled						
with punishment	0	0	10	7	10	5
Total	35	88	116	79	151	81

187

TABLE A.3
Meeting C (small group)—Model I.

	Students (N = 52)		Staff (N = 31)	
	N	%	N	%
Advocacy-no inquiry	24	46	9	29
Attribution with				
no data	16	31	8	26
no testing				
Inquiry with				
no advocacy	8	15	11	36
Attribution *with*				
data	3	6	1	3
without testing				
Total	51	100	29	100

TABLE A.4
Meeting B—Model I.

	Staff (N = 32)		Student (N = 66)		Total (N = 98)	
	N	%	N	%	N	%
Advocacy without inquiry	9	28	30	45	39	40
Attribution						
without data	10	31	18	27	28	29
without testing						
Task control	1	3	0	0	1	1
Controlling						
inquiry	2	6	1	2	3	3
Advocacy coupled						
with punishment	1	3	0	0	1	1
Total	23	72	49	74	72	73

TABLE A.5
Meeting B—Mixed Model

	Staff (N = 32)		Student (N = 66)		Total (N = 98)	
	N	%	N	%	N	%
Inquiry without advocacy	0	0	4	6	4	4
Attribution *with*						
data	10	31	13	20	23	23
without testing						
Total	10	31	17	26	27	27

References

Abelson, R. P., & Zimbardo, P. G. *Canvassing for peace*. Ann Arbor, Mich.: Society for the Psychological Study of Social Issues, 1970.

Adizes, I., & Borgese, E. M. *Self-management: New dimensions to democracy*. Santa Barbara, Calif.: ABC-CLIO Press, 1975.

Alderfer, C. P., & Brown, L. D. *Learning from changing* (Vol. 19). Beverly Hills, Calif.: Sage Publications, 1975.

Allport, G. W. *The person in psychology*. Boston: Beacon Press, 1969.

Altman, I. Environmental psychology and social psychology. *Personality and Social Psychology Bulletin, 1*(2), 1976, 96-113.

Argyris, C., & Argyris, D. Moral reasoning and moral action: Some preliminary questions. Mimeographed, Harvard University, 1979.

Argyris, C. *How normal science methodology makes leadership research less additive and less applicable*. Mimeographed, Harvard University, 1978.

Argyris, C. Organizational learning and management information systems. *Accounting, Organizations, and Society, 2*(4), 1977, 113-123.

Argyris, C. *Increasing leadership effectiveness*. New York: Wiley-Interscience, 1976. (a)

Argyris, C. Theories of action that inhibit individual learning. *American Psychologist, 31*(9), 1976, 638-654. (b)

Argyris, C. Single-loop and double-loop models in research on decision-making. *Administrative Science Quarterly, 21*, 1976, 363-375. (c)

Argyris, C. Dangers in applying results from experimental social psychology. *American Psychologist, 30*(4), 1975, 469-485.

Argyris, C. *Behind the front page*. San Francisco: Jossey-Bass, 1974. (a)

Argyris, C. Alternative schools: A behavioral analysis. *Teachers College Record, 75*(4), 1974, 429-452. (b)

Argyris, C. Some limits of rational man organizational theory. *Public Administration Review, 33*(3), 1973, 253-267.

Argyris, C. *The applicability of organizational sociology*. New York: Cambridge University Press, 1972. (a)

Argyris, C. Do personal growth laboratories represent an alternative culture? *Journal of Applied Behavioral Science, 8*(1), 1972, 7-28. (b)

Argyris, C. *Management and organizational development*. New York: McGraw-Hill, 1971.

Argyris, C. *Intervention theory and method*. Reading, Mass.: Addison-Wesley, 1970.

Argyris, C. The incompleteness of social psychological theory: Examples from small group, cognitive consistency, and attribution research. *American Psychologist*, 24(10), 1969, 893-907.

Argyris, C. Some unintended consequences of rigorous research. *Psychological Bulletin*, 70(3), 1968, 185-197.

Argyris, C. Today's problems with tomorrow's organizations. *Journal of Management Studies*, 4(1), 1967, 31-55. (a)

Argyris, C. On the future of laboratory education. *Journal of Applied Behavioral Science*, 3(2), 1967, 153-183. (b)

✓ Argyris, C. *Organization and innovation*. Homewood, Ill.: Irwin, 1965.

Argyris, C. *Interpersonal competence and organizational effectiveness*. Homewood, Ill.: Irwin, 1962.

Argyris, C. *Understanding organizational behavior*. Homewood, Ill.: Dorsey Press, 1960.

Argyris, C., & Schön, D. *Organizational learning*. Reading, Mass.: Addison-Wesley, 1978.

Argyris, C., & Schön, D. *Theory in practice*. San Francisco: Jossey-Bass, 1974.

Aronson, E. *The social animal*. San Francisco: Freeman, 1972.

Asplund, J. On the concept of value relevance. In J. Israel & H. Tajfel (Eds.), *The context of social psychology*. New York: Academic Press, 1972.

Bandler, R., & Grinder, J. *The structure of magic*. Palo Alto, Calif.: Science and Behavior Books, 1975.

Bandura, A. Self-efficacy: Toward a unifying theory of behavioral change. *Psychological Review*, 84(2), 1977, 191-215.

Bardach, E. The implementation game: What happens after a bill becomes a law. Cambridge, Mass.: MIT Press, 1977.

Barker, R. G. Explorations in psychological ecology. *American Psychologist*, 20, 1965, 1-14.

Barker, R., Dembo, T., & Lewin, K. Frustration and regression. *University of Iowa Studies in Child Welfare*, 1, 1941, 1-43.

Barker, R. G., & Wright, H. F. *Midwest and its children*. New York: Harper & Row, 1955.

Berger, P., & Luckmann, T. *The social construction of reality*. Garden City, N. Y.: Doubleday, 1967.

Billig, M. The new social psychology and "fascism." *European Journal of Social Psychology*, 7(4), 1977, 393-432.

Blake, R. R., & Mouton, J. S. *Building a dynamic corporation through grid organization development*. Reading, Mass.: Addison-Wesley, 1969.

Blau, P. M. A formal theory of differentiation in organizations. *American Sociological Review*, 35(2), 1970, 201-218.

Bloom, M. *The paradox of helping*. New York: Wiley, 1975.

Blum, J. L., & Naylor, J. C. *Industrial psychology*. New York: Harper & Row, 1968.

Brenner, M., Marsh, P., & Brenner, M. *The social contexts of method*. New York: St. Martin's Press, 1978.

Broadbent, D. E. *Decision and stress*. New York: Academic Press, 1971.

Brown, R. (eds.). *New directions in psychology*. New York: Holt, Rinehart & Winston, 1962.

Brugger, W. *Democracy and organization in the Chinese industrial enterprise (1948-1953)*. New York: Cambridge University Press, 1976.

Bruner, J. S., Oliver, R. R., Greenfield, P. M. *Studies in cognitive growth*. New York: Wiley, 1966.

Brunswick, E. Representative designs and probabilistic theory in a functional psychology. *Psychological Review*, 62, 1955, 193-217.

Burns, T., & Stalker, G. M. *The management of innovation*. London: Tavistock, 1961.

Campbell, D. T., & Stanley, J. C. *Experimental and quasi-experimental design for research*. Skokie, Ill.: Rand McNally, 1963.

Cartwright, D. Determinants of scientific progress: The case of research on the risky shift. *American Psychologist, 28*(3), 1973, 222-232.

Cartwright, D. Lewinian theory as a contemporary systematic framework. In S. Koch (Ed.), *Psychology: A study of a science* (Vol. 2). New York: McGraw-Hill, 1959.

Cazden, C. B., & John, V. P. Learning in American Indian Children. In M. L. W. Wax, S. Diamond, & F. O. Gearing (Eds.), *Anthropological perspectives on education*. New York: Basic Books, 1971.

Chemers, M. M., & Fiedler, F. E. The effectiveness of leadership training: A reply to Argyris. *American Psychologist, 33*(4), 1978, 391-394.

Cicourel, A. *Cognitive sociology*. New York: Penguin, 1973.

Cohen, M. D., & March, J. G. *Leadership and ambiguity: The American college president*. New York: McGraw-Hill, 1974.

Cohen, Y. A. The shaping of men's minds: Adaptations to imperatives of culture. In M. L. Wax, S. Diamond, & F. O. Gearing (Eds.), *Anthropological perspectives on education*. New York: Basic Books, 1971.

Coleman, J. S. *Policy research in the social sciences*. Morristown, N. J.: General Learning Press, 1972.

Collins, L. *The use of models in social science*. London: Tavistock, 1976.

Cook, T. D., & Campbell, D. T. The design and conduct of quasi-experiments and true experiments in field settings. In M. Dunnette (Ed.), *Handbook of industrial and organizational psychology*. Skokie, Ill.: Rand McNally, 1976.

Cronback, L. J., & Suppes, P. *Research for tomorrow's schools*. New York: Macmillan, 1969.

Dale, A., & Payne, R. *Consulting interventions using structured instruments: A critique* (Working paper 76-57). Brussels: European Institute for Advanced Studies in Management, 1976.

deCharms, R. *Enhancing motivation*. New York: Irvington, 1976.

deCharms, R. *Personal causation*. New York: Academic Press, 1968.

Deutch, M., & Hornstein, H. A. *Applying social psychology*. Hillsdale, N. J.: Lawrence Erlbaum, 1975.

Deutsch, M., & Collins, M. E. Interracial housing. In W. Peterson (Ed.), *American social patterns*. Garden City, N. Y.: Doubleday, 1965.

Deutsch, M., & Krauss, R. M. *Theories in social psychology*. New York: Basic Books, 1965.

Dobyns, H., Doughty, P. L., & Lasswell, H. D. *Peasants, power and applied social change*. Beverly Hills, Calif.: Sage Publications, 1971.

Dubin, R. Assaulting the Tower of Babel. *Contemporary Psychology, 20*(11), 1976, 881-882.

Dunnette, M. D., & Campbell, J. P. *Development of the Penney Career Index: Final technical reports*. Mimeographed, University of Minnesota, 1969.

Easton, L. D., & Guddar, K. H. (Eds.). *Writings on the young Marx in philosophy and society*. Garden City, N. Y.: Doubleday, 1967.

Edwards, A. L. Experiments: Their planning and execution. In G. Lindzcy (Ed.), *Handbook of social psychology*. Reading, Mass.: Addison-Wesley, 1954.

Festinger, L. *A theory of cognitive dissonance*. New York: Harper & Row, 1957.

Festinger, L. Laboratory experiments. In L. Festinger & D. Katz (Eds.), *Research methods in the behavioral sciences*. New York: Holt, Rinehart & Winston, 1953.

Feyerabend, P. K. Against Method: Outline of an anarchistic theory of knowledge. In M. Radner & S. Winokur (Eds.), *Analyses of theories and methods of physics and psychology. Minnesota Studies in the Philosophy of Science* (Vol. IV). Minneapolis: University of Minnesota Press, 1975.

Fiedler, F. E., & Chemers, M. M. *Leadership and effective management*. Glenview, Ill.: Scott, Foresman, 1974.

Fiedler, F. E., Chemers, M. M. with L. Makar. *Leader match: Second experimental version*. Mimeographed, University of Washington, Seattle, 1975.

Finkelman, D. Science and psychology. *American Journal of Psychology, 91* (2), 1978, 179-199.

Fleischman, E. A. Twenty years of consideration and structure. In E. Fleishman & J. G. Hunt (Eds.), *Current development in the study of leadership*. Carbondale: Southern Illinois University Press, 1973.

French, J. R. P., Jr. A formal theory of social power. *Psychological Review, 63*(3), 1956, 181-194.

French, J. R. P., Jr., Israel, J., & As, D. An experiment on participations in a Norwegian factory. *Human Relations, 13*, 1960, 3-20.

French, J. R. P., Jr., Kay, E., & Meyer, H. Participation and the appraisal system. *Human Relations, 20*, 1966, 3-20.

Fromkin, H. L., & Streufert, S. Laboratory experiments. In M. Dunnette (Ed.), *Handbook of industrial and organizational psychology*. Skokie, Ill.: Rand McNally, 1976.

Geertz, C. *The interpretation of cultures*. New York: Basic Books, 1973.

George, A. L. et al. *Towards a more soundly based foreign policy: making better use of information* (Commission on the Organization of the Government for the Conduct of Foreign Policy, Vol. II, Appendix D, 022-000-00112-4). Washington, D.C.: U.S. Government Printing Office, 1975.

Gergen, K. J. *Toward generative theory*. Mimeographed, Swathmore College, 1978.

Ginsberg, G. P. (Ed.). *Emerging strategies in social psychological research*, London: Wiley, 1978.

Ginsberg, G. P. Role-playing and role performance in social psychological research. In M. Brenner, P. Marsh, & M. Brenner (Eds.), *The social context of method*. New York: St. Martin's Press, 1978.

Guest, R. *Organizational change: The effect of successful leadership*. Homewood, Ill.: Irwin-Dorsey, 1962.

Guest, R., Hersey, P., & Blanchard, K. *Organizational change through effective leadership*. Englewood Cliffs, N. J.: Prentice-Hall, 1977.

Habermas, J. *Knowledge and human interests*. London: Heinemann, 1972.

Harré, R., & Secord, P. *The explanation of social behavior*. Oxford: Blackwell, 1972.

Heider, F. *The psychology of interpersonal relations*. New York: Wiley, 1958.

Heller, K., & Manahan, J. *Psychology and community change*. Homewood, Ill.: Dorsey Press, 1977.

Helmrick, R. Applied social psychology: The unfilled promise. *Personality and Social Psychology Bulletin*, 1975, 548-560.

Hethy, L., & Mako, C. Work performance, interests, powers and enrichment. *European Economic Review, 5*, 1974, 141-157.

Hymar, S., & Roosevelt, F. Comment: Symposium: Economics of the New Left. *Quarterly Journal of Economics, LXXXVI*(4), 1972, 655-683.

Israel, J. Stipulations and construction in the social science. In J. Israel & H. Tajfel (Eds.), *The context of social psychology*. New York: Academic Press, 1972.

Janis, I. L. *Victims of group think*. Boston: Houghton Miflin, 1972.

Jones, E. E., & Davis, K. E. From acts to dispositions. In L. Berkowitz (Ed.), *Advances in experimental social psychology* (Vol. 2). New York: Academic Press, 1965.

Jones, E. E., & Gerard, H. B. *Foundation of social psychology*. New York: Wiley, 1967.

Kagan, J. Motives and Development. *Journal of Personality and Social Psychology, 22*(1), 1972, 51-66.

Kaplan, A. *The conduct of inquiry.* New York: Intext, 1964.

Kelley, G. *The psychology of personal constructs.* New York: Norton, 1955.

Kelley, H. H. *Attribution in social interaction.* Morristown, N. J.: General Learning Press, 1971.

Kiesler, S. B., & Turner, C. F. *Fundamental research and the process of education.* Washington, D.C.: National Institute of Education, 1977.

Kohlberg, L., Kauffman, K., Scharf, P., & Hickey, J. *The just community approach to corrections: A manual* (Part I). Cambridge, Mass.: Moral Education Research Foundation, Harvard University, 1974.

Korman, A. K. Consideration, initiation structure, and organizational criteria: A review. *Personnel Psychology, 19*(4), 1966, 349-361.

Kuhn, T. S. *The structure of scientific revolution* (2nd ed.). Chicago: University of Chicago Press, 1970.

Lammers, C. J. Self-management and participation: Two concepts of decentralization in organizations. *Organization and Administrative Sciences, 5*(4), 1974, 17-33.

Langer, E. J., & Dweck, C. S. *Personal politics.* Englewood Cliffs, N. J.: Prentice-Hall, 1973.

Lazarsfeld, P. F., & Rietz, J. G. *An introduction to applied sociology.* Amsterdam: Elsevier, 1975.

Levinson, H. *Organizational diagnosis.* Cambridge, Mass.: Harvard University Press, 1972.

Lewin, K. *Field theory in social science.* New York: Harper & Row, 1951.

Lewin, K. Formalization and progress in psychology. In K. Lewin, R. Lippitt, & S. K. Escalona (Eds.), *Studies in topological and vector psychology I.* University of Iowa Studies in Child Welfare, University of Iowa Press, XVI, No. 3, No. 380, 1940, 9-42.

Lewin, K., Lippitt, R., & White, R. K. Patterns of aggressive behavior in experimentally created social climates. *Journal of Social Psychology, 10,* 1939, 271-301.

Lippitt, R. An experimental study of the effect of democratic and authoritarian group atmospheres. In K. Lewin, R. Lippett, & S. K. Escalona (Eds.), *Studies in topological and vector psychology, I. Studies in Child Welfare, 16*(3), No. 380, University of Iowa Press, 1940, 45-195.

Lippitt, R., & White, R. K. The "social climate" of children's groups. In R. Barker, J. Kounin, & H. F. Wright (Eds.) *Child behavior and development.* New York: McGraw-Hill, 1943.

Love, C. A., & March, J. G. *An introduction to models in the social sciences.* New York: Harper & Row, 1975.

Lowen, A., Hrapchak, W. J., & Kavanagh, J. M. Consideration and initiating structure: An experimental investigation of leadership traits. *Administrative Science Quarterly, 14*(2), 1969, 238-253.

Mann, F. C., Indik, B. P., & Vroom, V. H. *The productivity of work groups.* Survey Research Center, Institute for Social Research, University of Michigan, Organizational Studies Series 1, Report r, 1963.

Marglin S. A. *What do bosses do?* (Part I). *Review of Radical Politics and Economics* (RRPE), *4*(2), 1974.

Marglin, S. A. *What do bosses do?* (Part II). *Review of Radical Politics and Economics* (RRPE), *7*(1), 1975.

Matejko, A. Work and management. In R. Dubin, (Ed.), *Handbook of work, organizations and society.* Skokie, Ill.: Rand McNally, 1976.

Mayer, R. R. *Social planning and social change.* Englewood Cliffs, N. J.: Prentice-Hall, 1972.

McClelland, D. C. Managing motivation to expand human freedom. *American Psychologist, 33*(3), 1978, 201-210.

McClelland, D. C. *Power: The inner experience.* New York: Irvington, 1975.

McClelland, D. C., & Burnham, D. H. Power to the great motivator. *Harvard Business Review, 54*(2), 1976, 100-110.

McClelland, D. C., & Winter, D. G. *Motivating economic achievement.* New York: Free Press, 1971.

McGuire, W. J. The yin and yang of progress in social psychology: Seven koans. *Journal of Personality and Social Psychology, 26,* 1973, 446-456.

McGuire, W. M. Inducing resistance to persuasion. In L. Berkowitz (Ed.), *Advances in Experimental Social Psychology* (Vol. 1). New York: Academic Press, 1964.

Meissner, M. The language of work. In R. Dubin (Ed.), *Handbook of work, organization and society.* Skokie, Ill.: Rand McNally, 1976.

Meltzer, B. N., Petras, J. W., & Reynolds, L. T. *Symbolic interactionism: Genesis, varieties and criticism.* London: Routledge & Kegan Paul, 1975.

Menzel, H. Meaning—who needs it? In M. Brenner, P. Marsh, & M. Brenner (Eds.), *The social context of method.* New York: St. Martin's Press, 1978.

Milgram, S. *Obedience to authority.* New York: Harper & Row, 1974.

Miller, G. Psychology as a means of promoting human welfare. *American Psychologist,* 1969, *24,* 1063-1075.

Miller, G. A. The magical number seven, plus or minus two: Some limits on our capacity for processing information. *Psychological Review,* 1956, *63,* 81-96.

Mitroff, I. I. *The subjective side of science.* Amsterdam: Elsevier, 1974.

Mitroff, I. I., & Kelmann, R. H. The varieties of social science experience. Mimeographed, University of Pittsburgh, 1978.

Morse, J., & Lorsch, J. Beyond Theory Y. *Harvard Business Review,* 1970, 61.

Moscovici, S. Society and theory in social psychology. In J. Israel and H. Tajfel (Eds.), *The context of social psychology.* New York: Academic Press, 1972.

Neustadt, R., & Fineberg, H. V. *The swine flu affair.* Washington, D.C.: U.S. Department of Health, Education, and Welfare, 1978.

Nord, W. Job satisfaction reconsidered. *American Psychologist, 32*(12), 1977, 1026-1035.

Nord, W. The failure of current applied behavioral science: A Marxian perspective. *Journal of Applied Behavioral Science, 10*(4), 1974, 557-578.

Normann, R. *Management for growth.* Chichester: Wiley-Interscience, 1977.

Normann, R. *A personal quest for methodology.* Scandinavian Institute for Administrative Research, Stockholm, 1973.

Oakeshott, M. *Experience and its modes.* New York: Cambridge University Press, 1966.

Obradovic, J. Workers participation: Who participates? *Industrial Relations, 14*(1), 1975, 32-44.

Oh, T. K. Theory Y in the People's Republic of China. *California Management Review, XIX*(2), 1977, 77-84.

Orne, T. M. On the social psychology of the psychology experiment with particular reference to demand characteristics and their implications. *American Psychologist, 17,* 1962, 776-783.

Perrow, C. *Organizational analysis: A sociological view.* Belmont, Calif.: Wadsworth Publishing Co., 1970.

Phillips, D. *Abandoning method.* San Francisco: Jossey-Bass, 1973.

Polanyi, M. *The tacit dimension,* Garden City, N. Y.: Doubleday, 1967.

Power, C., & Reimer, J. Moral atmosphere: An educational bridge between moral judgment and action. In W. Damon (Ed.), *New directions for child development: Moral development.* San Francisco: Jossey-Bass, in press.

Reason, P. Explorations in the development of social praxis: Ideas for a programme of research. Mimeograph, Center for the Study of Organizational Change and Development, University of Bath, 1978.

Rhenman, E. *Organization theory for long-range planning.* New York: Wiley, 1973.

Ring, K. Experimental social psychology: Some sober questions about frivolous values. *Journal of Experimental Social Psychology, 13*, 1967, 113-123.

Rowbottom, R. *Social analysis.* London: Heinemann, 1977.

Rubin, Z. *Liking and loving.* New York: Holt, Rinehart & Winston, 1973.

Rychlak, J. F. *A philosophy of science for personality theory.* Boston: Houghton Mifflin, 1968.

Salancik, G. R., & Pfeffer, J. A social information processing approach to job attitudes and task designs. *Administrative Science Quarterly, 23*(2), 1978, 224-253.

Sampson, E. E. Psychology and the American ideal. *Journal of Personality and Social Psychology, 35*(11), 1977, 767-782.

Sampson, E. E. On justice as equality. *Journal of Social Issues, 31*, 1975, 45-64.

Schlenker, B. R. Social psychology and science. *Journal of Personality and Social Psychology, 4*(29), 1974, 1-115.

Schurmann, F. *Ideology and organization* (2nd ed.). Berkeley: University of California Press, 1968.

Schutz, A. *The phenomenology of the social world.* Evanston, Ill.: Northwestern University Press, 1967.

Scribner, S., & Cole, M. Cognitive consequences of formal and informal education. *Science, 182*(4112), 1973, 553-559.

Secord, P. F., & Backman, C. W. An interpersonal approach to personality. In B. A. Maher (Ed.), *Progress in experimental personality research.* New York: Academic Press, 1964.

Simon, H. *The science of the artificial.* Cambridge, Mass.: MIT Press, 1969.

Stebbing, L. S. *A modern introduction to logic.* New York: Crowell, 1943, 325.

Stephenson, T. E. Organizational development: A critique. *Journal of Management Studies, 12*(3), 1975, 249-265.

Stogdill, R. M. *Handbook of leadership.* New York: Free Press, 1974.

Sweezy, P. Comment: Symposium: Economics of the new left. *Quarterly Journal of Economics, 86*(4), 658-664.

Tannebaum, A. S., Kavcic, B., Rosner, M., Vianello, M., & Wieser, G. *Hierarchy in organizations.* San Francisco: Jossey-Bass, 1974.

Taylor, J. C. Job satisfaction and quality of working life: A reassessment. *Journal of Occupational Psychology, 50*, 1977, 243-252.

Thomas, D. S. An attempt to develop precise measurements in the social behavior field. *Sociologies, 8*, 1933, 436-456.

Thompson, D. *Organizations in Action.* New York: McGraw-Hill, 1967.

Vanek, J. with the assistance of C. Gunn. *The theory and practice of self-management: An American perspective.* Mimeographed, Department of Economics, Cornell University, No. 140, 1977.

Varela, J. A. *Psychological solutions to social problems.* New York: Academic Press, 1971.

Von Neumann, J. *The computer and the brain.* New Haven, Conn.: Yale University Press, 1958.

Wagner, H. M. The design of production and inventory systems for multiwarehouse companies. *Operations Research, 22*(2), 1974, 278-291.

Wagner, H. M. The ABC of OR. *Operations Research, 19*(6), 1971, 1259-1281.

Walton, R. E. *Work innovations at Topeka: After six years.* Mimeographed, Graduate School of Business. Harvard University, 1976.

Warr, P. Aided experiments in social psychology. *Bulletin of British Psychology Society, 30*, 1977, 2-8.

Warr, P. Toward a more human psychology. *Bulletin of British Psychology Society, 26*, 1973, 1-8.

Wasserman, E. R. Implementing Kohlberg's "just community" concept in an alternative high school. *Social Education, 32*, 1976.

Watzlawick, P., Veavin, J. H., & Jackson, D. D. *Pragmatics of human communications*. New York: Norton, 1967.

Wegner, D. M., & Vallacher, R. R. *Implicit psychology*. New York: Oxford University Press, 1977.

Weick, K. E. Laboratory experimentation with organizations: A Reappraisal. *Academy of Management Review*, 1977. (a)

Weick, K. E. Organization design: Organizations as self-designing systems. *Organizational Dynamics, 6*, 1977, 31-46. (b)

Weick, K. E. *The social psychology of organizing*. Reading, Mass.: Addison-Wesley, 1969.

Weick, K. E. Laboratory experimentation with organizations. In James G. March, *Handbook of organizations*. Skokie, Ill.: Rand McNally, 1965.

Weizenbaum, J. *Computer power and human reason*. San Francisco: Freeman, 1976.

Wexler, D., & Rice, L. *Innovations in client-centered therapy*. New York: Wiley-Interscience, 1974.

White, R. W. Motivation reconsidered: The concept of competence. *Psychological Review, 66*, 1959, 297-333.

Whyte, M. K. Bureaucracy and modernization in China: The Maoist critique. *American Sociological Review, 38*(2), 1973, 149-173.

Wildavsky, A. The self-evaluation organization. *Public Administration Review, XXXII*(5), 1972, 509-520.

Willems, E. P. Planning a rationale for naturalistic research. In E. P. Willems & H. L. Raush (Eds.), *Naturalistic viewpoints in psychological research*. New York: Holt, Rinehart & Winston, 1969.

Willems, E. P., & Raush, H. L. (Eds.). *Naturalistic viewpoints in psychological research*. New York: Holt, Rinehart & Winston, 1969.

Woods, P., & Hammersley, M. *School experiences explorations in the sociology of education*. New York: St. Martin's Press, 1977.

Zadek, L. A. A fuzzy set theoretic interpretation of linguistic hedges. *Journal of Cybernetics, 2*, 1972, 4-34.

Zelditch, M., Jr., & Hopkins, T. K. Laboratory experiments with organizations. A. Etzioni (Ed.), *Complex organizations*. Holt, Rinehart & Winston, 1961.

Zimbardo, P. The tactics and ethics of persuasion. In B. T. King & E. McGinnies (Eds.), *Attitudes, conflict and social change*. New York: Academic Press, 1972.

Zimbardo, P., & Ebbesen, E. B. *Influencing attitudes and changing behavior*. Reading, Mass.: Addison-Wesley, 1969.

Zuniga, R. The experimenting society and radical social reform: The role of the social scientist in Chile's Unidad popular experience. *American Psychologist, 30*(1), 1975, 99-115.

Author Index

Subject Index